THE `-GOD `-BOOK OF `-NUMEROLOGY!~'

PREVIOUS BOOKS:

THE `-GOD `-BOOK OF `-NUMEROLOGY!~'

DWAYNE W. ANDERSON

THE `-GOD `-BOOK OF `-NUMEROLOGY!-'

iUniverse books may be ordered through booksellers or by contacting:

iUniverse
1663 Liberty Drive
Bloomington, IN 47403
www.iuniverse.com
844-349-9409

ISBN: 978-1-6632-0779-1 (sc)
ISBN: 978-1-6632-0777-7 (hc)
ISBN: 978-1-6632-0778-4 (e)

Library of Congress Control Number: 2020916235

Print information available on the last page.

iUniverse rev. date: 08/27/2020

WITHOUT a `-DOUBT, OUR LIVES are `-ETCHED; and, `-ARTICULATED in `-TIME' to an `-EVENTUALITY; of `-GOD'S VERY OWN `-PURPOSE, to `-OUR `-VERY `-OWN PURPOSE of `-BEING; in the `-EXISTENCE/EXPANSE of `-TIME!!!~' OUR `-LIVES; are an `-ARTICULATION of `-MEANINGS, of '# `-NUMBERS!!!~' ALREADY `-PROVEN through `-**R**ECIPROCAL-**S**EQUENCING-**N**UMEROLOGY-**RSN**; and, **R**ECIPROCAL-**S**EQUENCED-**I**NVERSED-**R**EALITIES-**RSIR**!!!~' ENJOY the `-READS!!!~'

THE `-MARTIN'S!!!~'

MARTIN LUTHER (GERMAN PROFESSOR of THEOLOGY)
`-**BIRTH/YEAR** = (`-14**83**) = (43) (18) = (43 + 18) = (`-**61**)!!!~'

MARTIN LUTHER (GERMAN PROFESSOR of THEOLOGY)
`-**DEATH/YEAR** = (`-**1546**) = (15 + 46) = (`-**61**)!!!~'

MARTIN LUTHER KING, JR. (CIVIL RIGHTS MINISTER)
`-**BIRTH/YEAR** = (`-19**29**) = (99) (12) = (99 (-) 12) = (`-**87**)!!!~'

MARTIN LUTHER KING, JR. (CIVIL RIGHTS MINISTER)
`-**DEATH/YEAR** = (`-**1968**) = (19 + 68) = (`-**87**)!!!~'

I; think, `-IT'S `-TIME; for `-EVERYONE, to `-WAKE `-UP!!!~'"

The REAL PROPHET of DOOM
(Kismet) - INTRODUCTION -PENDULUM FLOW - III
by Dwayne W. Anderson

"PLAYBOY'S HUGH HEFNER'S `-BIRTHDAY = (4/9/1926)!!!~' TAKE the (`-1) from (1926); and, `-ADD `-IT to (`-926) = (926 + 1) = (`-927) = `-EQUALS = "HIS DAY of `-DEATH" = (SEPTEMBER 27ᵗʰ)!!!~' HE `-DIED on (9/27/2017) = `-EQUALS = (`-194) DAYS away from `-HIS VERY OWN `-BIRTHDAY!!!~' (`-194) = RECIPROCAL (INVERSE) = (`-491) = `-EQUALS = "THE VERY `-FIRST (`-3) (`-THREE) (`-#'S) of `-HIS `-BIRTHDAY (491)" = `-EQUALS = "AN (ALL-IN-ONE-#-NUMBER)" = (491) = (`-49) & (`-91) = "HIS VERY OWN `-BIRTHDAY; and, `-HIS VERY OWN `-AGE of `-DEATH"!!!~' *DEATH/YEAR* = `-EQUALS = (`-2017) = (`-17) = RECIPROCAL (INVERSE) = (`-71) = (71 + 20) = (`-91) = "HIS VERY OWN `-AGE of `-DEATH"!!!~'

NASA's *"HIDDEN FIGURES"* MARY JACKSON'S `-BIRTHDAY = (4/9/1921)!!!~' SHE `-DIED on (2/11/2005) = (2 + 11 + 20 + 05) = (`-38) = RECIPROCAL (INVERSE) = (`-83) = "HER VERY OWN `-AGE of `-DEATH"!!!~' SHE `-DIED (`-308) DAYS AWAY from *`-HER `-BIRTHDAY!!!~'* (`-38) = RECIPROCAL (INVERSE/MIRROR) = (`-83)!!!~' `-BIRTH/ YEAR = (`-1921) = (1 + 9 + 1) (`-2) = 11(2) = RECIPROCAL (`-MIRROR) = (2)(11) = "HER VERY OWN `-DAY of `-DEATH" = (FEBRUARY 11ᵗʰ)!!!~'

ACTOR TAB HUNTER was `-BORN on (**7**/**11**/**1931**) = (7 + 11 + 19 + 31) = (`-**68**) = RECIPROCAL (INVERSE/MIRROR) = (`-**86**) = "HIS VERY OWN `-AGE of `-DEATH!!!~' HE `-DIED (**7**/**8**/2018)!!!~' `-BIRTH/DAY = (**7**/**11**) = (7 x 11) = (`-**77**) = "HE DIED the `-VERY `-NEXT `-DAY on (`-**78**) = (JULY 8th)!!!~' HE `-DIED (`-**362**) DAYS AWAY from `-HIS `-BIRTHDAY = (3 x 62) = (`-**186**) = (86 x 1) = (`-**86**) = "HIS VERY OWN `-AGE of `-DEATH"!!!~'

AMERICAN BROADCASTER **HUGH DOWNS** was on (**20**/**20**); AND, `-**DIED** in (`-**20**/**20**)!!!~' BIRTH/DAY = (**2/14/1921**) = (2 + 14 + 19 + 21) = (`-**56**)!!!~' DIED on (**7/1/2020**) = (7 + 1 + 20 + 20) = (`-**48**) = (4 + 8) = (`-**12**) = RECIPROCAL (INVERSE/MIRROR) = (`-**21**) = "FLIP the (`-**2**) OVER to a (`-**7**)" = (`-**71**) = "HIS VERY OWN `-**DAY** of `-**DEATH** = (JULY 1st)!!!~' *BIRTH/YEAR* = (`-**1921**) = (9 (-) 2) / (1 x 1) = (**7/1**) = "HIS VERY OWN `-**DAY** of `-**DEATH**" = (JULY 1st)!!!~' *BIRTHDAY* = (**2/14**) = (14 / divided by / 2) = (`-**7**) x 1 = "MONTH of `-DEATH"!!!~' DIED (`-**228**) DAYS AWAY from HIS `-BIRTHDAY = (2 x 28) = (`-**56**) = "HIS VERY OWN `-**BIRTH/DAY** # `-**NUMBER** (`-**56**)"!!!~' HIS `-AGE of `-DEATH = (`-**99**) = RECIPROCAL (INVERSE/MIRROR) = (`-**66**) = (99 + 66) = (`-**165**) = (65 x 1) = (`-**65**) = RECIPROCAL (INVERSE/MIRROR) = (`-**56**) = "HIS VERY OWN `-**BIRTH/DAY** # `-**NUMBER** (`-**56**)!!!~'

DWAYNE W. ANDERSON'S `-**MOTHER** was `-**BORN** in (`-**1944**) = (19 + 44) = (`-**63**) = DWAYNE W. ANDERSON'S MOTHER'S `-AGE of `-DEATH = `-*EQUALED* = (`-63)!!!~'

AMERICAN ACTRESS **RITA HAYWORTH** was `-**BORN** in (`-19/18) = (19 + 18) = (`-**37**) = "SHE had a (`-**37**) YEAR ACTING CAREER"!!!~' `-**DIED** in (`-*19/87*) at the `-**AGE** of (`-**68**)!!!~' (87 (-) 19 = (`-**68**) = "**AGE of** `-**DEATH**"!!!~' (**5/14**) DAY of `-DEATH!!!~' (**5/14**) **FRANK SINATRA'S DAY of** `-**DEATH** in (`-*1998*)!!!~' (19 + 98) = (`-**117**) = (17 x 1) = (`-**17**) = AMERICAN ACTRESS **RITA HAYWORTH** was `-**BORN** on the (`-**17**th)!!!~' SHE `-**DIED** (`-**156**) DAYS AWAY from `-**HER** `-**BIRTH/DAY** at the `-**HEIGHT** of (**5' 6**")!!!~'

JUNE POINTER from the MUSICAL GROUP "THE POINTER SISTERS" had a `-**BIRTHDAY** of (**11/30**) = (11 + 30) = (`-**41**)!!!~' Her `-DEATH/DAY was (**4/11**/2006) = (4 + 11 + 20 + 06) = (`-**41**)!!!~'

BONNIE POINTER from the MUSICAL GROUP "THE POINTER SISTERS" had a `-**BIRTH/YEAR** of (`-**1950**) = (19 + 50) = (`-**69**) = BONNIE POINTER `-**DIED** at the `-**AGE** of (`-**69**)!!!~'

SHE `-DIED on (**6/8**/2020) = (**6** + **8** + 20 + 20) = (`-**54**)!!!~' **HER** `-**SISTER** JUNE POINTER had a `-**BIRTHDAY** of (**11/30/1953**) = (11 + 30 + 19 + 53) = (`-**113**) = (11/3) = "**PART of** `-**BIRTHDAY**"!!!~' BIRTHDAY # `-NUMBER (`-**113**) + **JUNE POINTER'S DEATH/DAY # `-NUMBER** of (`-**41**) = (`-**154**) = (54 x 1) = (`-**54**) = **HER** `-**SISTER** *BONNIE POINTER'S* **DEATH/ DAY #** `-**NUMBER** = (`-**EQUALS**) = (`-**54**)!!!~'

SEE the `-**LINKS** between `-**SISTERS**!!!~'

BASEBALL'S DON BAYLOR was `-**BORN** in (`-**1949**) = (19 + 49) = (`-**68**) = DON BAYLOR had `-**DIED** at the `-**AGE** of (`-**68**)!!!~' DON BAYLOR'S **BIRTHDAY** was (**6/28**) = (6 x 28) = (`-**168**) = (68 x 1) = (`-**68**) = DON BAYLOR `-**DIED** at the `-**AGE** of (`-**68**)!!!~'

AMERICAN SINGER GLEN CAMPBELL had a `-**BIRTHDAY** of (**4/22/1936**) = (4 + 22 + 19 + 36) = (`-**81**) = GLEN CAMPBELL had `-DIED at the `-AGE of (`-**81**) at (`-**108**) DAYS away from `-**HIS LAST `-BIRTHDAY!!!~'** HE was `-BORN in (`-**36**) = (3 x 6) = (`-**18**) = RECIPROCAL (MIRROR) = (`-**81**) = **"AGE of `-DEATH"** for **AMERICAN SINGER GLEN CAMPBELL!!!~'** GLEN CAMPBELL'S `-**BIRTHDAY** was (***APRIL 22nd***) / (**4/22**) = (4 x 22) = (`-**88**) = **&; GLEN CAMPBELL** `-**DIED** (`-**EXACTLY**) on the # `-NUMBER of (`-**88**) = **HIS** `-**DEATH/DAY was "AUGUST (8th)"!!!~'**

ACTRESS MAGDA GABOR'S BIRTHDAY was (**6/11**/1915)!!!~' **BIRTHDAY = (6/11) = (6 x 11) = (`-66) = EQUALS = "HER VERY OWN DEATH/DAY"** of (**6/6/1997**)!!!~' (**1915**) = (95 + 1 + 1) = (`-**97**) = **"YEAR of `-DEATH from YEAR of `-BIRTH"!!!~'** (**66**) = RECIPROCAL (INVERSE/MIRROR) = (`-**99**) = (9 x 9) = (`-**81**) = **"AGE of `-DEATH for `-MAGDA GABOR"!!!~'**

SEE the `-MANY `-PATTERNS!!!~'

/|\ BOOK TITLE: `-GOD is `-the MATHEMATICIAN-'"!!!~' /|
by Dwayne W. Anderson

CHEF FLOYD CARDOZ `-***AGE of `-DEATH*** = (`-**59**) /|\ (`-***BIRTH 10/02/19/60***) (`-***DEATH: 3/25/20/20***)!!!~'

5

`-**BIRTH** = (10 x 2) (-) (19 + 60) = (`-**20**) (-) (`-**79**) = (`-**59**) = `-**AGE** of `-**DEATH** (`-**59**)!!!~'

`-**DEATH**= (3/25/20/20) = (3) + (52) + (2) + (2) = (`-**59**) = `-**AGE** of `-**DEATH** (`-**59**)!!!~'

FORMER CHAIR (CARTER-REAGAN) of the FEDERAL RESERVE PAUL VOLCKER (AGE of `-DEATH) = (`-**92**) (BIRTH: **SEPTEMBER 5**, 19**27**) (DEATH: **DECEMBER 8, 2019**)!!!~'

(*) DEATH/DAY # `-NUMBER = (12 + 8 + 20 + 19) = **59** = RECIPROCAL (MIRROR) = (`-**95**) = `-**BIRTH/DAY** = (**SEPTEMBER 5**th)!!!~'

COUNTRY MUSIC STAR TROY GENTRY was `-BORN (**4/5**/1967) = (4 + 5 + 19 + 67) = (`-**95**) = (9 x 5) = (`-**45**) & `-DIED on (9/8/2017) = (9 + 8 + 20 + 17) = (`-**54**) = RECIPROCAL (INVERSE/ MIRROR) = (`-**45**) = "**HIS VERY OWN** `-**BIRTHDAY**" = (**APRIL 5**th)!!!~'

POLISH COMPOSER KRZYSZTOF PENDERECKI (`-**86**) (BIRTH: NOVEMBER **23**, 19**33**) (DEATH: **MARCH 29**, 2020)!!!~'

(*) `-**BIRTHDAY** # `-**NUMBER** = (11 + 23 + 19 + 33) = (`-**86**) = `-**AGAIN, ANOTHER** `-**INDIVIDUAL** had `-**IT to where their** `-**BIRTHDAY** # `-**NUMBER** = `-**EQUALS** = "**THEIR** `-**ACTUAL** `-**AGE** of `-**DEATH** (`-**86**)"!!!~'

AMERICAN RAPPER CHYNNA ROGERS (AGE of `-DEATH) = (`-**25**) (BIRTH: **AUGUST 19, 19<u>94</u>**) (DEATH: APRIL 8, 2020)!!!~' **APRIL 8** = (`-**48**) = (8 + 20 + 20)!!!~'

(*) `-**REVERSE** `-**SEQUENCE** on `-*HER* `-*BIRTHDAY #* `-*NUMBER* = (94 (-) 19 (-) 19 (-) 8) = (`-**48**) = `-**HER** VERY OWN `-**DEATH/DAY** (**4/8**) = "(APRIL **8**th)"!!!~'

`-**DEATH/DAY** # `-**NUMBER** = (4 + 8 + 20 + 20) = (`-**52**) = RECIPROCAL (INVERSE/MIRROR) = (`-**25**) = "**AGE** of `-**DEATH** for **AMERICAN RAPPER CHYNNA ROGERS** (`-**25**)"!!!~'

(EXCERPT from `-MY `-PREVIOUS `-BOOK):

**NEW BOOK /||\ REAL MESSAGES
of `-GOD I, II; & III-!!!~' /||**
by Dwayne W. Anderson

<u>The # `-**NUMBER** (`-**168**)!!!~'</u>

<u>#1</u>/PRESIDENT GEORGE WASHINGTON'S `-**PRODUCT of** `-**DEATH** from `-**DAY of** `-**DEATH** = (`-**168**)!!!~'

<u>#2</u>/PRESIDENT JOHN ADAMS `-**PRODUCT of** `-**DEATH** from `-**DAY of** `-**DEATH** = (`-**28**)!!!~' <u>#3</u>/PRESIDENT THOMAS JEFFERSON `-**PRODUCT of** `-**DEATH** from `-**DAY of** `-**DEATH** = (`-**28**)!!!~'

<u>#4</u>/PRESIDENT JAMES MADISON `-**PRODUCT of** `-**DEATH** from `-**DAY of** `-**DEATH** = (`-**168**)!!!~'

<u>#5</u>/PRESIDENT JAMES MONROE `-**PRODUCT of** `-**DEATH** from `-**DAY of** `-**DEATH** = (`-**28**)!!!~' (28 + 28 + 28) = (`-**84**)!!!~' (`-84) x 2) = (`-**168**)!!!~'

#6/PRESIDENT JOHN QUINCY ADAMS `-DAY of `-DEATH (2/**23**) = (2**2** x **3**) = (`-**66**)!!!~' (`-**66**) for the (`-**6TH**) PRESIDENT = (`-**666**)!!!~' DEATH/DAY # `-NUMBER = (`-**91**)!!!~'

`-BORN JULY 11ᵗʰ, 1**767** = (7 + 11 + 17 + 67) = (`-**102**) /|\ `-DIED FEBRUARY **23**ʳᵈ, 1**848** = (2 + 23 + 18 + 48) = `-(`-**91**)-"

(67 (-) 17 (-) 11 (-) 7) = (`-**32**) = -a PROPHETIC # `-NUMBER!!!~' (102 + 32) = (`-**134**)!!!~' (34 x 2) = (`-**68**)!!!~'

`-**1767** = (17 + 67) = `-**84** = **RECIPROCAL** = `-**48** = **DIED** in the **YEAR** of (`-**48**)!!!~'

#7/PRESIDENT ANDREW JACKSON `-DAY of `-DEATH = JUNE(**6**) **8** = (`-**6/8**) = (6 x 8) = `-**48** = RECIPROCAL = `-**84**!~'

`-AND; `-HE `-**DIED** on the `-**DAY** of (**6/8**)!!!~' DEATH/DAY # `-NUMBER = `-(`-**77**)-"!!!~'

`-BORN MARCH 15ᵗʰ, 17**67** = (3 + 15 + 17 + 67) = (`-**102**) (SAME as **#6/**PRESIDENT) /|\ `-DIED **JUNE** 8ᵗʰ, 1845 = (6 + 8 + 18 + 45) = (`-**77**)

(67 (-) 17 (-) 15 (-) 3) = (`-**32**) = -a PROPHETIC # `-NUMBER!!!~' (102 + 32) = (`-**134**)!!!~' (34 x 2) = (`-**68**)!!!~'

`-ADD UP `-**DEATH/DAY** # `-**NUMBERS** for **#6** & **#7** = (**91** (ADAMS) + **77** (JACKSON)) = (`-**168**)!!!~'/|\ FROM `-BIRTH to `-BIRTH for these `-TWO `-PRESIDENTS; IT `-EQUALS (`-**168**) (Read Below) for PRESIDENTS **#6** & **#7**, `-Too!!!~' From `-**BIRTH** to `-**BIRTH**; and, from `-**DEATH** to `-**DEATH** = `-**EQUALS** = (`-**168**)!!!~'

THERE ARE (`-**247**) DAYS `-**IN-BETWEEN** from `-BIRTH to `-BIRTH with **#6/**PRESIDENT JOHN QUINCY ADAMS &

#**7**/PRESIDENT ANDREW JACKSON!!!~' (`-**247**) = (24 x 7) = (`-**168**)!!!~'

#**8**/PRESIDENT MARTIN VAN BUREN `-PRODUCT of `-DEATH from `-DAY of `-DEATH = (`-**168**)!!!~' #**8**/MARTIN VAN BUREN `-DAY of `-DEATH = JULY 24$^{th}$ = (**7**/**24**) = (7 x 24) = `-**168**!~' `-RECIPROCAL (MIRROR) (**7**/**24**) of **6**/ PRESIDENT JOHN QUINCY ADAMS & #**7**/PRESIDENT ANDREW JACKSON!!!~' (`-**247**) = (**24** x **7**) = (`-**168**)!!!~' #**6**, #**7**, & #**8** `-PRESIDENTS (`-ALL) `-ADD `-UP `-TOGETHER (**6**-to-**8**)!!!~' AGAIN, the `-TIME `-BETWEEN `-BIRTHS (#**6**, #**7**) PRESIDENTS (`-**24** x **7**) = `-EQUALS = the `-RECIPROCAL (MIRROR) = "To the `-DAY of `-DEATH /|\ of the `-VERY `-NEXT `-PRESIDENT #**8**/PRESIDENT MARTIN VAN BUREN (**7** x **24**)"!!!~'

#**9**/PRESIDENT WILLIAM HENRY HARRISON `-DIED at the `-AGE of (`-**68**)!~'

`-BORN FEBRUARY 9$^{th}$, 17**73** /|\ `-DIED APRIL **4**th, 18**41** /|\ (41 (-) 18) = (`-**23**) = -a PROPHETIC # `-NUMBER!!!~'

`-BIRTH = (2 + 9 + 17 + **73**) = `-**101** /|\ `-DEATH = (4 + 4 + 18 + 41) = `-**67**

(101 + 67) = (`-**168**)!!!~'

#**12**-PRESIDENT ` = ZACHARY TAYLOR `-BORN NOVEMBER 24th, 17**84** /|\ `-DIED JULY 9th, 18**50**!!!~'

(11 + 24 + 17 + 84) = (`-**136**)!!!~' /|\ (7 + 9 + 18 + 50) = (`-**84**) = DEATH/DAY # `-NUMBER = `-EQUALS = "YEAR of `-BIRTH (`-**84**)!!!~' (84 + 84) = (`-**168**)!!!~'

(84 (-) 17 (-) 24 (-) 11) = (`-**32**) = -a **PROPHETIC # `-NUMBER!!!**`~'
(136 + 32) = (`-**168**)!!!~'

`-**DIED** in (`-**1850**) = (18 + 50) = (`-**68**)!!!~'

The Prophet!~'
Mediator/Arbitrator: Dwayne W. Anderson

`-**DIED** at the `-**AGE** of (`-**33**)!!!~'

ACTRESS NAYA RIVERA'S `-**BIRTHDAY** = (1/12/19/**87**) = (1 +
12 + 19 + **87**) = (`-**119**)!!!~'

(1**98**7) = (9/8) (1/7) = (9 + 8) = 1**7** /|\ (1 + 7) = **8** /|\ (**178**) = "**DAY
of `-DEATH**"!!!~'

(**1/7**) = "WAS `-**BORN** in (`-**1**) (**JANUARY**); and, `-**DIED** in (`-**7**)
(**JULY**)"!!!~'

ACTRESS NAY RIVERA'S `-**DEATH/DAY** = (**7**/**8**/20/20) = (**7** +
8 + 20 + 20) = (`-**55**)!!!~' (55) = (**23** + **32**)!!!~'

(119 (-) 55) = (`-**64**) = (2 x 32) = (`-**232**) =
RECIPROCAL-SEQUENCING-NUMEROLOGY-RSN!!!~'

(119 + 55) = (`-**174**) = (17 x 4) = (`-**68**) = "**The** `-**MARK**"!!!~'

ACTRESS NAYA RIVERA `-**DIED** (`-1**78**) DAYS AWAY from
`-**HER** `-**BIRTHDAY!!!**~'

(366 (-) 1**78**) = (`-**188**)!!!~'

`-**BORN** in (`-**87**) = RECIPROCAL (INVERSE/MIRROR) = (`-**78**) = `-**DIED** on (`-**7/8**) with (`-1**78**) DAYS BETWEEN `-**BIRTH**; and, `-**DEATH!!!**~'

FRAGMENTED `-**BIRTH/DAY** # `-**NUMBER** = (1 + 1 + 2 + 1 + 9 + **8** + **7**) = (`-**29**)!!!~'

FRAGMENTED `-**DEATH/DAY** # `-**NUMBER** = (**7** + **8** + 2 + 0 + 2 + 0) = (`-**19**)!!!~'

(29 + 19) = (`-**48**) = RECIPROCAL (INVERSE/MIRROR) = (`-**84**)!!!~'

(48 + 84) = (`-**132**) = (32 x 1) = (`-**32**) = -a PROPHETIC # `-NUMBER!!!~'

`-**DIED** at the `-**AGE** of (`-**85**)!!!~'

SOCCER PLAYER JACK CHARLTON `-**BIRTHDAY** = (**5/8**/19/35) = (**5** + **8** + 19 + 35) = (`-**67**)!!!~'

`-**BIRTH/DAY** = (**5/8**) = (`-**58**) = RECIPROCAL (INVERSE/ MIRROR) = (`-**85**) = `-**AGE of** `-**DEATH for SOCCER PLAYER JACK CHARLTON** (`-**85**)!!!~'

(1**935**) = (935 (-) 1) = (**934**) = 9(3 + 4) = **9**(**7**) = RECIPROCAL (INVERSE/MIRROR) = **7**(**9**) = `-**DIED** the `-VERY `-NEXT `-DAY `-AFTERWARDS!!!~'

SOCCER PLAYER JACK CHARLTON `-**DEATH/DAY** = (7/10//20/20) = (7 + 10 + 20 + 20) = (`-**57**) = "WAS `-**BORN** in (`-**5**) (**MAY**); and, `-**DIED** in (`-**7**) (**JULY**)"!!!~'

II

(67 (-) 57) = (`-**10**)!!!~'

(67 + 57) = (`-**124**) = (24 (-) 1) = (`-**23**) = -a PROPHETIC # `-NUMBER!!!~'

SOCCER PLAYER JACK CHARLTON `-**DIED** (`-**63**) DAYS AWAY from `-**HIS** `-**BIRTHDAY!!!~'**

(365 (-) 63) = (`-**302**) = (32 + 0) = (`-**32**) = -a PROPHETIC # `-NUMBER!!!~'

`-**BORN** on (`-**5/8**) = RECIPROCAL (INVERSE/MIRROR) = (`-**85**) = "**AGE of** `-**DEATH**" for SOCCER PLAYER JACK CHARLTON!!!~' `-**DEATH/DAY** # `-NUMBER = (`-**57**) -(**NEXT # `-NUMBER = `-EQUALS** = (`-**58**)- while being `-MARRIED in (`-19**58**) to PAT KEMP!!!~' **JACK CHARLTON** was `-**MARRIED** for (`-**62**) **YEARS**; and, was (**6' 2**") in (`-**HEIGHT**)!!!~'

FRAGMENTED `-**BIRTH/DAY** # `-NUMBER = (5 + 8 + 1 + 9 + 3 + 5) = (`-**31**)!!!~'

FRAGMENTED `-**DEATH/DAY** # `-NUMBER = (7 + 1 + 0 + 2 + 0 + 2 + 0) = (`-**12**)!!!~'

(31 + 12) = (`-**43**) = RECIPROCAL (INVERSE/MIRROR) = (`-**34**)!!!~'

`-**DIED** at the `-**AGE** of (`-**37**)!!!~'

AUSTRALIAN MUSICIAN INXS' MICHAEL HUTCHENCE `-**BIRTHDAY** = (**1/22**/19/60) = (**1** + **22** + 19 + 60) = (`-**102**)!!!~' `-**BIRTH/DAY** = (**1/22**) = (1 + 22) = (`-**23**) = -a PROPHETIC # `-NUMBER!!!~'

`-**BIRTH/DAY** = (**1/22**) = (**ALL-IN-ONE-#-NUMBER**) = (1 + 2) (2) = (`-**32**) = "FLIP the (`-**2**) OVER to a (`-**7**)" = (`-**37**) = "**AGE of** `-**DEATH for AUSTRALIAN MUSICIAN INXS' MICHAEL HUTCHENCE** (`-**37**)"!!!~'

(**196**0) = (96 + 1) = (**97**) = "**YEAR of** `-**DEATH**"!!!~'

`-**BORN**; and, `-**DIED** on (`-**22**) / `-*DIVIDED* `-*by* (`-**2**) = (`-**11**) = (**ALL-IN-ONE-#-NUMBER**) = (`-**111**) = "WAS `-**BORN** in (`-**1**) (**JANUARY**); and, `-**DIED** in (`-**11**) (**NOVEMBER**)"!!!~'

AUSTRALIAN MUSICIAN INXS' MICHAEL HUTCHENCE `-**DEATH/DAY** = (**11/22**/19/97) = (**11** + **22** + 19 + 97) = (`-**149**) = (14 + 9) = (`-**23**) = -a PROPHETIC # `-NUMBER!!!~' (14 x 9) = (`-**126**)!!!~'

(149 (-) 102) = (`-**47**)!!!~'

(149 + 102) = (`-**251**)!!!~'

AUSTRALIAN MUSICIAN INXS' MICHAEL HUTCHENCE `-**DIED** (`-**61**) DAYS AWAY from `-**HIS** `-**BIRTHDAY!!!~'**

(365 (-) 61) = (`-**304**)!!!~'

`-**BORN** on (`-**1/22**) = "**AND; JUST** `-**ADD** a `-**ONE** (`-**1**)" = (**11/22**) = "**DAY of** `-**DEATH**"!!!~' `-**BIRTH/YEAR** = (`-**1960**) as `-**OUTLINED** `-**ABOVE** = `-**EQUALS** = (`-**97**) = "**YEAR of** `-**DEATH**"!!!~'

FRAGMENTED `-**BIRTH/DAY** # `-**NUMBER** = (**1** + **2** + **2** + **1** + 9 + 6 + 0) = (`-**21**)!!!~'

FRAGMENTED `-**DEATH/DAY** # `-**NUMBER** = (1 + **1** + **2** + **2** + **1** + 9 + 9 + 7) = (`-**32**) = "FLIP the (`-**2**) OVER to a (`-**7**)"

= (`-37) = "AGE of `-DEATH for AUSTRALIAN MUSICIAN INXS' MICHAEL HUTCHENCE (`-37)" = -a PROPHETIC # `-NUMBER!!!~'

(21 + 32) = (`-53) = RECIPROCAL (INVERSE/MIRROR) = (`-35) = "TWO `-YEARS `-AWAY from `-AGE of `-DEATH for AUSTRALIAN MUSICIAN INXS' MICHAEL HUTCHENCE (`-37)"!!!~'

`-**DIED** at the `-**AGE** of (`-**57**)!!!~'

ACTRESS KELLY PRESTON `-**BIRTHDAY** = (10/13/19/62) = (10 + 13 + 19 + 62) = (`-**104**)!!!~' `-**BIRTH/DAY** = (**10/13**) = (10 + 13) = (`-**23**) = -a PROPHETIC # `-NUMBER!!!~'

(1**962**) = (9 (-) 2) (6 (-) 1) = (**7**) (**5**) = (`-**75**) = RECIPROCAL (INVERSE/MIRROR) = (`-**57**) = "AGE of `-DEATH for `-ACTRESS KELLY PRESTON"!!!~'

(`-**59**) = "TWO `-YEARS `-AWAY from `-AGE of `-DEATH for ACTRESS KELLY PRESTON (`-**57**)!!!~'

ACTRESS KELLY PRESTON `-**DEATH/DAY** = (7/12/20/20) = (7 + 12 + 20 + 20) = (`-**59**) = (5 x 9) = (`-**45**)!!!~' "WAS `-**BORN** in (`-**10**) (**OCTOBER**); and, `-**DIED** in (`-**7**) (**JULY**)"; and, (**7/10**) `-**DIED** TWO `-DAYS `-LATER"!!!~'

(104 (-) 59) = (`-**45**)!!!~'

(104 + 59) = (`-**163**) = (63 x 1) = (`-**63**)!!!~'

(`-**6**) = RECIPROCAL (INVERSE/MIRROR) = (`-**9**)!!!~'

ACTRESS KELLY PRESTON `-**DIED** (`-**93**) DAYS AWAY from `-**HER** `-**BIRTHDAY!!!~'**

(365 (-) 93) = (`-**272**) = **RECIPROCAL-SEQUENCING-NUMEROLOGY-RSN!!!~'**

(`-**272**) = "FLIP ONE (`-**2**) OVER to a (`-**7**)" = (2 (-) 7) (7) = (`-**57**) = "**AGE of `-DEATH for `-ACTRESS KELLY PRESTON**"!!!~'

FRAGMENTED `-**BIRTH/DAY** # `-**NUMBER** = (1 + 0 + 1 + 3 + 1 + 9 + 6 + 2) = (`-**23**) = -a PROPHETIC # `-NUMBER!!!~'

FRAGMENTED `-**DEATH/DAY** # `-**NUMBER** = (7 + 1 + 2 + 2 + 0 + 2 + 0) = (`-**14**)!!!~'

(23 + 14) = (`-**37**) = RECIPROCAL (INVERSE/MIRROR) = (`-**73**)!!!~'

(73 (-) 37) = (`-**36**) = "FLIP the (`-**6**) OVER to a (`-**9**)" = (`-**39**) = RECIPROCAL (INVERSE/MIRROR) = (`-**93**) = "**DAYS in `-DEATH `-AWAY from `-BIRTHDAY**"!!!~'

`-**DIED** at the `-**AGE** of (`-**27**)!!!~'

BENJAMIN KEOUGH (LISE MARIE PRESLEY'S SON) `-**BIRTHDAY** = (10/21/19/92) = (10 + 21 + 19 + 92) = (`-**142**)!!!~' (2) (14 / 2) = (`-**27**) = "**AGE of `-DEATH**"!!!~'

(1**9**9**2**) = (1 + 9) (9 + 2) = (**10**) (**11**) = `-EQUALS = (**OCTOBER 11**[th])!!!~'

(1**9**9**2**) = (9 (-) 2) (1 + 9) = (**7**) (**10**) = `-EQUALS = (**JULY 10**[th]) = "**DIED `-TWO `-DAYS `-LATER**"!!!~'

BENJAMIN KEOUGH (LISE MARIE PRESLEY'S SON) `-**DEATH/DAY** = (7/12/20/20) = (7 + 12 + 20 + 20) = (`-**59**)!!!~' "WAS `-**BORN** in (`-**10**) (**OCTOBER**); and, `-**DIED** in (`-**7**) (**JULY**)"; and, (**7/10**) `-**DIED** TWO `-**DAYS** `-**LATER**"!!!~'

`-**DEATH/DAY** = (**7/12**) = RECIPROCAL (INVERSE/MIRROR) = (**21/7**) = (27 x 1) = (`-**27**) = "**AGE of** `-**DEATH for BENJAMIN KEOUGH (LISE MARIE PRESLEY'S SON**)!!!~'

(142 (-) 59) = (`-**83**)!!!~'

(142 + 59) = (`-**201**) = (21 + 0) = (`-**21**) = "**WAS** `-**BORN** on the (`-**21**ˢᵗ)"!!!~'

BENJAMIN KEOUGH (LISE MARIE PRESLEY'S SON) `-**DIED** (`-**101**) DAYS AWAY from `-**HIS** `-**BIRTHDAY**!!!~'

(365 (-) 101) = (`-**264**) = (64 x 2) = (`-**128**) = (28 (-) 1) = (`-**27**) = "**AGE of** `-**DEATH for BENJAMIN KEOUGH (LISE MARIE PRESLEY'S SON**)!!!~'

Was `-**BORN** on a (`-**21**ˢᵗ); and, `-**DIED** on a (`-**12**ᵗʰ)!!!~' (`-**21**) = RECIPROCAL (INVERSE/MIRROR) = (`-**12**)!!!~'

FRAGMENTED `-**BIRTH/DAY** # `-**NUMBER** = (1 + 0 + 2 + 1 + 1 + 9 + 9 + 2) = (`-**25**) = "**TWO** `-**YEARS** `-**AWAY** from `-**AGE of** `-**DEATH for BENJAMIN KEOUGH (LISE MARIE PRESLEY'S SON**) (`-**27**)!!!~'

FRAGMENTED `-**DEATH/DAY** # `-**NUMBER** = (7 + 1 + 2 + 2 + 0 + 2 + 0) = (`-**14**)!!!~'

(25 + 14) = (`-**39**) = RECIPROCAL (INVERSE/MIRROR) = (`-**93**)!!!~'

(93 (-) 39) = (`-**54**) / `-*DIVIDED* `-*by* (`-**2**) = (`-**27**) = "AGE of `-DEATH for BENJAMIN KEOUGH (LISE MARIE PRESLEY'S SON)!!!~'

`-**DIED** at the `-**AGE** of (`-**58**)!!!~'

AMERICAN SCHOOLTEACHER MARY KAY LETOURNEAU `-**BIRTHDAY** = (1/30/19/62) = (**1** + **30** + 19 + 62) = (`-**112**)!!!~'

(1**962**) = (9 (-) 2) (6 (-) 1) = (**7**) (**5**) = (`-**75**) = RECIPROCAL (INVERSE/MIRROR) = (`-**57**) = "DIED the `-VERY `-NEXT `-YEAR at (`-**58**)"!!!~'

AMERICAN SCHOOLTEACHER MARY KAY LETOURNEAU `-**DEATH/DAY** = (7/6/20/20) = (**7** + **6** + 20 + 20) = (`-**53**)!!!~' "WAS `-**BORN** in (`-**1**) (**JANUARY**); and, `-**DIED** in (`-**7**) (**JULY**)"; and, (**7/1**) /|\ (7 (-) 1) = (`-**6**) = (`-**7/6**) = `-**DAY** of `-**DEATH**"!!!~'

(19 + 62 + 20 + 20) = (`-**121**) = "SWIPE 1" = `-BIRTH/DAY # `-NUMBER (`-**112**)!!!~'

(112 (-) 53) = (`-**59**)!!!~'

(112 + 53) = (`-**165**)!!!~'

AMERICAN SCHOOLTEACHER MARY KAY LETOURNEAU `-**DIED** (`-**158**) DAYS AWAY from `-**HER** `-**BIRTHDAY; WHILE** `-**DYING** at the `-**AGE** of (`-**58**)!!!~'

(366 (-) 158) = (`-**208**)!!!~'

`-**BIRTH** (**1/30**) = (1 + 30) = (`-**31**); and, `-**DEATH** (**7/6**) = (7 + 6) = (`-**13**)!!!~' (`-**31**) = RECIPROCAL (INVERSE/MIRROR) = (`-**13**)!!!~'

FRAGMENTED `-**BIRTH/DAY** # `-**NUMBER** = (1 + 3 + 0 + 1 + 9 + 6 + 2) = (`-**22**)!!!~'

FRAGMENTED `-**DEATH/DAY** # `-**NUMBER** = (7 + 6 + 2 + 0 + 2 + 0) = (`-**17**)!!!~'

(22 + 17) = (`-**39**) = RECIPROCAL (INVERSE/MIRROR) = (`-**93**)!!!~'

(93 + 39) = (`-**132**) = (32 x 1) = (`-**32**) = -a PROPHETIC # `-NUMBER!!!~'

`-**DIED** at the `-**AGE** of (`-**41**)!!!~'

CANADIAN ACTOR NICK CORDERO `-**BIRTHDAY** = (**9/17**/19/**78**) = (**9** + **17** + 19 + **78**) = (`-**123**)!!!~' (`-**123**) = (23 x 1) = (`-**23**) = -a PROPHETIC # `-NUMBER!!!~'

"WAS `-**BORN** on (`-**17**ᵗʰ); and, `-**DIED** in (`-**7**) (**JULY**)"; and, (**7/1**) /|\ (7 (-) 1) = (`-**6**) = (`-**7/6**) = `-**DAY** after `-**DEATH**"!!!~'

(1**978**) = (1 + 7) (9 + 8) = (**8**) (**17**) = `-*EQUALS* = (**AUGUST** 17ᵗʰ) = `-**BORN** the `-**NEXT** `-**MONTH**; and, (`-**81**7) = (87 x 1) = (`-**87**) = RECIPROCAL (INVERSE/MIRROR) = (`-**78**) = `-**BORN** in (`-**78**)!!!~'

(1**978**) = (8 + 1) (9 + 7) = (**9**) (**16**) = `-*EQUALS* = (**SEPTEMBER** 16ᵗʰ) = "**BORN** the `-**VERY** `-**NEXT** `-**DAY**"!!!~'

CANADIAN ACTOR NICK CORDERO `-**DEATH/DAY** = (**7**/**5**/20/20) = (**7** + **5** + 20 + 20) = (`-**52**)!!!~' "FLIP the (`-**2**) OVER to a (`-**7**)" = (`-**57**) = RECIPROCAL (INVERSE/MIRROR) = (`-**75**) = "**DAY** of `-**DEATH** for CANADIAN ACTOR NICK CORDERO"!!!~'

(123 (-) 52) = (`-**71**)!!!~'

(123 + 52) = (`-**175**) = (75 x 1) = (`-**75**) = (JULY 5th) = "**DAY** of `-**DEATH** for CANADIAN ACTOR NICK CORDERO"!!!~'

CANADIAN ACTOR NICK CORDERO `-**DIED** (`-**74**) DAYS AWAY from `-**HIS** `-**BIRTHDAY!!!**~' (`-**74**) = "**WHILE DYING on** (`-**75**)"!!!~'

(365 (-) 74) = (`-**291**) = (91 x 2) = (`-**182**) = (82 x 1) = (`-**82**) / `-*DIVIDED* `-*by* (`-**2**) = (`-**41**) = "**AGE** of `-**DEATH** for CANADIAN ACTOR NICK CORDERO (`-**41**)"!!!~'

`-**BIRTH/DAY** = (**9/17**) = (9 x 17) = (`-**153**)!!!~' `-**DEATH/DAY** = (**7/5**) = (7 x 5) = (`-**35**)!!!~' (`-**35**) = RECIPROCAL (INVERSE/MIRROR) = (`-**53**)!!!~'

/|\ FRAGMENTED `-**BIRTH/DAY** # `-**NUMBER** = (9 + 1 + 7 + 1 + 9 + **7** + **8**) = (`-**42**) = "**ONE** `-**YEAR** `-**AWAY** from `-**AGE** of `-**DEATH** for CANADIAN ACTOR NICK CORDERO (`-**41**)"!!!~' `-**DIED** in the `-**YEAR** `-**OF** (`-**42**)!!!~' /|\

FRAGMENTED `-**DEATH/DAY** # `-**NUMBER** = (**7** + **5** + 2 + 0 + 2 + 0) = (`-**16**)!!!~'

(42 + 16) = (`-**58**) = RECIPROCAL (INVERSE/MIRROR) = (`-**85**)!!!~'

(58 + 85) = (`-**143**) = (43 (-) 1) = (`-**42**) = "ONE `-YEAR `-AWAY from AGE of `-DEATH for CANADIAN ACTOR NICK CORDERO (`-**41**)"!!!~' `-**DIED** in the `-**YEAR** `-**OF** (`-**42**)!!!~'

`-**BIRTH/YEAR** = (`-**78**); and, `-**DEATH/DAY** = (`-**75**)!!!~'

(78 + 75) = (`-**153**) = "SEE `-**ABOVE**"!!!~'

`-**DIED** at the `-**AGE** of (`-**69**)!!!~'

ENGLISH SINGER/SONGWRITER DAVID BOWIE `-**BIRTHDAY** = (**1**/**8**/19/**47**) = (**1** + **8** + 19 + **47**) = (`-**75**)!!!~' (`-**47**) = RECIPROCAL (INVERSE/MIRROR) = (`-**74**)!!!~'

"WAS `-**BORN** in (`-**1**) (JANUARY); and, `-**DIED** in (`-**1**) (**JANUARY**)"; and, (**1/1**) = (`-**11**) = "**DIED** the `-**DAY** `-**BEFORE**"!!!~'

(19**47**) = (1 + 4) (9 + 7) = (**5**) (**16**) = (5 + 1) (6) = "**FLIP** the (`-**6**) OVER to a (`-**9**)" = (`-**69**) = "AGE of `-**DEATH** for ENGLISH SINGER/SONGWRITER **DAVID BOWIE** (`-**69**)"!!!~'

(19**47**) = (4 (-) 1) (9 (-) 7) = (**3**) (**2**) = `-*EQUALS* = (`-**32**) = -a PROPHETIC # `-NUMBER"!!!~'

ENGLISH SINGER/SONGWRITER DAVID BOWIE `-**DEATH/DAY** = (**1**/**10**/20/16) = (**1** + **10** + 20 + 16) = (`-**47**)!!!~' WAS `-**BORN** in (`-**47**)!!!~'

(75 (-) 47) = (`-**28**)!!!~'

(75 + 47) = (`-**122**) = (22 + 1) = (`-**23**) = -a PROPHETIC # `-NUMBER"!!!~'

ENGLISH SINGER/SONGWRITER DAVID BOWIE `-**DIED** (`-**2**) DAYS AWAY from `-**HIS** `-**BIRTHDAY!!!**~'

(365 (-) 2) = (`-**363**) = (33) (6) = (3 + 3) (6) = "**FLIP** the (`-**6**) OVER to a (`-**9**)" = (`-**69**) = "**AGE of** `-**DEATH** for ENGLISH SINGER/ SONGWRITER **DAVID BOWIE** (`-**69**)"!!!~'

FRAGMENTED `-**BIRTH/DAY** # `-**NUMBER** = (1 + 8 + 1 + 9 + 4 + 7) = (`-**30**)!!!~'

FRAGMENTED `-**DEATH/DAY** # `-**NUMBER** = (1 + 1 + 0 + 2 + 0 + 1 + 6) = (`-**11**)!!!~'

(30 + 11) = (`-**41**) = RECIPROCAL (INVERSE/MIRROR) = (`-**14**)!!!~'

`-**DIED** at the `-**AGE** of (`-**65**)!!!~'

AMERICAN ACTOR HARRY ANDERSON `-**BIRTHDAY** = (**10**/**14**/19/**52**) = (**10** + **14** + 19 + **52**) = (`-**95**)!!!~' (`-**95**) = RECIPROCAL (INVERSE/MIRROR) = (`-**59**)!!!~'

/|\ `-**BIRTH/DAY** # `-**NUMBER** = (`-**95**) = "FLIP the (`-**9**) OVER to a (`-**6**)" = (`-**65**) = `-**AGE of** `-**DEATH** for **AMERICAN ACTOR HARRY ANDERSON** (`-**65**)"!!!~' /|\

`-**BIRTH/DAY** = (**10/14**) = (10 + 14) = (`-**24**) = (6 x 4) = (`-**64**) = "**ONE** `-**YEAR** `-**AWAY** from `-**AGE of** `-**DEATH** for **AMERICAN ACTOR HARRY ANDERSON** (`-**65**)"!!!~'

"WAS `-**BORN** in (`-**10**) (OCTOBER); and, `-**DIED** in (`-**4**) (**APRIL**)"; and, (**10/4**) = `-**BIRTH/DAY** = (**10/14**)!!!~'

(19**52**) = (2 (-) 1) (9 + 5) = (**1**) (**14**) = `-*EQUALS* = **JUST** `-**ADD** a `-**ZERO** (`-**0**) = (**10/14**) = (**OCTOBER** 14th) = `-**BIRTH/DAY!!!**~'

(19**52**) = (1 + 5) (9 + 2) = (**6**) (**11**) = `-*EQUALS* = (**6 x 11**) = (`-**66**) = "**DIED** the `-**YEAR** `-**OF** /|\ for `-**AGE**"!!!~'

AMERICAN ACTOR HARRY ANDERSON `-**DEATH/DAY** = (**4/16**/20/18) = (**4** + **16** + 20 + 18) = (`-**58**)!!!~' `-**DEATH/DAY** = (**4/16**) = (46 x 1) = (`-**46**) = RECIPROCAL (INVERSE/MIRROR) = (`-**64**) = Was (**6' 4"**) in (`-**HEIGHT**)!!!~' `-**DEATH/DAY** = (**4/16**) = (4 + 1) (6) = (`-**56**) = RECIPROCAL (INVERSE/MIRROR) = (`-**65**) = "**AGE of** `-**DEATH for AMERICAN ACTOR HARRY ANDERSON** (`-**65**)"!!!~'

`-**DEATH/DAY** = (**4/16**) = RECIPROCAL (INVERSE/MIRROR) = (`-**61/4**) = (61 + 4) = (`-**65**) = "**AGE of** `-**DEATH for AMERICAN ACTOR HARRY ANDERSON** (`-**65**)"!!!~'

(95 (-) 58) = (`-**37**)!!!~'

(95 + 58) = (`-**153**) = (53 x 1) = (`-**53**) = RECIPROCAL (INVERSE/ MIRROR) = (`-**35**)!!!~'

AMERICAN ACTOR HARRY ANDERSON `-**DIED** (`-**184**) DAYS AWAY from `-**HIS** `-**BIRTHDAY!!!**~' (`-**184**) = (14 x 8) = (`-**112**) / `-2 = (`-**56**) = RECIPROCAL (INVERSE/MIRROR) = (`-**65**) = "**AGE of** `-**DEATH for AMERICAN ACTOR HARRY ANDERSON** (`-**65**)"!!!~'

(365 (-) 184) = (`-**181**)!!!~'

`-**BIRTH/DAY** = (**10/14**) = (10 (-) 1) (4) = (**9/4**) /|\ `-**DEATH/DAY** = (**4/16**) = (4 x 1) (6) = "**FLIP** the (`-**6**) OVER to a (`-**9**)" = (**4/9**) = (`-**RECIPROCAL/INVERSE/MIRRORS**-`)!!!~'

`-**BIRTH/DAY** = (**10/14**) /|\ `-**DEATH/DAY** = (**4/16**) = (4 + 6) (1) = (**10/1**) = "FIRST (`-**3**) `-THREE `-DIGITS of `-**BIRTH/DAY**"!!!~'

FRAGMENTED `-**BIRTH/DAY** # `-**NUMBER** = (1 + 0 + 1 + 4 + 1 + 9 + 5 + 2) = (`-**23**) = -a PROPHETIC # `-**NUMBER**!!!~'

FRAGMENTED `-**DEATH/DAY** # `-**NUMBER** = (4 + 1 + 6 + 2 + 0 + 1 + 8) = (`-**22**)!!!~'

(23 + 22) = (`-**45**) = RECIPROCAL (INVERSE/MIRROR) = (`-**54**)!!!~'

`-**DIED** at the `-**AGE** of (`-**80**)!!!~'

CIVIL RIGHTS LEADER REPRESENTATIVE JOHN LEWIS `-**BIRTHDAY** = (**2/21**/19/**40**) = (**2** + **21** + *19* + **40**) = (`-**82**)!!!~' (`-**82**) = RECIPROCAL (INVERSE/MIRROR) = (`-**28**)!!!~' `-**BORN** in (`-**40**); and, `-**DIED** in (**20** + **20**)!!!~'

(`-**82**) = "TWO `-YEARS `-AWAY from `-AGE of `-DEATH for CIVIL RIGHTS LEADER REPRESENTATIVE JOHN LEWIS (`-**80**)"!!!~'

`-**BIRTH/DAY** = (**2/21**) = (2 + 21) = (`-**23**) = -a PROPHETIC # `-**NUMBER**!!!~'

WAS `-MARRIED in (`-**68**); and, `-ELECTED to `-CONGRESS in (`-**86**)!!!~' (`-**86**) = RECIPROCAL (INVERSE/MIRROR) = (`-**68**)!!!~' MARRIED from (`-19**68** to 20**12**) to LILLIAN MILES!!!~' (68 + 12) = (`-**80**) = "AGE of `-DEATH for CIVIL RIGHTS LEADER REPRESENTATIVE JOHN LEWIS (`-**80**)"!!!~'

"WAS `-**BORN** in (`-**2**) (FEBRUARY); and, `-**DIED** in (`-**7**) (**JULY**)"; and, (**2/7**) = (7 (-) 2) = (`-**5**) = "The `-**HAND** of `-**GOD**"!!!~'

(**1940**) = (9 (-) 0) (1 + 4) = (**9**) (**5**) = `-*EQUALS* = (**95**) = "**AGE** of `-**DEATH** of CIVIL RIGHTS LEADER **C. T. VIVIAN** who had `-**DIED** on the `-VERY `-SAME `-DAY as CIVIL RIGHTS LEADER REPRESENTATIVE JOHN LEWIS" (**7**/1**7**) of (**20/20**)!!!~'

C.T. VIVIAN was `-**BORN** in (`-**24**); and, `-**DIED** on (**7/17**) = (7 + 17) = (`-**24**)!!!~'

C.T. VIVIAN was `-**BORN** on (7/30/19/24) = (7 + 30 + 19 + 24) = (`-**80**) = "**AGE** of `-**DEATH** for CIVIL RIGHTS LEADER REPRESENTATIVE JOHN LEWIS (`-**80**)"!!!~'

(**1940**) = (10) (9 + 4) = (**10**) (**13**) = `-*EQUALS* = (**10 + 13**) = (`-**23**) = -a PROPHETIC # `-NUMBER!!!~'

CIVIL RIGHTS LEADER REPRESENTATIVE JOHN LEWIS `-**DEATH/DAY** = (**7**/1**7**/20/20) = (**7** + **17** + 20 + 20) = (`-**64**)!!!~' (`-**64**) = (`-**2**) x (`-**32**) = (`-**232**) = **RECIPROCAL-SEQUENCING-NUMEROLOGY-RSN**!!!~'

`-**DEATH/DAY** = (**7/17**) = (7 x 17) = (`-**119**) = RECIPROCAL (INVERSE/MIRROR) = (`-**911**)!!!~'

(82 (-) 64) = (`-**18**)!!!~'

(82 + 64) = (`-**146**) = (46 x 1) = (`-**46**) = RECIPROCAL (INVERSE/ MIRROR) = (`-**64**) = `-**DEATH/DAY** # `-**NUMBER**!!!~'

CIVIL RIGHTS LEADER REPRESENTATIVE JOHN LEWIS `-**DIED** (`-**147**) DAYS AWAY from `-**HIS** `-**BIRTHDAY**!!!~' (`-**147**)

= (47 (-) 1) = (`-**46**) = RECIPROCAL (INVERSE/MIRROR) = (`-**64**) = `-**DEATH/DAY** # `-**NUMBER!!!**~'

(**147**) = (17 x 4) = (`-**68**) = WAS `-**MARRIED** in (`-**68**)!!!~'

(366 (-) 147) = (`-**219**) = "REMEMBER (`-**2**) (`-**19's**) for `-FRAGMENTED `-BIRTH/DAY # `-NUMBER; and, `-FRAGMENTED `-DEATH/DAY # `-NUMBERS `-BELOW"!!!~'

NON-LEAP YEAR for CIVIL RIGHTS LEADER REPRESENTATIVE JOHN LEWIS = `-EQUALS = (`-**146**) = "DAYS AWAY from `-BIRTH/DAY to `-DEATH/DAY = `-BIRTH/DAY # `-NUMBER & `-DEATH/DAY # `-NUMBER /|\ `-ADDED `-UP `-TOGETHER /|\ = (`-**146**)"!!!~'

`-**BIRTH/DAY** = (**2/21**) = "**FLIP** the (`-**2**) OVER to a (`-**7**)" = `-**DEATH/DAY** = (**7/71**) = "**SWIPE 1**" = (**7/17**) = `-**DEATH/DAY!!!**~'

FRAGMENTED `-**BIRTH/DAY** # `-**NUMBER** = (2 + 2 + 1 + 1 + 9 + 4 + 0) = (`-**19**)!!!~'

FRAGMENTED `-**DEATH/DAY** # `-**NUMBER** = (7 + 1 + 7 + 2 + 0 + 2 + 0) = (`-**19**)!!!~'

(19 + 19) = (`-**38**) = RECIPROCAL (INVERSE/MIRROR) = (`-**83**) = "**THREE** `-**YEARS** `-**AWAY** from `-**AGE** of `-**DEATH** for **CIVIL RIGHTS LEADER REPRESENTATIVE JOHN LEWIS** (`-**80**)"!!!~'

`-**DIED** at the `-**AGE** of (`-**90**)!!!~'

AMERICAN COMEDIAN DON RICKLES `-**BIRTHDAY** = (**5**/**8**/19/**26**) = (**5** + **8** + 19 + **26**) = (`-**58**)!!!~' `-**BIRTHDAY #** `-**NUMBER** (`-**58**) = `-**EQUALS** = `-**BIRTH/DAY** of (**5/8**)!!!~'

(`-**58**) = RECIPROCAL (INVERSE/MIRROR) = (`-**85**) = "**FIVE** `-**YEARS** `-**AWAY** from `-**AGE** of `-**DEATH** for AMERICAN COMEDIAN DON RICKLES (`-**90**)!!!~'

MARRIED to BARBARA RICKLES from (`-1965 to `-2017) = (2017 (-) 1965) = (`-**52**) / `-*DIVIDED* `-*by* (`-**2**) = (`-**26**) = "**WAS** `-**BORN** in (`-**26**)"!!!~'

"WAS `-**BORN** in (`-**5**) (MAY); and, `-**DIED** in (`-**4**) (**APRIL**)"; and, (**5/4**) = RECIPROCAL (INVERSE/MIRROR) = (**4/5**) = "AMERICAN COMEDIAN DON RICKLES **DIED** the `-VERY `-NEXT `-DAY (**4/6**)"!!!~' (45 + 45) = (`-**90**) = "**AGE** of `-**DEATH** for AMERICAN COMEDIAN DON RICKLES (`-**90**)"!!!~'

`-**BIRTH/DAY** = (**5/8**); and, `-**DEATH/DAY** = (**4/6**) = (5 + 8 + 4 + 6) = (`-**23**) = RECIPROCAL (INVERSE/MIRROR) = (`-**32**) = -a PROPHETIC # `-**NUMBER**!!!~'

(**19**2**6**) = (9 (-) 6) (1 + 2) = (**3**) (**3**) = `-*EQUALS* = **JUST** `-**ADD** a `-**THREE** (`-**3**) = (**333**) = `-*DAYS* `-*AWAY* from `-**BIRTH/DAY** to `-**DEATH/DAY**!!!~'

AMERICAN COMEDIAN DON RICKLES `-**DEATH/DAY** = (**4/6**/20/17) = (**4** + **6** + 20 + 17) = (`-**47**)!!!~' `-**DIED** the `-**DAY** `-**BEFORE** (**4/6**)!!!~'

(58 (-) 47) = (`-**11**)!!!~'

(58 + 47) = (`-**105**) = (15 + 0) = (`-**15**) = (15 + 11) = (`-**26**) = **"YEAR of `-BIRTH (`-26)"!!!~'**

AMERICAN COMEDIAN DON RICKLES `-**DIED** (`-**32**) DAYS AWAY from `-**HIS** `-**BIRTHDAY!!!~'** (`-**32**) = -a PROPHETIC # `-NUMBER!!!~'

(365 (-) 32) = (`-**333**)!!!~'

`-**BIRTHDAY** # `-**NUMBER** (`-**58**) = `-**EQUALS** = `-**BIRTH/ DAY** of (**5/8**)!!!~'

`-**DEATH/DAY** = (**4/6**) = `-**BIRTH/YEAR** = (**1926**) = (19 + 26) = (`-**45**); and, `-**DEATH/DAY** # `-**NUMBER** = (`-**47**) = AMERICAN COMEDIAN DON RICKLES `-**DIED RIGHT** in `-**BETWEEN** (45,(**46**),47)!!!~'

FRAGMENTED `-**BIRTH/DAY** # `-**NUMBER** = (5 + 8 + 1 + 9 + 2 + 6) = (`-**31**) = RECIPROCAL (INVERSE/MIRROR) = (`-**13**) = **"A VERY PIVOTAL # `-NUMBER"!!!~'**

FRAGMENTED `-**DEATH/DAY** # `-**NUMBER** = (4 + 6 + 2 + 0 + 1 + 7) = (`-**20**)!!!~'

(31 + 20) = (`-**51**) = RECIPROCAL (INVERSE/MIRROR) = (`-**15**)!!!~'

`-**DIED** at the `-**AGE** of (`-**90**)!!!~'

AMERICAN SINGER/SONGWRITER CHUCK BERRY `-**BIRTHDAY** = (**10/18**/19/**26**) = (**10** + **18** + 19 + **26**) = (`-**73**)!!!~'

`-**BIRTH/DAY** = (**10/18**) = RECIPROCAL (INVERSE/MIRROR) = (**81/01**) = (**ALL-IN-ONE-#-NUMBER**) = (8 + 1) (1 x 0) = (`-**90**) = "**AGE of** `-**DEATH** for AMERICAN SINGER/SONGWRITER CHUCK BERRY (`-**90**)"!!!~'

`-**BIRTH/DAY** = (**10/18**) = (10 x 18) = (`-**180**) / (`-**2**) = (`-**90**) = "**AGE of** `-**DEATH** for AMERICAN SINGER/SONGWRITER CHUCK BERRY (`-**90**)"!!!~'

MARRIED to THEMETTA SUGGS from (`-1948 to `-2017) = (2017 (-) 1948) = (`-**69**) = (**YIN/YANG**) = (6 + 9) = (`-**15**)!!!~'

(6 x 9) = (`-**54**) = RECIPROCAL (INVERSE/MIRROR) = (`-**45**) x `-*TIMES* (`-**2**) = (`-**90**) = "**AGE of** `-**DEATH** for AMERICAN SINGER/SONGWRITER CHUCK BERRY (`-**90**)"!!!~'

"WAS `-**BORN** in (`-**10**) (OCTOBER); and, `-**DIED** in (`-**3**) (**MARCH**)"; and, (**10/3**) = (OCTOBER 3rd) = (`-**15**) DAYS AWAY from `-HIS `-**BIRTH/DAY**!!!~' RECIPROCAL (INVERSE/MIRROR) = (**3/10**) = (MARCH 10th) = (`-**8**) DAYS AWAY from `-HIS `-**DEATH/DAY**!!!~' (15 + 8) = (`-**23**) = -a PROPHETIC # `-NUMBER!!!~'

`-**BIRTH/YEAR** = (`-**1926**) = (19 + 26) = (`-**45**) = (45 x (`-**2**) = (`-**90**) = "**AGE of** `-**DEATH** for AMERICAN SINGER/SONGWRITER CHUCK BERRY (`-**90**)"!!!~'

(**1926**) = (9 + 6) (1 + 2) = (**15**) (**3**) = `-*EQUALS* = (15 x 3) = (`-**45**) x (`-2) = (`-**90**) = "**AGE of** `-**DEATH** for AMERICAN SINGER/SONGWRITER CHUCK BERRY (`-**90**)"!!!~'

AMERICAN SINGER/SONGWRITER CHUCK BERRY `-**DEATH/DAY** = (**3/18**/20/17) = (**3** + **18** + 20 + 17) = (`-**58**)!!!~'

`-**DEATH/DAY** = (**3/18**) = (3 x 18) = (`-**54**) = (6 x 9) = (`-**69**)!!!~'

`-**DEATH/YEAR** = (`-20/1**7**) = (**ALL-IN-ONE-#-NUMBER**) = (2 + 7) (0 x 1) = (`-**90**) = "**AGE of** `-**DEATH for AMERICAN SINGER/SONGWRITER CHUCK BERRY** (`-**90**)"!!!~'

(73 (-) 58) = (`-**15**)!!!~'

(73 + 58) = (`-**131**) = (13 x 1) = (`-**13**) = "A VERY PIVOTAL # `-NUMBER"!!!~'

AMERICAN SINGER/SONGWRITER CHUCK BERRY `-**DIED** (`-**151**) DAYS AWAY from `-**HIS** `-**BIRTHDAY**!!!~' (`-**151**) = **RECIPROCAL-SEQUENCING-NUMEROLOGY-RSN**!!!~'

(365 (-) 151) = (`-**214**) = (21 x 4) = (`-**84**) = RECIPROCAL (INVERSE/MIRROR) = (`-**48**) = "WAS `-**MARRIED** to THEMETTA SUGGS **in** (`-19**48**)"!!!~'

(365 (-) 151) = (`-**214**) = (14 x 2) = (`-**28**) = FRAGMENTED `-**BIRTH/DAY** # `-**NUMBER** (`-**28**)!!!~'

WAS `-**BORN** on an (`-**18**th); and, `-**DIED** on an (`-**18**th)!!!~'

FRAGMENTED `-**BIRTH/DAY** # `-**NUMBER** = (1 + 0 + 1 + 8 + 1 + 9 + 2 + 6) = (`-**28**) = RECIPROCAL (INVERSE/MIRROR) = (`-**82**)!!!~'

FRAGMENTED `-**DEATH/DAY** # `-**NUMBER** = (3 + 1 + 8 + 2 + 0 + 1 + 7) = (`-**22**)!!!~'

(28 + 22) = (`-**50**) = RECIPROCAL (INVERSE/MIRROR) = (`-**05**)!!!~'

(50 + 05) = (`-**55**) = (`-**23**) + (`-**32**)!!!~'

AMERICAN SINGER/SONGWRITER **CHUCK BERRY** was a (`-**RECIPROCAL/INVERSE/MIRROR**) of AMERICAN COMEDIAN **DON RICKLES!!!**~'

`-**PLEASE; GO** `-**BACK; and,** `-**REVIEW!!!**~'

`-**DIED** at the `-**AGE** of (`-**87**)!!!~'

AMERICAN MUSICIAN LITTLE RICHARD `-**BIRTHDAY** = (**12**/**5**/*19*/**32**) = (**12** + **5** + *19* + **32**) = (`-**68**)!!!~' (`-**68**) = RECIPROCAL (INVERSE/MIRROR) = (`-**86**) = **"ONE `-YEAR `-AWAY from `-AGE of `-DEATH for AMERICAN MUSICIAN LITTLE RICHARD (`-87)"**!!!~'

`-**PART** of `-**BIRTH/DAY** = (**5/19**) = (59 x 1) = (`-**59**) = (**5/9**) = `-**DEATH/DAY** = (MAY 9th)!!!~'

MARRIED to ERNESTINE CAMPBELL from (`-19**59** to `-19**63**) = (1963 (-) 1959) = (`-**4**)!!!~' WAS `-**MARRIED** in (`-**59**); and, `-**DIED** on (**5/9**)!!!~'

"WAS `-**BORN** in (`-**12**) (DECEMBER); and, `-**DIED** in (`-**5**) (**MAY**)"; and, (**12/5**) = `-**BIRTH/DAY** = (**DECEMBER 5th**)!!!~'

`-**BIRTH/DAY** = (**12/5**); and, `-**DEATH/DAY** = (**5/9**) = (12 + 5 + 5 + 9) = (`-**31**) = RECIPROCAL (INVERSE/MIRROR) = (`-**13**) = **"A VERY PIVOTAL # `-NUMBER"**!!!~'

(**19**_**32**_) = (92) (-) (1 + 3) = (**92 (-) 4**) = `-*EQUALS* = (`-**88**) = `-**YEAR** of `-**DEATH!!!**~'

AMERICAN MUSICIAN LITTLE RICHARD `-**DEATH/DAY** = (**5**/**9**/20/20) = (**5** + **9** + 20 + 20) = (`-**54**)!!!~' `-**DIED** `-**FIVE** `-**DAYS** `-**LATER** (**5/9**)!!!~'

(`-**54**) = RECIPROCAL (INVERSE/MIRROR) = (`-**45**) = `-**DEATH/DAY** = (**5** x **9**) = (`-**5/9**)!!!~'

(68 (-) 54) = (`-**14**)!!!~'

(68 + 54) = (`-**122**) = (22 + 1) = (`-**23**) = -a PROPHETIC # `-NUMBER!!!~'

AMERICAN MUSICIAN LITTLE RICHARD `-**DIED** (`-**156**) DAYS AWAY from `-**HIS** `-**BIRTHDAY**!!!~' (15 x 6) = (`-**90**) = "**THREE** `-**YEARS** `-**AWAY from** `-**AGE of** `-**DEATH for** **AMERICAN MUSICIAN LITTLE RICHARD** (`-**87**)"!!!~'

(`-**156**) = (56 x 1) = (`-**56**) = (8 x 7) = (`-**87**) = "**AGE of** `-**DEATH** **for AMERICAN MUSICIAN LITTLE RICHARD** (`-**87**)"!!!~'

(366 (-) 156) = (`-**210**) = (21 + 0) = (`-**21**) = RECIPROCAL (INVERSE/MIRROR) = (`-**12**)!!!~'

FRAGMENTED `-**BIRTH/DAY** # `-**NUMBER** = (1 + 2 + 5 + 1 + 9 + 3 + 2) = (`-**23**) = RECIPROCAL (INVERSE/MIRROR) = (`-**32**) = -a PROPHETIC # `-NUMBER **&** `-**HE was** `-**BORN in** (`-**32**)"!!!~'

FRAGMENTED `-**DEATH/DAY** # `-**NUMBER** = (5 + 9 + 2 + 0 + 2 + 0) = (`-**18**) = RECIPROCAL (INVERSE/MIRROR) = (`-**81**)!!!~'

(23 + 18) = (`-**41**) = RECIPROCAL (INVERSE/MIRROR) = (`-**14**)!!!~'

(41 + 14) = (`-**55**) = (`-**23**) + (`-**32**)!!!~'

`-**DIED** at the `-**AGE** of (`-**88**)!!!~'

AMERICAN JOURNALIST JIMMY BRESLIN `-**BIRTHDAY** = (**10/17**/19/**28**) = (**10** + **17** + 19 + **28**) = (`-**74**) = RECIPROCAL (INVERSE/MIRROR) = (`-**47**)!!!~'

`-**BIRTH/YEAR** = (`-**1928**) = (19 + 28) = (`-**47**) = RECIPROCAL (INVERSE/MIRROR) = (`-**74**) = `-**BIRTH/DAY** # `-**NUMBER** (`-**74**)!!!~'

`-**BIRTH/DAY** = (**10/17**) = (10 x 17) = (`-**170**) = (17 + 0) = (`-**17**) = "**DAY of** `-**BIRTH** (`-**17**[th]); and, `-**YEAR of** `-**DEATH** (`-**17**)"!!!~'

MARRIED to RONNIE ELDRIDGE from (`-19**82** to `-20**17**) = (2017 (-) 1982) = (`-**35**) = RECIPROCAL (INVERSE/MIRROR) = (`-**53**)!!!~'

"WAS `-**BORN** in (`-**10**) (OCTOBER); and, `-**DIED** in (`-**3**) (**MARCH**)"; and, (**10/3**) = (OCTOBER 3rd) = (`-**14**) DAYS AWAY from `-HIS `-**BIRTH/DAY**!!!~' RECIPROCAL (INVERSE/MIRROR) = (**3/10**) = (MARCH 10[th]) = (`-**9**) DAYS AWAY from `-HIS `-**DEATH/DAY**!!!~' (14 + 9) = (`-**23**) = -a PROPHETIC # `-**NUMBER**!!!~'

(**19**2**8**) = (98) (12) = `-*EQUALS* = (98 (-) 12) = (`-**86**) = RECIPROCAL (INVERSE/MIRROR) = (`-**68**) = "**The** `-**MARK**"!!!~'

MARRIED `-in (`-**82**) = RECIPROCAL (INVERSE/MIRROR) = (`-**28**) = `-**BORN** in (`-**28**) = **2**(**8**'s) = (`-**88**) = **"AGE of `-DEATH for AMERICAN JOURNALIST JIMMY BRESLIN** (`-**88**)"!!!~'

AMERICAN JOURNALIST JIMMY BRESLIN `-**DEATH/DAY** = (**3**/**19**/20/17) = (**3** + **19** + 20 + 17) = (`-**59**)!!!~'

`-**DEATH/DAY** = (**3/19**) = (3 x 19) = (`-**57**) = (5 x 7) = (`-**35**) = "WAS `-**MARRIED** to RONNIE ELDRIDGE for (`-**35**) `-**YEARS**"!!!~'

(74 (-) 59) = (`-**15**)!!!~'

(74 + 59) = (`-**133**) = (13 x 3) = (`-**39**)!!!~'

AMERICAN JOURNALIST JIMMY BRESLIN `-**DIED** (`-**153**) DAYS AWAY from `-**HIS** `-**BIRTHDAY**!!!~' (`-**153**) = (53 x 1) = (`-**53**) = RECIPROCAL (INVERSE/MIRROR) = (`-**35**) = "**MARRIED** for (`-**35**) YEARS to RONNIE ELDRIDGE"!!!~'

(365 (-) 153) = (`-**212**) = (21 x 2) = (`-**42**) = **"The `-MARK"**!!!~'

FRAGMENTED `-**BIRTH/DAY** # `-**NUMBER** = (1 + 0 + 1 + 7 + 1 + 9 + 2 + 8) = (`-**29**) = RECIPROCAL (INVERSE/MIRROR) = (`-**92**)!!!~'

FRAGMENTED `-**DEATH/DAY** # `-**NUMBER** = (3 + 1 + 9 + 2 + 0 + 1 + 7) = (`-**23**) = RECIPROCAL (INVERSE/MIRROR) = (`-**32**) = -a PROPHETIC # `-**NUMBER**!!!~'

(29 + 23) = (`-**52**) = RECIPROCAL (INVERSE/MIRROR) = (`-**25**)!!!~'

AMERICAN JOURNALIST JIMMY BRESLIN was a (`-**RECIPROCAL/INVERSE/MIRROR**) of AMERICAN SINGER/SONGWRITER **CHUCK BERRY**!!!~'

`-**PLEASE;** **GO** `-**BACK;** and, `-**REVIEW**!!!~'

`-**DIED** at the `-**AGE** of (`-**53**)!!!~'

SINGER/SONGWRITER GEORGE MICHAEL `-**BIRTHDAY** = (**6**/**25**/19/**63**) = (**6** + **25** + 19 + **63**) = (`-**113**) = (13 x 1) = (`-**13**) = "A VERY PIVOTAL # `-NUMBBER"!!!~'

`-**BIRTH/DAY** = (**6/25**) = RECIPROCAL (INVERSE/MIRROR) = (**52/6**) = (`-**52.6**) = ROUNDED UP = (`-**53**) = `-**AGE of** `-**DEATH** for **SINGER/SONGWRITER GEORGE MICHAEL** (`-**53**)"!!!~'

`-**BIRTH/DAY** = (**6/25**) = (6 + 25) = (`-**31**) = RECIPROCAL (INVERSE/MIRROR) = (`-**13**) = "A VERY PIVOTAL # `-NUMBER"!!!~'

"WAS `-**BORN** in (`-**6**) (JUNE); and, `-**DIED** in (`-**12**) (DECEMBER)"; and, (**6/12**) = (JUNE 12th) = (`-**13**) DAYS AWAY from `-HIS `-**BIRTH/DAY**!!!~' RECIPROCAL (INVERSE/ MIRROR) = (**12/6**) = (DECEMBER 6$^{th}$) = (`-**19**) DAYS AWAY from `-HIS `-**DEATH/DAY**!!!~' (13 + 19) = (`-**32**) = -a PROPHETIC # `-**NUMBER**!!!~'

(**19**6**3**) = (9 + 3) (1 + 6) = `-*EQUALS* = (12) (7) = (12) (2 + 5) = `-*EQUALS* = (**12/25**) = `-**DEATH/DAY** (DECEMBER 25th)!!!~'

SINGER/SONGWRITER GEORGE MICHAEL `-**DEATH/ DAY** = (**12/25**/20/16) = (**12** + **25** + 20 + 16) = (`-**73**)!!!~'

`-**DEATH/DAY** = (**12/25**) = (12 + 25) = (`-**37**) = RECIPROCAL (INVERSE/MIRROR) = (`-**73**) = `-**DEATH/DAY** # `-**NUMBER** (`-**73**)!!!~'

34

(113 (-) 73) = (`-**40**)!!!~'

(113 + 73) = (`-**186**) = (86 x 1) = (`-**86**) = RECIPROCAL (INVERSE/ MIRROR) = (`-**68**) = "The `-**MARK**"!!!~'

SINGER/SONGWRITER GEORGE MICHAEL `-**DIED** (`-**182**) DAYS AWAY from `-**HIS** `-**BIRTHDAY**!!!~' (`-**182**) = (18 x 2) = (`-**36**) = RECIPROCAL (INVERSE/MIRROR) = (`-**63**) = "WAS `-**BORN** in (`-**63**)"!!!~'

(365 (-) 182) = (`-**183**) = (18 x 3) = (`-**54**) = `-**DIED** at the `-**AGE** of (`-**53**)!!!~'

WAS `-**BORN** on a (`-**25**th); and, `-**DIED** on a (`-**25**th)!!!~'

(`-**25**) = RECIPROCAL (INVERSE/MIRROR) = (`-**52**) = "**ONE `-YEAR `-AWAY from `-AGE of `-DEATH for SINGER/ SONGWRITER GEORGE MICHAEL** (`-**53**)"!!!~'

FRAGMENTED `-**BIRTH/DAY** # `-**NUMBER** = (6 + 2 + 5 + 1 + 9 + 6 + 3) = (`-**32**) = RECIPROCAL (INVERSE/MIRROR) = (`-**23**) = -a PROPHETIC # `-**NUMBER**!!!~'

FRAGMENTED `-**DEATH/DAY** # `-**NUMBER** = (1 + 2 + 2 + 5 + 2 + 0 + 1 + 6) = (`-**19**) = RECIPROCAL (INVERSE/MIRROR) = (`-**91**)!!!~'

(32 + 19) = (`-**51**) = RECIPROCAL (INVERSE/MIRROR) = (`-**15**)!!!~'

(51 + 15) = (`-**66**)!!!~' (`-**66**) (-) (`-**53**) = (`-**13**) = "A VERY PIVOTAL # `-**NUMBER**"!!!~'

(51 + 15) = (`-**66**) = (6 x 6) = (`-**36**) = RECIPROCAL (INVERSE/ MIRROR) = (`-**63**) = `-**YEAR** of `-**BIRTH** (`-**63**)!!!~'

(32 + 19) = (`-**51**) = "**TWO** `**-YEARS** `**-AWAY** from `**-AGE** of `**-DEATH** for SINGER/SONGWRITER GEORGE MICHAEL (`-**53**)"!!!~'

(91 (-) 23) = (`-**68**) = "The `-**MARK**"!!!~'

`-**DIED** at the `-**AGE** of (`-**62**)!!!~'

AMERICAN TELEVISION ACTRESS BEA BENADERET `-**BIRTHDAY** = (**4/4**/19/**06**) = (**4** + **4** + 19 + **06**) = (`-**33**)!!!~'

"WAS `-**BORN** in (`-**4**) (APRIL); and, `-**DIED** in (`-**10**) (OCTOBER)"; and, (**4/10**) = (APRIL 10ᵗʰ) = (`-**6**) DAYS AWAY from `-HER `-**BIRTH/DAY**!!!~' RECIPROCAL (INVERSE/ MIRROR) = (**10/4**) = (OCTOBER 4ᵗʰ) = (`-**9**) DAYS AWAY from `-HER `-**DEATH/DAY**!!!~' (6 x 9) = (`-**54**) = "**AGE of `-DEATH of `-HER `-HUSBAND /|\ EUGENE TWOMBLY (`-54**)"!!!~'

(**19**06) = (0 + 6) (1 (-) 9) = `-*EQUALS* = (6) (8) = `-*EQUALS* = (**68**) = `-**DEATH/YEAR** for AMERICAN TELEVISION ACTRESS BEA BENADERET & `-HER `-HUSBAND EUGENE TWOMBLY (`-19**68**)!!!~'

AMERICAN TELEVISION ACTRESS BEA BENADERET `-**DEATH/DAY** = (**10/13**/19/**68**) = (**10** + **13** + 19 + **68**) = (`-**110**)!!!~'

`-**DEATH/DAY** = (**10/13**) = (10 + 13) = (`-**23**) = RECIPROCAL (INVERSE/MIRROR) = (`-**32**) = -a PROPHETIC # `-NUMBER!!!~'

(110 (-) 33) = (`-**77**) = (77 x 2) = (`-**154**) = (54 x 1) = (`-**54**) = "**AGE of `-DEATH of `-HER `-HUSBAND /|\ EUGENE TWOMBLY (`-54**)"!!!~'

(110 + 33) = (`-**143**) = (43 x 1) = (`-**43**) = RECIPROCAL (INVERSE/ MIRROR) = (`-**34**) = (43 + 34) = (`-**77**) = "SEE `-ABOVE"!!!~'

WAS `-**BORN** on a (`-**4**ᵗʰ); and, `-**DIED** on a (`-**13**ᵗʰ) = (**4/13**) = (43 x 1) = (`-**43**) = "SEE `-ABOVE"!!!~'

AMERICAN TELEVISION ACTRESS BEA BENADERET `-**DIED** (`-**173**) DAYS AWAY from `-**HER** `-**BIRTHDAY**!!!~' (`-**173**) = (17 x 3) = (`-**51**) = RECIPROCAL (INVERSE/MIRROR) = (`-**15**)!!!~' (51 + 15) = (`-**66**) = 2(6's) = (`-**26**) = RECIPROCAL (INVERSE/MIRROR) = (`-**62**) = "**AGE of `-DEATH for AMERICAN TELEVISION ACTRESS BEA BENADERET** (`-**62**)"!!!~'

(365 (-) 173) = (`-**192**) = "FLIP the (`-**9**) OVER to a (`-**6**)" = (`-**162**) = (62 x 1) = (`-**62**) = "**AGE of `-DEATH for AMERICAN TELEVISION ACTRESS BEA BENADERET** (`-**62**)"!!!~'

FRAGMENTED `-**BIRTH/DAY** # `-**NUMBER** = (4 + 4 + 1 + 9 + 0 + 6) = (`-**24**) = RECIPROCAL (INVERSE/MIRROR) = (`-**48**) = (6 x 8) = (`-**68**) = `-**DEATH/YEAR** for AMERICAN TELEVISION ACTRESS BEA BENADERET (`-19**68**)!!!~'

FRAGMENTED `-**DEATH/DAY** # `-**NUMBER** = (1 + 0 + 1 + 3 + 1 + 9 + 6 + 8) = (`-**29**) = RECIPROCAL (INVERSE/MIRROR) = (`-**92**) = "FLIP the (`-**9**) OVER to a (`-**6**)" = (`-**62**) = "**AGE of `-DEATH for AMERICAN TELEVISION ACTRESS BEA BENADERET** (`-**62**)"!!!~'

(24 + 29) = (`-**53**) = RECIPROCAL (INVERSE/MIRROR) = (`-**35**)!!!~'

(53 + 35) = (`-**88**) = 2(8's) = (`-**28**) = RECIPROCAL (INVERSE/ MIRROR) = (`-**82**) = "**SEE** `-**BELOW**"!!!-'

`-**DIED** at the `-**AGE** of (`-**54**)!!!-'

EUGENE TWOMBLY /|\ SOUND EFFECTS TECHNICIAN in RADIO and MOTION PICTURES and `-HUSBAND of AMERICAN TELEVISION ACTRESS BEA BENADERET `-**BIRTHDAY** = (**4**/**27**/19/**14**) = (**4** + **27** + 19 + **14**) = (`-**64**)!!!-'

`-**BIRTH/DAY** = (**4/27**) = (4 x 27) = (`-**108**) / `-***DIVIDED*** `-*by* (`-**2**) = (`-**54**) = "AGE of `-DEATH for EUGENE TWOMBLY (`-**54**)"!!!-'

"WAS `-**BORN** in (`-**4**) (APRIL); and, `-**DIED** in (`-**10**) (OCTOBER)"; and, (**4/10**) = (APRIL 10ᵗʰ) = (`-**17**) DAYS AWAY from `-HIS `-**BIRTH/DAY**!!!-' RECIPROCAL (INVERSE/ MIRROR) = (**10/4**) = (OCTOBER 4ᵗʰ) = (`-**13**) DAYS AWAY from `-HIS `-**DEATH/DAY**!!!-' (17 x 13) = 1(173) = (`-**173**) = "**WIFE** `-**DIED** this `-**MANY DAYS AWAY** from `-HER `-BIRTHDAY (`-**173**); and, HUSBAND `-DIED this `-MANY DAYS AWAY from `-HIS `-BIRTHDAY (`-173)"!!!-'

WHEN `-WIFE is (`-**173**) DAYS AWAY in REVERSE DIRECTION `-HUSBAND is (`-**192**) DAYS AWAY in REVERSE DIRECTION!!!-' WHEN `-WIFE is (`-**192**) DAYS AWAY in FORWARD DIRECTION `-HUSBAND is (`-**173**) DAYS AWAY in FORWARD DIRECTION on `-DAYS AWAY from `-BIRTH to `-DEATH!!!-' HUSBAND & WIFE are (`-RECIPROCALS/ INVERSE/MIRRORS) of `-EACH `-OTHER!!!-'

`-HUSBAND & `-WIFE were `-BOTH `-BORN in (`-4) (APRIL); and, `-BOTH `-WIFE & `-HUSBAND `-DIED in (`-10) (OCTOBER)!!!~'

(19̲14) = (19) (14) = (19 + 14) = `-EQUALS = (33̲) = `-WIFE'S `-BIRTH/DAY # `-NUMBER (`-33̲) for AMERICAN TELEVISION ACTRESS BEA BENADERET!!!~'

EUGENE TWOMBLY /|\ SOUND EFFECTS TECHNICIAN in RADIO and MOTION PICTURES and `-HUSBAND of AMERICAN TELEVISION ACTRESS BEA BENADERET `-DEATH/DAY = (10̲/17̲/19/68̲) = (10̲ + 17̲ + 19 + 68̲) = (`-114̲)!!!~'

`-DEATH/DAY = (10̲/17̲) = (10 + 17) = (`-27̲) = `-DAY of `-BIRTH (`-27̲ᵗʰ)!!!~'

(114 (-) 64) = (`-50̲) = (5 + 0) = (`-5̲) = "THE `-HAND of `-GOD"!!!~'

(114 + 64) = (`-178̲) = (78 (-) 1) = (`-77̲) = (77 x 2) = (`-154̲) = (54 x 1) = (`-54̲) = "AGE of `-DEATH for EUGENE TWOMBLY (`-54̲)"!!!~'

EUGENE TWOMBLY /|\ SOUND EFFECTS TECHNICIAN in RADIO and MOTION PICTURES and `-HUSBAND of AMERICAN TELEVISION ACTRESS BEA BENADERET `-DIED (`-173̲) DAYS AWAY from `-HIS `-BIRTHDAY; just as `-HIS `-WIFE `-DID /|\ ACTRESS BEA BENADERET!!!~' (`-173̲) = (17 x 3) = (`-51̲) = RECIPROCAL (INVERSE/MIRROR) = (`-15̲)!!!~' (51 + 15) = (`-66̲) = 2(6's) = (`-26̲) = RECIPROCAL (INVERSE/MIRROR) = (`-62̲) = "AGE of `-DEATH for AMERICAN TELEVISION ACTRESS BEA BENADERET (`-62̲)"!!!~'

(365 (-) 173) = (`-**192**) = "FLIP the (`-**9**) OVER to a (`-**6**)" = (`-**162**) = (62 x 1) = (`-**62**) = "AGE of `-DEATH for AMERICAN TELEVISION ACTRESS BEA BENADERET (`-**62**)"!!!~'

FRAGMENTED `-**BIRTH/DAY** # `-NUMBER = (4 + 2 + 7 + 1 + 9 + 1 + 4) = (`-**28**) = RECIPROCAL (INVERSE/MIRROR) = (`-**82**)!!!~' (82 (-) 28) = (`-**54**) = "**AGE** of `-**DEATH** for EUGENE TWOMBLY /|\ SOUND EFFECTS TECHNICIAN in RADIO and MOTION PICTURES and `-HUSBAND of AMERICAN TELEVISION ACTRESS BEA BENADERET"!!!~'

FRAGMENTED `-**DEATH/DAY** # `-NUMBER = (1 + 0 + 1 + 7 + 1 + 9 + 6 + 8) = (`-**33**) = "**BIRTH/DAY #** `-**NUMBER** of `-WIFE AMERICAN TELEVISION ACTRESS BEA BENADERET"!!!~'

(28 + 33) = (`-**61**) = RECIPROCAL (INVERSE/MIRROR) = (`-**16**) = (61 (-) 16) = (`-**45**) = RECIPROCAL (INVERSE/MIRROR) = (`-**54**) = "AGE of `-DEATH for EUGENE TWOMBLY /|\ SOUND EFFECTS TECHNICIAN in RADIO and MOTION PICTURES and `-HUSBAND of AMERICAN TELEVISION ACTRESS BEA BENADERET"!!!~'

BEA BENADERET (`-**62**) & EUGENE TWOMBLY (`-**54**) = (62 + 54) = (`-**116**) = (11 x 6) = (`-**66**) = 2(6's) = (`-**26**) = RECIPROCAL (INVERSE/MIRROR) = (`-**62**) = "AGE of `-DEATH for AMERICAN TELEVISION ACTRESS BEA BENADERET (`-**62**)"!!!~'

BEA BENADERET (`-**62**) & EUGENE TWOMBLY (`-**54**) = (62 + 54) = (`-**116**) = RECIPROCAL (INVERSE/MIRROR) = (**611**) = (61 + 1) = (`-**62**) = "AGE of `-DEATH for AMERICAN TELEVISION ACTRESS BEA BENADERET (`-**62**)"!!!~'

`-**DIED** at the `-**AGE** of (`-**56**)!!!~'

(`-**56**) = (5 x 6) = (`-**30**) = "**DAY of `-BIRTH** (`-**30**)"!!!~'

AMERICAN ACTRESS MEREDITH MACRAE `-**BIRTHDAY** = (**5**/**30**/19/**44**) = (**5** + **30** + 19 + **44**) = (`-**98**)!!!~'

`-**BIRTH/DAY** = (**5/30**) = (53 + 0) = (`-**53**) = "**THREE `-YEARS `-AWAY from `-AGE of `-DEATH for AMERICAN ACTRESS MEREDITH MACRAE** (`-**56**)"!!!~'

"WAS `-**BORN** in (`-**5**) (MAY); and, `-**DIED** in (`-**7**) (JULY)"; and, (**5/7**) = (MAY 7th) = (`-**23**) DAYS AWAY from `-HER `-**BIRTH/ DAY!!!~'** RECIPROCAL (INVERSE/MIRROR) = (**7/5**) = (JULY 5[th]) = (`-**9**) DAYS AWAY from `-HER `-**DEATH/DAY!!!~'** (23 + 9) = (`-**32**) = -a PROPHETIC # `-NUMBER!!!~'

(1**9**4**4**) = (1 + 4) (9 (-) 4) = `-*EQUALS* = (5) (5) = `-*EQUALS* = (**55**) = (`-**23**) + (`-**32**) & = **SHE `-DIED the `-VERY `-NEXT `-YEAR at the `-AGE of** (`-**56**)!!!~'

AMERICAN ACTRESS MEREDITH MACRAE `-**DEATH/ DAY** = (**7**/**14**/20/**00**) = (**7** + **14** + 20 + **00**) = (`-**41**) = RECIPROCAL (INVERSE/MIRROR) = (`-**14**) = "**DAY of `-DEATH**"!!!~'

/|\ `-**DEATH/DAY** = (**7/14**) = (7 x 14) = (`-**98**) = `-**HER `-VERY `-OWN `-BIRTH/DAY** # `-**NUMBER** (`-**98**)!!!~' /|\

(98 (-) 41) = (`-**57**) = (5 x 7) = (`-**35**) = RECIPROCAL (INVERSE/ MIRROR) = (`-**53**) = `-**BIRTH/DAY** was (**5/3**0)!!!~'

(98 + 41) = (`-**139**)!!!~'

AMERICAN ACTRESS MEREDITH MACRAE `-**DIED** (`-**45**) DAYS AWAY from `-**HER `-BIRTHDAY!!!~'**

(365 (-) 45) = (`-**320**) = (32 + 0) = (`-**32**) = -a PROPHETIC # `-NUMBER!!!~'

FRAGMENTED `-**BIRTH/DAY** # `-**NUMBER** = (5 + 3 + 0 + 1 + 9 + 4 + 4) = (`-**26**) = RECIPROCAL (INVERSE/MIRROR) = (`-**62**) = `-**AGE** of `-**DEATH** for AMERICAN TELEVISION ACTRESS BEA BENADERET (`-**62**)!!!~' THEY `-**BOTH** `-**DIED** of `-CANCER; and, `-**BOTH** were `-**MOTHER** & `-**DAUGHTER** on PETTICOAT JUNCTION!!!~'

FRAGMENTED `-**DEATH/DAY** # `-**NUMBER** = (7 + 1 + 4 + 2 + 0 + 0 + 0) = (`-**14**) = RECIPROCAL (INVERSE/MIRROR) = (`-**41**) = "DAY of `-**DEATH** (`-**14**); and, `-**RECIPROCAL (INVERSE/ MIRROR)** = `-**EQUALS** = "DEATH/DAY # `-NUMBER (`-**41**)"!!!~'

(26 + 14) = (`-**40**) = RECIPROCAL (INVERSE/MIRROR) = (`-**04**)!!!~'

(40 + 04) = (`-**44**) = "AMERICAN ACTRESS MEREDITH MACRAE WAS `-**BORN** in (`-**44**)"!!!~'

AMERICAN ACTRESS MEREDITH MACRAE (`-**2,000**) `-**DIED** (`-**32**) `-**YEARS** `-AFTER AMERICAN TELEVISION ACTRESS BEA BENADERET (`-**1,968**)!!!~'

`-**DIED** at the `-**AGE** of (`-**75**)!!!~'

(`-**75**) = RECIPROCAL (INVERSE/MIRROR) = (`-**57**)!!!~'

(75 + 57) = (`-**132**) = (32 x 1) = (`-**32**) = -a PROPHETIC # `-NUMBER!!!~'

AMERICAN ACTOR MIKE MINOR `-**BIRTHDAY** = (**12**/**7**/19/**40**) = (**12** + **7** + 19 + **40**) = (`-**78**) = (7 x 8) = (`-**56**) = "SEE `-BELOW"!!!~'

(`-**78**) = "THREE `-YEARS `-AWAY from `-AGE of `-DEATH for AMERICAN ACTOR MIKE MINOR (`-**75**)"!!!~'

`-**BIRTH/DAY** = (**12**/**7**) = RECIPROCAL (INVERSE/MIRROR) = (**7**/**21**) = (72 + 1) = (`-**73**) = "TWO `-YEARS `-AWAY from `-AGE of `-DEATH for AMERICAN ACTOR MIKE MINOR (`-**75**)"!!!~'

"WAS `-**BORN** in (`-**12**) (DECEMBER); and, `-**DIED** in (`-**1**) (JANUARY)"; and, (**12**/**1**) = (DECEMBER 1st) = (`-**6**) DAYS AWAY from `-HIS `-**BIRTH/DAY**!!!~' RECIPROCAL (INVERSE/MIRROR) = (**1**/**12**) = (JANUARY 12th) = (`-**16**) DAYS AWAY from `-HIS `-**DEATH/DAY**!!!~' (6 + 16) = (`-**22**)!!!~'

(**1940**) = (90) (14) = (90 (-) 14) = `-*EQUALS* = (**76**) = "IN the `-YEAR of `-DEATH (`-**76**) for AMERICAN ACTOR MIKE MINOR"!!!~'

AMERICAN ACTOR MIKE MINOR `-**DEATH/DAY** = (**1**/**28**/20/**16**) = (**1** + **28** + 20 + **16**) = (`-**65**) = RECIPROCAL (INVERSE/MIRROR) = (`-**56**) = "**AGE** of `-**DEATH** of `-INITIAL `-LOVE `-INTEREST on PETTICOAT JUNCTION AMERICAN ACTRESS MEREDITH MACRAE (`-**56**)"!!!~'

`-**DEATH/DAY** = (**128**) = & `-**BIRTHDAY** (`-**127**) = "JUST `-**ONE** (`-**1**) # `-**NUMBER** (`-**OFF**)"!!!~'

(78 (-) 65) = (`-**13**) = "A VERY PIVOTAL # `-NUMBER"!!!~'

(78 + 65) = (`-**143**) = (43 + 1) = (`-**44**) = "**AMERICAN ACTRESS MEREDITH MACRAE** was `-**BORN** in (`-**44**)"!!!~'

/|\ AMERICAN ACTOR MIKE MINOR `-**DIED** (`-**52**) DAYS AWAY from `-**HIS** `-**BIRTHDAY**!!!~' (`-**52**) = RECIPROCAL (INVERSE/MIRROR) = (`-**25**) = "FLIP the (`-**2**) OVER to a (`-**7**)" = (`-**75**) = "**AGE** of `-**DEATH** for **AMERICAN ACTOR MIKE MINOR** (`-**75**)"!!!~' /|\

(365 (-) 52) = (`-**313**) = "**#35/PRESIDENT JOHN F. KENNEDY** # `-**NUMBER**"!!!~'

FRAGMENTED `-**BIRTH/DAY** # `-**NUMBER** = (1 + 2 + 7 + 1 + 9 + 4 + 0) = (`-**24**) = RECIPROCAL (INVERSE/MIRROR) = (`-**42**) = "The `-**MARK**"!!!~'

FRAGMENTED `-**DEATH/DAY** # `-**NUMBER** = (1 + 2 + 8 + 2 + 0 + 1 + 6) = (`-**20**) = RECIPROCAL (INVERSE/MIRROR) = (`-**02**)!!!~' (20 + 02) = (`-**22**) = "**SEE** `-**ABOVE**"!!!~'

(24 + 20) = (`-**44**) = "**AMERICAN ACTRESS MEREDITH MACRAE** was `-**BORN** in (`-**44**)"; and, `-**THEY** `-**BOTH** `-**DIED** of `-**CANCER**!!!~'

`-**DIED** at the `-**AGE** of (`-**76**)!!!~'

AMERICAN ACTOR EDGAR BUCHANAN (WHO PLAYED UNCLE JOE CARSON on PETTICOAT JUNCTION) `-**BIRTHDAY** = (3/**20**/19/**03**) = (**3** + **20** + 19 + **03**) = (`-**45**)!!!~'

`-**BIRTH/DAY** = (3/**20**) = "FLIP the (`-**2**) OVER to a (`-**7**)" = (3/**70**) = RECIPROCAL (INVERSE/MIRROR) = (**07/3**) = (73 + 0) =

(`-73) = "THREE `-YEARS `-AWAY from `-AGE of `-DEATH for AMERICAN ACTOR EDGAR BUCHANAN (`-76)"!!!~'

"WAS `-BORN in (`-3) (MARCH); and, `-DIED in (`-4) (APRIL)"; and, (3/4) = (MARCH 4th) = (`-16) DAYS AWAY from `-HIS `-BIRTH/DAY!!!~' RECIPROCAL (INVERSE/MIRROR) = (4/3) = (APRIL 3rd) = (`-1) DAYS AWAY from `-HIS `-DEATH/DAY!!!~' (16 x 1) = (`-16) = (4 x 4) = (`-4/4) = `-DEATH/DAY for AMERICAN ACTOR EDGAR BUCHANAN!!!~'

(1903) = (90) (13) = (90 (-) 13) = `-EQUALS = (77) = `-DIED the `-YEAR of `-AGE `-PRIOR of (`-76)!!!~'

AMERICAN ACTOR EDGAR BUCHANAN `-DEATH/DAY = (4/4/19/79) = (4 + 4 + 19 + 79) = (`-106) = (16 + 0) = (`-16) = (4 x 4) = (4/4) = `-DEATH/DAY!!!~'

(106 (-) 45) = (`-61) = RECIPROCAL (INVERSE/MIRROR) = (`-16) = (61 + 16) = (`-77) = `-DIED the `-YEAR of `-AGE `-PRIOR (`-76)!!!~'

(106 + 45) = (`-151) = (15 x 1) = (`-15) = "DIED this `-MANY `-DAYS AWAY from `-HIS `-BIRTH/DAY"!!!~'

AMERICAN ACTOR EDGAR BUCHANAN `-DIED (`-15) DAYS AWAY from `-HIS `-BIRTHDAY!!!~' (`-15) = RECIPROCAL (INVERSE/MIRROR) = (`-51)!!!~'

(365 (-) 15) = (`-350) = (35 + 0) = (`-35) = RECIPROCAL (INVERSE/MIRROR) = (`-53)!!!~'

FRAGMENTED `-BIRTH/DAY # `-NUMBER = (3 + 2 + 0 + 1 + 9 + 0 + 3) = (`-18) = RECIPROCAL (INVERSE/MIRROR) = (`-81)!!!~'

FRAGMENTED `-**DEATH/DAY** # `-**NUMBER** = (4 + 4 + 1 + 9 + 7 + 9) = (`-**34**) = RECIPROCAL (INVERSE/MIRROR) = (`-**43**)!!!~'

(34 + 43) = (`-**77**) = "**ONE** `-**YEAR** `-**AWAY** from `-**AGE** of `-**DEATH** for AMERICAN ACTOR EDGAR BUCHANAN (`-**76**)"!!!~'

(18 + 34) = (`-**52**) = RECIPROCAL (INVERSE/MIRROR) = (`-**25**) = "FLIP the (`-**2**) OVER to a (`-**7**)" = (`-**75**) = "**AGE** of `-**DEATH** for AMERICAN ACTOR MIKE MINOR (`-**75**)"!!!~' BOTH `-**PLAYED** on `-**PETTICOAT** `-**JUNCTION**!!!~'

DEATH/DAY = (**4/4/19/79**) = `-REVERSE `-SEQUENCE = (79 (-) 19 (-) 4 (-) 4) = (`-**52**) = RECIPROCAL (INVERSE/MIRROR) = (`-**25**) = "FLIP the (`-**2**) OVER to a (`-**7**)" = (`-**75**) = "**AGE** of `-**DEATH** for AMERICAN ACTOR MIKE MINOR (`-**75**)"!!!~' BOTH `-**PLAYED** on `-**PETTICOAT** `-**JUNCTION**!!!~'

AMERICAN ACTOR EDGAR BUCHANAN (WHO PLAYED UNCLE JOE CARSON on PETTICOAT JUNCTION) `-**DIED** on (**4/4**) the `-**BIRTH/DAY** (**4/4**) of AMERICAN TELEVISION ACTRESS BEA BENADERET (WHO `-PLAYED WIDOW KATE BRADLEY with `-HER (`-3) DAUGHTERS) on `-**PETTICOAT** `-**JUNCTION**"!!!~'

`-**DIED** at the `-**AGE** of (`-**62**)!!!~'

AMERICAN SINGER/SONGWRITER SONNY BONO `-**BIRTHDAY** = (**2/16/19/35**) = (**2** + **16** + 19 + **35**) = (`-**72**)!!!~'

/|\ `-**BIRTH/DAY** = (**2/16**) = (26 x 1) = (`-**26**) = RECIPROCAL (INVERSE/MIRROR) = (`-**62**) = "**AGE of `-DEATH for AMERICAN SINGER/SONGWRITER SONNY BONO** (`-**62**)"!!!~' /|\

"WAS `-**BORN** in (`-**2**) (FEBRUARY); and, `-**DIED** in (`-**1**) (JANUARY)"; and, (**2/1**) = (FEBRUARY 1st) = (`-**15**) DAYS AWAY from `-HIS `-**BIRTH/DAY**!!!~' RECIPROCAL (INVERSE/ MIRROR) = (**1/2**) = (JANUARY 2$^{nd}$) = (`-**3**) DAYS AWAY from `-HIS `-**DEATH/DAY**!!!~' (15 x 3) = (`-**45**) = RECIPROCAL (INVERSE/MIRROR) = (`-**54**) = `-**BIRTH/YEAR** = (19 + 35) = (`-**54**)!!!~'

(19**35**) = (1 + 5) (9 (-) 3) = (6) (6) = `-*EQUALS* = (**66**) = 2(6's) = (`-**26**) = RECIPROCAL (INVERSE/MIRROR) = (`-**62**) = "**AGE of `-DEATH for AMERICAN SINGER/SONGWRITER SONNY BONO** (`-**62**)"!!!~'

AMERICAN SINGER/SONGWRITER SONNY BONO `-**DEATH/DAY** = (**1/5**/19/**98**) = (**1** + **5** + 19 + **98**) = (`-**123**) = (23 x 1) = (`-**23**) = -a PROPHETIC # `-NUMBER!!!~'

`-**DEATH/DAY** # `-**NUMBER** in `-**REVERSE** = (98 (-) 19 (-) 5 (-) 1) = (`-**73**) = "**JUST `-ONE** (`-**1**) # `-**NUMBER** (`-**OFF**)" from `-**HIS** `-**BIRTH/DAY** # `-**NUMBER** = (`-**72**)!!!~'

(`-**31**) **DAYS** in the `-**MONTH** of (`-**JANUARY**) = (31 (-) 5) = (`-**26**) = RECIPROCAL (INVERSE/MIRROR) = (`-**62**) = "**AGE of `-DEATH for AMERICAN SINGER/SONGWRITER SONNY BONO** (`-**62**)"!!!~'

(123 (-) 72) = (`-**51**) = RECIPROCAL (INVERSE/MIRROR) = (`-**15**) = (51 + 15) = (`-**66**) = 2(6's) = (`-**26**) = RECIPROCAL (INVERSE/ MIRROR) = (`-**62**) = "**AGE of `-DEATH for AMERICAN SINGER/SONGWRITER SONNY BONO** (`-**62**)"!!!~'

(123 + 72) = (`-**195**) = "FLIP the (`-**9**) OVER to a (`-**6**)" = (`-**165**) = (65 + 1) = (`-**66**) = 2(6's) = (`-**26**) = RECIPROCAL (INVERSE/ MIRROR) = (`-**62**) = "**AGE of `-DEATH for AMERICAN SINGER/SONGWRITER SONNY BONO** (`-**62**)"!!!~'

AMERICAN SINGER/SONGWRITER SONNY BONO `-**DIED** (`-**42**) DAYS AWAY from `-**HIS** `-**BIRTHDAY!!!~'** (`-**42**) = "The `-**MARK**"!!!~'

(365 (-) 42) = (`-**323**) = **RECIPROCAL-SEQUENCING- NUMEROLOGY-RSN**!!!~'

FRAGMENTED `-**BIRTH/DAY** # `-**NUMBER** = (2 + 1 + 6 + 1 + 9 + 3 + 5) = (`-**27**) = RECIPROCAL (INVERSE/MIRROR) = (`-**72**) = `-**BIRTH/DAY** # `-**NUMBER** of **AMERICAN SINGER/ SONGWRITER SONNY BONO** (`-**72**)!!!~'

FRAGMENTED `-**DEATH/DAY** # `-**NUMBER** = (1 + 5 + 1 + 9 + 9 + 8) = (`-**33**) = "**PETTICOAT JUNCTION**"!!!~'

(`-**33**) = (**33**) x (`-2) = (`-**66**) = "**SEE `-ABOVE & `-BELOW**"!!!~'

(27 + 33) = (`-**60**) = RECIPROCAL (INVERSE/MIRROR) = (`-**06**) = (60 + 06) = (`-**66**) = 2(6's) = (`-**26**) = RECIPROCAL (INVERSE/ MIRROR) = (`-**62**) = "**AGE of `-DEATH for AMERICAN SINGER/SONGWRITER SONNY BONO** (`-**62**)"!!!~'

`-**DIED** at the `-**AGE** of (`-**86**)!!!~'

AMERICAN ACTOR ANDY GRIFFITH `-**BIRTHDAY** = (**6**/**1**/19/**26**) = (**6** + **1** + 19 + **26**) = (`-**52**)!!!~'

`-**BIRTH/MONTH** & `-**BIRTH/YEAR** = (**6/26**) = "FLIP the (`-**6**) OVER to a (`-**9**)" = (**9/2**6) = (92 (-) 6) = (`-**86**) = "**AGE of `-DEATH for AMERICAN ACTOR ANDY GRIFFITH (`-86**)"!!!~'

"WAS `-**BORN** in (`-**6**) (JUNE); and, `-**DIED** in (`-**7**) (JULY)"; and, (**6/7**) = (JUNE 7th) = (`-**6**) DAYS AWAY from `-HIS `-**BIRTH/ DAY!!!~'** RECIPROCAL (INVERSE/MIRROR) = (**7/6**) = (JULY 6th) = (`-**3**) DAYS AWAY from `-HIS `-**DEATH/DAY!!!~'** (**6/3**) = `-AGE of `-DEATH = (`-**86**) (-) (`-**63**) = (`-**23**) = -a PROPHETIC # `-NUMBER!!!~'

(**192**6) = (1 + 9 (-) 2) (6) = (8) (6) = `-*EQUALS* = (**86**) = "**AGE of `-DEATH for AMERICAN ACTOR ANDY GRIFFITH (`-86**)"!!!~'

AMERICAN ACTOR ANDY GRIFFITH `-**DEATH/DAY** = (**7/3**/20/**12**) = (**7** + **3** + 20 + **12**) = (`-**42**) = "The `-**MARK**"!!!~'

(52 (-) 42) = (`-**10**) = RECIPROCAL (INVERSE/MIRROR) = (`-**01**)!!!~'

(52 + 42) = (`-**94**) = RECIPROCAL (INVERSE/MIRROR) = (`-**49**)!!!~'

(94 (-) 10) = (`-**84**)!!!~'

(49 (-) 01) = (`-**48**)!!!~'

(`-**84**) = RECIPROCAL (INVERSE/MIRROR) = (`-**48**) = (8 x 6) = (`-**86**) = "**AGE of `-DEATH for AMERICAN ACTOR ANDY GRIFFITH (`-86**)"!!!~'

AMERICAN ACTOR ANDY GRIFFITH `-**DIED** (`-**32**) DAYS AWAY from `-**HIS `-BIRTHDAY!!!~'** (`-**32**) = -a PROPHETIC # `-NUMBER!!!~'

(365 (-) 32) = (`-**333**)!!!~'

FRAGMENTED `-**BIRTH/DAY** # `-**NUMBER** = (6 + 1 + 1 + 9 + 2 + 6) = (`-**25**) = RECIPROCAL (INVERSE/MIRROR) = (`-**52**) = `-**BIRTH/DAY** # `-**NUMBER** of AMERICAN ACTOR ANDY GRIFFITH (`-**52**)!!!~'

FRAGMENTED `-**DEATH/DAY** # `-**NUMBER** = (7 + 3 + 2 + 0 + 1 + 2) = (`-**15**) = RECIPROCAL (INVERSE/MIRROR) = (`-**51**)!!!~'

(25 + 15) = (`-**40**) = RECIPROCAL (INVERSE/MIRROR) = (`-**04**) = (40 + 04) = (`-**44**)!!!~'

(**40.5** + **40.5**) = (`-**81**) = "**AGE** of `-**DEATH** for AMERICAN ACTOR **DON** **KNOTTS** (`-**81**)"!!!~'

`-**DIED** at the `-**AGE** of (`-**81**)!!!~'

AMERICAN ACTOR DON KNOTTS `-**BIRTHDAY** = (**7**/**21**/19/**24**) = (**7** + **21** + 19 + **24**) = (`-**71**)!!!~' (71 x 2) = (`-**142**) = (42 x 1) = (`-**42**) = `-**DEATH/DAY** # `-**NUMBER** for AMERICAN ACTOR ANDY GRIFFITH (`-**42**)!!!~'

/|\ `-**BIRTH/DAY** # `-**NUMBER** (`-**71**) + `-**BIRTH/DAY** (7 + 2 + 1) = (71 + 10) = (`-**81**) = `-**AGE** of `-**DEATH** for AMERICAN ACTOR DON KNOTTS (`-**81**)!!!~' /|\

`-**BIRTH/DAY** = (**7**/**21**) = (**ALL-IN-ONE-#-NUMBER**) = (7 + 1) (2) = (`-**82**) = "**ONE** `-**YEAR** `-**AWAY** from `-**AGE** of `-**DEATH** for AMERICAN ACTOR DON KNOTTS (`-**81**)!!!~'

`-**BIRTH/MONTH** & `-**BIRTH/YEAR** = (**7/24**) = (7 x 24) = (`-**168**) = (68 x 1) = (`-**68**) = RECIPROCAL (INVERSE/MIRROR) = (`-**86**) = "**AGE of `-DEATH for AMERICAN ACTOR ANDY GRIFFITH (`-86**)"!!!~'

"WAS `-**BORN** in (`-**7**) (JULY); and, `-**DIED** in (`-**2**) (FEBRUARY)"; and, (**7/2**) = (JULY 2ⁿᵈ) = (**"FIRST (`-2) NUMERALS of `-BIRTH/DAY"**) = (`-**19**) DAYS AWAY from `-HIS `-**BIRTH/DAY!!!~'** RECIPROCAL (INVERSE/MIRROR) = (**2/7**) = (FEBRUARY 7ᵗʰ) = (`-**17**) DAYS AWAY from `-HIS `-**DEATH/DAY!!!~'** (**19/17**) = (19 + 17) = (`-**36**) = RECIPROCAL (INVERSE/MIRROR) = (`-**63**) = `-AGE of `-DEATH for AMERICAN ACTOR ANDY GRIFFITH = (`-**86**) (-) (`-**63**) = (`-**23**) = -a PROPHETIC # `-NUMBER!!!~'

(19 x 17) = (`-**323**) = **RECIPROCAL-SEQUENCING-NUMEROLOGY-RSN!!!~'**

(**19**24) = (9 (-) 1) (4 (-) 2) = (8) (2) = `-*EQUALS* = (**82**) = "**ONE** (`-1) `-**YEAR** `-**AWAY** from `-**AGE** of `-**DEATH** for AMERICAN ACTOR DON KNOTTS (`-**81**)"!!!~' `-**DIED** in the `-**YEAR** of (`-**82**)!!!~'

(**19**24) = (9 (-) 1) (2 + 4) = (8) (6) = `-*EQUALS* = (**86**) = `-**AGE** of `-**DEATH** for AMERICAN ACTOR ANDY GRIFFITH (`-**86**)"!!!~'

AMERICAN ACTOR DON KNOTTS `-**DEATH/DAY** = (**2/24**/20/**06**) = (**2** + **24** + 20 + **06**) = (`-**52**) = `-**BIRTH/DAY** # `-**NUMBER** of AMERICAN ACTOR ANDY GRIFFITH (`-**52**)!!!~'

`-**DEATH/DAY** = (**2/24**) = RECIPROCAL (INVERSE/MIRROR) = (**42/2**) = (**ALL-IN-ONE-#-NUMBER**) = (4 x 2) (2) = (`-**82**) = "**ONE** (`-1) `-**YEAR** `-**AWAY** from `-**AGE** of `-**DEATH** for

AMERICAN ACTOR DON KNOTTS (`-81)"!!!~' `-DIED in the `-YEAR of (`-82)!!!~'

`-**DEATH/DAY** = (`-24ᵗʰ) = RECIPROCAL (INVERSE/MIRROR) = (`-42) = `-**DEATH/DAY** # `-**NUMBER of AMERICAN ACTOR ANDY GRIFFITH** (`-42)!!!~'

(71 (-) 52) = (`-19) = RECIPROCAL (INVERSE/MIRROR) = (`-91)!!!~'

(71 + 52) = (`-123) = (23 x 1) = (`-23) = -a PROPHETIC # `-NUMBER!!!~'

AMERICAN ACTOR DON KNOTTS `-**DIED** (`-147) DAYS AWAY from `-**HIS** `-**BIRTHDAY!!!~'** (`-147) = (14 x 7) = (`-98) = RECIPROCAL (INVERSE/MIRROR) = (`-89) = "FLIP the (`-9) OVER to a (`-6)" = (`-86) = "**AGE of `-DEATH for AMERICAN ACTOR ANDY GRIFFITH** (`-86)"!!!~'

(365 (-) 147) = (`-218) = (21 x 8) = (`-168) = (68 x 1) = (`-68) = RECIPROCAL (INVERSE/MIRROR) = (`-86) = "**AGE of `-DEATH for AMERICAN ACTOR ANDY GRIFFITH** (`-86)"!!!~'

FRAGMENTED `-**BIRTH/DAY** # `-**NUMBER** = (7 + 2 + 1 + 1 + 9 + 2 + 4) = (`-26) = RECIPROCAL (INVERSE/MIRROR) = (`-62)!!!~'

(26 + 26) = (`-52) = `-**BIRTH/DAY** # `-**NUMBER of AMERICAN ACTOR ANDY GRIFFITH** (`-52)!!!~'

(26 + 62) = (`-88) = 2(8's) = (`-28) = RECIPROCAL (INVERSE/MIRROR) = (`-82) = "**YEAR of `-DEATH for `-AGE for AMERICAN ACTOR DON KNOTTS** (`-81)"!!!~'

FRAGMENTED `-**DEATH/DAY** # `-**NUMBER** = (2 + 2 + 4 + 2 + 0 + 0 + 6) = (`-**16**) = RECIPROCAL (INVERSE/MIRROR) = (`-**61**)!!!~'

(26 + 16) = (`-**42**) = "**SEE** `-**ABOVE** for `-**BOTH** AMERICAN ACTOR **DON KNOTTS** (`-**24**) & AMERICAN ACTOR **ANDY GRIFFITH** (`-**42**)"!!!~'

(`-**24**) = RECIPROCAL (INVERSE/MIRROR) = (`-**42**)!!!~'

(42 (-) 24) = (`-**18**) = RECIPROCAL (INVERSE/MIRROR) = (`-**81**) = `-**AGE of** `-**DEATH for** AMERICAN ACTOR DON KNOTTS (`-**81**)!!!~'

`-**DIED** at the `-**AGE** of (`-**86**)!!!~'

AMERICAN TELEVISION ACTRESS FRANCES BAVIER `-**BIRTHDAY** = (**12**/**14**/19/**02**) = (**12** + **14** + 19 + **02**) = (`-**47**) = AMERICAN ACTOR DON KNOTTS `-**DIED** (`-**147**) DAYS AWAY from `-**HIS** `-**BIRTHDAY!!!**~'

/|\ `-**BIRTH/DAY** = (**12/14**) = (12 x 14) = (`-**168**) = (68 x 1) = (`-**68**) = RECIPROCAL (INVERSE/MIRROR) = (`-**86**) = "**AGE of** `-**DEATH for** AMERICAN TELEVISION ACTRESS FRANCES BAVIER & **AGE** of `-**DEATH for** AMERICAN ACTOR ANDY GRIFFITH (`-**86**)"!!!~' /|\

"WAS `-**BORN** in (`-**12**) (DECEMBER); and, `-**DIED** in (`-**12**) (DECEMBER)"; and, (**12/12**) = (DECEMBER 12th) = (`-**2**) DAYS AWAY from `-HER `-**BIRTH/DAY!!!**~' RECIPROCAL (INVERSE/MIRROR) = (**12/12**) = (DECEMBER 12$^{th}$) = (`-**6**) DAYS AWAY from `-HER `-**DEATH/DAY!!!**~' (**2/6**) = "FLIP the

('-**6**) OVER to a ('-**9**)" = (92 (-) 6) = ('-**86**) = "**AGE of** '-**DEATH for**
AMERICAN TELEVISION ACTRESS FRANCES BAVIER &
AGE of '-**DEATH for AMERICAN ACTOR ANDY GRIFFITH**
('-**86**)"!!!-'

(1**90**2) = (90) (1 + 2) = (90) (3) = (90 (-) 3) = '-*EQUALS* = (**87**)
= "**ONE** ('-**1**) '-**YEAR** '-**AWAY from** '-**AGE of** '-**DEATH for**
AMERICAN TELEVISION ACTRESS FRANCES BAVIER ('-
86)"!!!-' '-**DIED in the** '-**YEAR of** ('-**87**)!!!-'

(**19**02) = (9 (-) 1) (2 + 0) = (8) (2) = '-*EQUALS* = (**82**) = '-**YEAR**
of '-**DEATH for AMERICAN ACTOR DON KNOTTS WHO**
'-**DIED at** ('-**81**)!!!-'

AMERICAN TELEVISION ACTRESS FRANCES BAVIER
'-**DEATH/DAY** = (**12**/**06**/19/**89**) = (**12** + **06** + 19 + **89**) = ('-**126**) =
"**JUST** '-**ADD a** '-**ZERO** ('-**0**)" = '-**DEATH/DAY** of AMERICAN
TELEVISION ACTRESS FRANCES BAVIER ('-**12/06**)!!!-'

'-**DEATH/DAY** = (**12/06**) = (**ALL-IN-ONE-#-NUMBER**) = (2 +
6) (1 + 0) = ('-**81**) = '-**AGE of** '-**DEATH for AMERICAN ACTOR**
DON KNOTTS WHO '-**DIED at the** '-**AGE of** ('-**81**)!!!-'

'-**BIRTH/DAY** = ('-**12/14**) = (12 + 14) = ('-**26**) = "**SEE** '-**ABOVE**
TWICE" = "FLIP the ('-**6**) OVER to a ('-**9**)" = (92 (-) 6) = ('-**86**) =
"**AGE of** '-**DEATH for AMERICAN TELEVISION ACTRESS**
FRANCES BAVIER & **AGE of** '-**DEATH for AMERICAN**
ACTOR ANDY GRIFFITH ('-**86**)"!!!-'

/|\ '-**DEATH/YEAR** = ('-**89**) = "FLIP the ('-**9**) OVER to a ('-**6**)"
= ('-**86**) = "**AGE of** '-**DEATH for AMERICAN TELEVISION**
ACTRESS FRANCES BAVIER & **AGE of** '-**DEATH for**
AMERICAN ACTOR ANDY GRIFFITH ('-**86**)"!!!-' /|\

`-**DEATH/DAY** # `-**NUMBER** in `-**REVERSE** = (89 (-) 19 (-) 06 (-) 12) = (`-**52**) = `-**BIRTH/DAY** # `-**NUMBER** of AMERICAN ACTOR ANDY GRIFFITH (`-**52**)!!!~'

(126 (-) 47) = (`-**79**) = RECIPROCAL (INVERSE/MIRROR) = (`-**97**)!!!~'

(126 + 47) = (`-**173**) = (73 x 1) = (`-**73**)!!!~'

AMERICAN TELEVISION ACTRESS FRANCES BAVIER `-**DIED** (`-**8**) DAYS AWAY from `-**HER** `-**BIRTHDAY!!!**~'

(365 (-) 8) = (`-**357**) = (35 + 7) = (`-**42**) = `-**DEATH/DAY** # `-**NUMBER** of AMERICAN ACTOR ANDY GRIFFITH (`-**42**) = RECIPROCAL (INVERSE/MIRROR) = (`-**24**) = `-**DEATH/ DAY** of AMERICAN ACTOR DON KNOTTS (`-**24**)!!!~'

FRAGMENTED `-**BIRTH/DAY** # `-**NUMBER** = (1 + 2 + 1 + 4 + 1 + 9 + 0 + 2) = (`-**20**) = RECIPROCAL (INVERSE/MIRROR) = (`-**02**)!!!~'

FRAGMENTED `-**DEATH/DAY** # `-**NUMBER** = (1 + 2 + 0 + 6 + 1 + 9 + 8 + 9) = (`-**36**) = RECIPROCAL (INVERSE/MIRROR) = (`-**63**)!!!~'

(20 + 36) = (`-**56**)!!!~'

`-**AGE** of `-**DEATH** for **FRANCES BAVIER** (`-**86**) (-) (`-**63**) = (`-**23**) = -a PROPHETIC # `-NUMBER!!!~'

`-**DIED** at the `-**AGE** of (`-**91**)!!!~'

AMERICAN ACTOR MIKE CONNERS `-**BIRTHDAY** = (**8**/**15**/19/**25**) = (**8** + **15** + 19 + **25**) = (`-**67**)!!!~'

`-**BIRTH/DAY** = (**8/15**) = (**ALL-IN-ONE-#-NUMBER**) = (8 + 1) (5) = (`-**95**) = "**FOUR** `-**YEARS** `-**AWAY** from `-**AGE** of `-**DEATH** for AMERICAN ACTOR MIKE CONNERS (`-**91**)!!!~'

`-**BIRTH/DAY** = (**8/15**) = (8 + 15) = (`-**23**) = -a PROPHETIC # `-NUMBER!!!~'

"WAS `-**BORN** in (`-**8**) (AUGUST); and, `-**DIED** in (`-**1**) (JANUARY)"; and, (**8/1**) = (AUGUST 1st) = (**"FIRST** (`-**2**) NUMERALS of `-HIS `-BIRTH/DAY"**) = (`-**14**) DAYS AWAY from `-HIS `-**BIRTH/DAY**!!!~' RECIPROCAL (INVERSE/ MIRROR) = (**1/8**) = (JANUARY 8th) = (`-**18**) DAYS AWAY from `-HIS `-**DEATH/DAY**!!!~' (14/18) = (14 + 18) = (`-**32**) = -a PROPHETIC # `-NUMBER!!!~'

(1**9**2**5**) = (9 (-) 2) (1 + 5) = (7) (6) = `-*EQUALS* = (**76**) = RECIPROCAL (INVERSE/MIRROR) = (`-**67**) = `-**BIRTH/DAY** # `-**NUMBER** of AMERICAN ACTOR MIKE CONNERS (`-**67**)!!!~'

`-**DEATH/YEAR** = (`-**2**01**7**) = (2 + 7) (1 + 0) = (9) (1) = `-*EQUALS* = (`-**91**) = "AGE of `-**DEATH** for AMERICAN ACTOR MIKE CONNERS (`-**91**)!!!~'

AMERICAN ACTOR MIKE CONNERS `-**DEATH/DAY** = (**1**/**26**/20/**17**) = (**1** + **26** + 20 + **17**) = (`-**64**) = (2 x 32) = (`-**232**) = **RECIPROCAL-SEQUENCING-NUMEROLOGY-RSN**!!!~'

`-**DEATH/DAY** = (**1/26**) = RECIPROCAL (INVERSE/MIRROR) = (**62/1**) = "FLIP the (`-**6**) OVER to a (`-**9**)" = (**92/1**) = (92 (-) 1)

= (`-91) = "AGE of `-DEATH for AMERICAN ACTOR MIKE CONNERS (`-91)!!!~'

(67 (-) 64) = (`-3)!!!~'

(67 + 64) = (`-131) = (13 x 1) = (`-13) = "A VERY PIVOTAL # `-NUMBER"!!!~'

AMERICAN ACTOR MIKE CONNERS `-DIED (`-201) DAYS AWAY from `-HIS `-BIRTHDAY!!!~'

(365 (-) 201) = (`-164) = (64 x 1) = (`-64) = `-HIS `-VERY `-OWN `-DEATH/DAY # `-NUMBER!!!~'

FRAGMENTED `-BIRTH/DAY # `-NUMBER = (8 + 1 + 5 + 1 + 9 + 2 + 5) = (`-31) = RECIPROCAL (INVERSE/MIRROR) = (`-13) = "A VERY PIVOTAL # `-NUMBER"!!!~'

/|\ FRAGMENTED `-DEATH/DAY # `-NUMBER = (1 + 2 + 6 + 2 + 0 + 1 + 7) = (`-19) = RECIPROCAL (INVERSE/MIRROR) = (`-91) = "AGE of `-DEATH for AMERICAN ACTOR MIKE CONNERS (`-91)!!!~' /|\

(31 + 19) = (`-50) = (5 + 0) = (`-5) = "THE `-HAND of `-GOD-'"!!!~'

`-DIED at the `-AGE of (`-40)!!!~'

AMERICAN ACTOR PAUL WALKER `-BIRTHDAY = (9/12/19/73) = (9 + 12 + 19 + 73) = (`-113) = (13 x 1) = "A VERY PIVOTAL # `-NUMBER"!!!~'

`-**BIRTH/DAY** = (**9/12**) = (91 / `-*DIVIDED* `-*by* (`-**2**) = (`-**45.5**) = "(`-**5.5**) `-YEARS `-AWAY from `-AGE of `-DEATH for AMERICAN ACTOR PAUL WALKER (`-**40**)!!!~'

`-**DEATH/YEAR** = (`-**19/73**) = (73 (-) 19) = (`-**54**) = RECIPROCAL (INVERSE/MIRROR) = (`-**45**) = "(`-**5**) `-YEARS `-AWAY from `-AGE of `-DEATH for AMERICAN ACTOR PAUL WALKER (`-**40**)!!!~'

"WAS `-**BORN** in (`-**9**) (SEPTEMBER); and, `-**DIED** in (`-**11**) (NOVEMBER)"; and, (**9/11**) = (SEPTEMBER 11th) = ("FIRST (`-**2**) NUMERALS of `-HIS `-**BIRTH/DAY**") /|\ (ALMOST `-HIS `-EXACT `-**BIRTHDAY**) = (`-**1**) DAYS AWAY from `-HIS `-**BIRTH/DAY**!!!~' RECIPROCAL (INVERSE/MIRROR) = (**11/9**) = (NOVEMBER 9$^{th}$) = (`-**21**) DAYS AWAY from `-HIS `-**DEATH/DAY**!!!~' (**1/21**) = RECIPROCAL-**S**EQUENCING-**N**UMEROLOGY-**RSN**!!!~'

`-**BIRTH/DAY** = (**9/12**) = (9 + 12) = (`-**21**)!!!~' (91 x 2) = (`-**182**) = (82 x 1) = (`-**82**) / `-*DIVIDED* `-*by* (`-**2**) = (`-**41**) = `-NEAR `-AGE of `-DEATH (`-**40**)!!!~'

(1**973**) = "FLIP the (`-**9**) OVER to a (`-**6**)" & "FLIP the (`-**7**) OVER to a (`-**2**) = (**1623**) = (16 + 23) = (`-**39**) = "DIED of `-AGE upon the `-NEXT `-YEAR; at the `-AGE of (`-**40**)"!!!~'

`-**DEATH/YEAR** = (`-**2013**) = (2 + 3 (-) 1) (0) = (4) (0) = `-*EQUALS* = (`-**40**) = "AGE of `-DEATH for AMERICAN ACTOR PAUL WALKER (`-**40**)!!!~'

AMERICAN ACTOR PAUL WALKER `-**DEATH/DAY** = (**11/30**/20/**13**) = (**11** + **30** + 20 + **13**) = (`-**74**)!!!~'

`-**DEATH/DAY** = (**11/30**) = (11 + 30) = (`-**41**) = "**ONE `-YEAR `-AWAY** from `-**AGE** of `-**DEATH** for AMERICAN ACTOR PAUL WALKER (`-**40**)"!!!~'

(113 (-) 74) = (`-**39**) = "**DIED of `-AGE upon the `-NEXT `-YEAR; at the `-AGE of (`-40**)"!!!~'

(113 + 74) = (`-**187**) = RECIPROCAL (INVERSE/MIRROR) = (**781**) = (78 + 1) = (`-**79**) = "**DIED this `-MANY `-DAYS `-AWAY from `-HIS `-VERY `-OWN `-BIRTH/DAY!!!**~'

AMERICAN ACTOR PAUL WALKER `-**DIED** (`-**79**) DAYS AWAY from `-**HIS `-BIRTHDAY!!!**~'

(365 (-) 79) = (`-**286**) = (28 x 6) = (`-**168**) = (68 x 1) = (`-**68**) = "The `-**MARK**"!!!~'

FRAGMENTED `-**BIRTH/DAY** # `-**NUMBER** = (9 + 1 + 2 + 1 + 9 + 7 + 3) = (`-**32**) = RECIPROCAL (INVERSE/MIRROR) = (`-**23**) = -a PROPHETIC # `-NUMBER!!!~'

FRAGMENTED `-**DEATH/DAY** # `-**NUMBER** = (1 + **1** + **3** + 0 + 2 + 0 + **1** + **3**) = (`-**11**)!!!~'

(32 + 11) = (`-**43**) = RECIPROCAL (INVERSE/MIRROR) = (`-**34**)!!!~'

(`-**43**) = "**THREE `-YEARS `-AWAY** from `-**AGE** of `-**DEATH** for AMERICAN ACTOR PAUL WALKER (`-**40**)!!!**~'

/|\ `-**BIRTH/DAY** # `-**NUMBER** in `-**REVERSE** = (73 (-) 19 (-) 12 (-) 9) = (`-**33**)!!!~'

`-**DEATH/YEAR** = (`-**20/13**) = (20 + 13) = (`-**33**)!!!~' /|\

`-**DIED** at the `-**AGE** of (`-**104**)!!!~'

BRITISH/AMERICAN ACTRESS OLIVIA DE HAVILLAND `-**BIRTHDAY** = (**7**/**1**/19/**16**) = (**7** + **1** + 19 + **16**) = (`-**43**)!!!~'

"WAS `-**BORN** in (`-**7**) (JULY); and, `-**DIED** in (`-**7**) (JULY)"; and, (**7/7**) = (JULY 7th) = (`-**6**) DAYS AWAY from `-HER `-**BIRTH/DAY**!!!~' RECIPROCAL (INVERSE/MIRROR) = (**7/7**) = (JULY 7th) = (`-**19**) DAYS AWAY from `-HER `-**DEATH/DAY**!!!~' (**6/19**) = (6 x 19) = (`-**114**) = "(`-**10**) AWAY from `-**AGE** of `-**DEATH** (`-**104**)" = "**REPLACE** the (`-**1**) WITH an (`-**0**) from (`-**10**)"!!!~'

(1**9**16) = (96) (11) = (96 + 11) = `-*EQUALS* = (**107**) = "**THREE** `-**YEARS** `-**AWAY** from **AGE** of `-**DEATH** for BRITISH/AMERICAN ACTRESS OLIVIA DE HAVILLAND (`-**104**)"!!!~'

`-**DEATH/YEAR** = (`-**2020**) = (2 + 2) (0/0) = "**REPLACE** the (`-**1**) WITH an (`-**0**)" = "AGE of `-DEATH for BRITISH/AMERICAN ACTRESS OLIVIA DE HAVILLAND (`-**104**)"!!!~'

BRITISH/AMERICAN ACTRESS OLIVIA DE HAVILLAND `-**DEATH/DAY** = (**7**/**26**/20/**20**) = (**7** + **26** + 20 + **20**) = (`-**73**)!!!~'

`-**DEATH/DAY** = (**7/26**) = (7 + 26) = (`-**33**)!!!~'

(73 (-) 43) = (`-**30**)!!!~'

(73 + 43) = (`-**116**) = "TWELVE (`-**12**) `-YEARS `-AWAY from **AGE** of `-**DEATH** for BRITISH/AMERICAN ACTRESS OLIVIA DE HAVILLAND (`-**104**)"!!!~'

`-**BIRTH/DAY** # `-**NUMBER** for BRITISH/AMERICAN ACTRESS OLIVIA DE HAVILLAND = (`-**43**) = (4 x 3) = (`-**12**)!!!~'

BRITISH/AMERICAN ACTRESS OLIVIA DE HAVILLAND `-**DIED** (`-**25**) DAYS AWAY from `-**HER** `-**BIRTHDAY!!!**~' (`-**25**) = RECIPROCAL (INVERSE/MIRROR) = (`-**52**)!!!~'

(365 (-) 25) = (`-**340**) = (34 + 0) = (`-**34**) = RECIPROCAL (INVERSE/ MIRROR) = (`-**43**) = `-**BIRTH/DAY #** `-**NUMBER for BRITISH/ AMERICAN ACTRESS OLIVIA DE HAVILLAND** (`-**43**)!!!~'

/|\ FRAGMENTED `-**BIRTH/DAY #** `-**NUMBER** = (7 + 1 + 1 + 9 + 1 + 6) = (`-**25**) = `-**DIED** this `-**MANY** `-**DAYS AFTER** `-**HER** `-**VERY** `-**OWN** `-**BIRTH/DAY** (`-**25**) = RECIPROCAL (INVERSE/MIRROR) = (`-**52**) x `-*TIMES* (`-*2)* = (`-**104**) = "**AGE of** `-**DEATH for BRITISH/AMERICAN ACTRESS OLIVIA DE HAVILLAND** (`-**104**)"!!!~' /|\

FRAGMENTED `-**DEATH/DAY #** `-**NUMBER** = (7 + 2 + 6 + 2 + 0 + 2 + 0) = (`-**19**) = RECIPROCAL (INVERSE/MIRROR) = (`-**91**)!!!~'

(25 + 19) = (`-**44**)!!!~' (`-**60**) `-**YEARS** `-**AWAY from** `-**AGE of** `-**DEATH at** (`-**104**)!!!~'

AMERICAN ACTOR CLARK GABLE `-**DIED in** (`-**19**60)!!!~'

`-**DIED** at the `-**AGE** of (`-**59**)!!!~'

AMERICAN ACTOR CLARK GABLE `-**BIRTHDAY** = (**2/1**/19/**01**) = (**2** + **1** + 19 + **01**) = (`-**23**) = -a PROPHETIC # `-**NUMBER!!!**~'

"WAS `-**BORN** in (`-**2**) (FEBRUARY); and, `-**DIED** in (`-**11**) (NOVEMBER)"; and, (**2/11**) = (FEBRUARY 11th) = (**"FIRST (`- 2) NUMERALS of** `-**BIRTH/DAY"**) = (`-**10**) DAYS AWAY from

`-HIS `-**BIRTH/DAY!!!**~' RECIPROCAL (INVERSE/MIRROR)
= (**11/2**) = (NOVEMBER 2nd) = ('-**14**) DAYS AWAY from `-HIS
`-**DEATH/DAY!!!**~' (**10/14**) = (104 x 1) = ('-**104**) = "**AGE of**
`-**DEATH for BRITISH/AMERICAN ACTRESS OLIVIA DE
HAVILLAND** (`-**104**)"!!!~'

(1**901**) = "FLIP the ('-**9**) OVER to a ('-**6**)" = (6 (-) 1) (9 x 1) = ('-**59**)
= "**AGE of** `-**DEATH for AMERICAN ACTOR CLARK GABLE**
(`-**59**)!!!~'

`-**DEATH/YEAR** = ('-1**960**) = (6 (-) 1) (9 + 0) = (5) (9) = `-*EQUALS*
= (`-**59**) = "**AGE of** `-**DEATH for AMERICAN ACTOR CLARK
GABLE** (`-**59**)!!!~'

AMERICAN ACTOR CLARK GABLE `-**DEATH/DAY** =
(**11/16**/19/**60**) = (**11** + **16** + 19 + **60**) = ('-**106**) = "**TWO** ('-**2**)
`-**YEARS** `-**AWAY from** the **AGE** of `-**DEATH for BRITISH/
AMERICAN ACTRESS OLIVIA DE HAVILLAND** (`-**104**)"!!!~'

(106 (-) 23) = ('-**83**)!!!~'

(106 + 23) = ('-**129**) = (12 x 9) = ('-**108**) = "**FOUR** ('-**4**) `-**YEARS**
`-**AWAY from** the **AGE** of `-**DEATH for BRITISH/AMERICAN
ACTRESS OLIVIA DE HAVILLAND** (`-**104**)"!!!~'

('-**129**) = (**12/9**) = ('-DECEMBER 9th) = `-**SUBTRACT** from
`-**DEATH/DAY** (**11/16**) = ('-**23**) `-**DAYS** = -a PROPHETIC #
`-**NUMBER!!!**~'

AMERICAN ACTOR CLARK GABLE `-**DIED** ('-**77**) DAYS
AWAY from `-**HIS** `-**BIRTHDAY!!!**~'

(365 (-) 77) = (`-**288**) = (88 x 2) = (`-**176**) = (76 + 1) = (`-**77**) = AMERICAN ACTOR CLARK GABLE `-**DIED** THIS `-MANY DAYS AWAY from `-**HIS** `-**BIRTHDAY!!!**~'

FRAGMENTED `-**BIRTH/DAY** # `-**NUMBER** = (2 + 1 + 1 + 9 + 0 + 1) = (`-**14**) = RECIPROCAL (INVERSE/MIRROR) = (`-**41**)!!!~'

(41 + 14) = (`-**55**) = (`-**23**) + (`-**32**)!!!~'

FRAGMENTED `-**DEATH/DAY** # `-**NUMBER** = (1 + 1 + 1 + 6 + 1 + 9 + 6 + 0) = (`-**25**) = FRAGMENTED `-**BIRTH/DAY** # `-**NUMBER of BRITISH/AMERICAN ACTRESS OLIVIA DE HAVILLAND** (`-**25**)"!!!~'

FRAGMENTED `-**DEATH/DAY** # `-**NUMBER** = (1 + 1 + 1 + 6 + 1 + 9 + 6 + 0) = (`-**25**) = RECIPROCAL (INVERSE/MIRROR) = (`-**52**)!!!~'

(14 + 25) = (`-**39**) = RECIPROCAL (INVERSE/MIRROR) = (`-**93**)!!!~'

(93 + 39) = (`-**132**) = (32 x 1) = (`-**32**) = -a PROPHETIC # `-NUMBER!!!~'

`-**DIED** at the `-**AGE** of (`-**98**)!!!~'

AMERICAN ACTOR/COMEDIAN CARL REINER `-**BIRTHDAY**=(**3/20**/19/**22**)=(**3**+**20**+19+**22**)=(`-**64**)=(2x32)=(`-**232**) = **RECIPROCAL-SEQUENCING-NUMEROLOGY-RSN**!!!~'

`-**BIRTH/DAY** = (**3/20**) = (32 + 0) = (`-**32**) = -a PROPHETIC # `-NUMBER!!!~'

WAS `-**MARRIED** to `-**WIFE ESTELLE REINER** for (`-**64**) `-**YEARS** from (1943-to-2008) = `-**EQUALS** `-**HIS** `-**BIRTH/DAY** # `-**NUMBER** (`-**64**)!!!~'

"WAS `-**BORN** in (`-**3**) (MARCH); and, `-**DIED** in (`-**6**) (JUNE)"; and, (**3/6**) = (MARCH 6th) = "**SON ACTOR/COMEDIAN ROB REINER'S** `-**BIRTH/DAY** (**3/6**)" = (`-**14**) DAYS AWAY from `-HIS `-**BIRTH/DAY**!!!~' RECIPROCAL (INVERSE/MIRROR) = (**6/3**) = (JUNE 3rd) = (`-**26**) DAYS AWAY from `-HIS `-**DEATH/DAY**!!!~' (**14/26**) = (14 + 26) = (`-**40**) /|\ (14 x 26) = (`-**364**) = (**ALL-IN-ONE-#-NUMBER**)!!!~'

(19**22**) = (9 + 2) (1 + 2) = (11) (3) = "**JUST** `-**ADD** a (`-**ZERO**) (`-**0**)" = (101) (-) 3) = `-*EQUALS* = (`-**98**) = "**AGE of** `-**DEATH for AMERICAN ACTOR/COMEDIAN CARL REINER** (`-**98**)"!!!~'

AMERICAN ACTOR/COMEDIAN CARL REINER `-**DEATH/DAY** = (**6/29**/20/**20**) = (**6** + **29** + 20 + **20**) = (`-**75**) = (7 x 5) = (`-**35**)!!!~'

`-**BIRTH/DAY** # `-**NUMBER** (`-**64**) = (6 x 4) = (`-**24**)!!!~'

(`-**35**) + (`-**24**) = (`-**59**) = RECIPROCAL (INVERSE/MIRROR) = (`-**95**) = "**ONE** `-**YEAR** `-**AWAY** from `-**HIS** `-**WIFE'S** `-**AGE of** `-**DEATH** (`-**94**)!!!~'

/|\ `-**DEATH/DAY** = (**6/29**) = RECIPROCAL (INVERSE/MIRROR) = (**92/6**) = (92 + 6) = (`-**98**) = "**AGE of** `-**DEATH for AMERICAN ACTOR/COMEDIAN CARL REINER** (`-**98**)"!!!~' /|\

(75 (-) 64) = (`-**11**)!!!~'

(75 + 64) = (`-**139**) = (13 x 9) = (`-**117**)!!!~'

AMERICAN ACTOR/COMEDIAN CARL REINER `-**DIED** (`-**101**) DAYS AWAY from `-**HIS** `-**BIRTHDAY!!!**~'

(365 (-) 101) = (`-**264**) = `-BIRTH/DAY # `-NUMBER = (`-**64**)!!!~'

FRAGMENTED `-**BIRTH/DAY** # `-**NUMBER** = (3 + 2 + 0 + 1 + 9 + 2 + 2) = (`-**19**) = RECIPROCAL (INVERSE/MIRROR) = (`-**91**)!!!~'

FRAGMENTED `-**DEATH/DAY** # `-**NUMBER** = (6 + 2 + 9 + 2 + 0 + 2 + 0) = (`-**21**) = RECIPROCAL (INVERSE/MIRROR) = (`-**12**)!!!~'

(19 + 21) = (`-**40**) = RECIPROCAL (INVERSE/MIRROR) = (`-**04**)!!!~'

(40 + 04) = (`-**44**) = "**WIFE'S ESTELLE REINER'S `-BIRTH/ DAY # `-NUMBER**"!!!~'

`-**DIED** at the `-**AGE** of (`-**94**)!!!~'

AMERICAN ACTRESS ESTELLE REINER `-**BIRTHDAY** = (**6/5**/19/**14**) = (**6** + **5** + 19 + **14**) = (`-**44**)!!!~'

`-**BIRTH/DAY** = (**6/5**) = "FLIP the (`-**6**) OVER to a (`-**9**)" = (**9/5**) = (`-**95**) = "**ONE `-YEAR `-AWAY from `-AGE of `-DEATH for AMERICAN ACTRESS ESTELLE REINER** (`-**94**)"!!!~'

WAS `-**BORN** on (`-**6/5**); and, was (`-**60**) DAYS AWAY from `-**HER** (`-**65**th) WEDDING ANNIVERSARY!!!~'

WAS `-**MARRIED** to `-HUSBAND CARL REINER for (`-**64**) `-**YEARS** from (1943-to-2008)!!!~'

"WAS `-**BORN** in (`-**6**) (JUNE); and, `-**DIED** in (`-**10**) (OCTOBER)"; and, (**6/10**) = (JUNE 10ᵗʰ) = (`-**5**) DAYS AWAY from `-HER `-**BIRTH/DAY!!!**~' RECIPROCAL (INVERSE/ MIRROR) = (**10/6**) = (OCTOBER 6ᵗʰ) = (`-**19**) DAYS AWAY from `-HER `-**DEATH/DAY!!!**~' (**5/19**) = (5 x 19) = (`-**95**) = "ONE `-**YEAR** `-**AWAY** from `-**HER** `-**VERY** `-**OWN** `-AGE of `-DEATH (`-**94**)!!!~'

(1**91**4) = (94) (1 x 1) = (94) (1) = (94 x 1) = `-EQUALS = (`-**94**) = "AGE of `-DEATH for AMERICAN ACTRESS ESTELLE REINER (`-**94**)"!!!~'

AMERICAN ACTRESS ESTELLE REINER `-**DEATH/DAY** = (**10/25**/20/**08**) = (**10** + **25** + 20 + **08**) = (`-**63**) = `-HUSBAND `-**DIED** in (`-**6**); and, was `-**BORN** in (`-**3**)!!!~'

(`-**63**) = RECIPROCAL (INVERSE/MIRROR) = (`-**36**) = "**SON** ACTOR/COMEDIAN ROB REINER was `-**BORN** on (`-**3/6**)"!!!~'

(63 (-) 44) = (`-**19**)!!!~'

(63 + 44) = (`-**107**)!!!~'

AMERICAN ACTRESS ESTELLE REINER `-**DIED** (`-**142**) DAYS AWAY from `-HER `-**BIRTHDAY!!!**~' (`-**142**) = (42 + 1) = (`-**43**) = "WAS `-**MARRIED** in (`-**43**)"!!!~'

(365 (-) 142) = (`-**223**) = (2 x 23) = (`-**46**) = RECIPROCAL (INVERSE/ MIRROR) = (`-**64**) = THE `-**BIRTH/DAY** # `-**NUMBER** = (`-**64**) of `-HER `-**HUSBAND ACTOR/COMEDIAN CARL REINER** (`-**64**)!!!~'

FRAGMENTED `-**BIRTH/DAY** # `-NUMBER = (6 + 5 + 1 + 9 + 1 + 4) = (`-**26**) = RECIPROCAL (INVERSE/MIRROR) = (`-**62**)!!!~'

FRAGMENTED `-**DEATH/DAY** # `-NUMBER = (1 + 0 + 2 + 5 + 2 + 0 + 0 + 8) = (`-**18**) = RECIPROCAL (INVERSE/MIRROR) = (`-**81**)!!!~'

(26 + 18) = (`-**44**) = "THE `-BIRTH/DAY # `-NUMBER of AMERICAN ACTRESS ESTELLE REINER (`-**44**)"!!!~'

HUSBAND'S **BIRTH/DAY** # `-NUMBER (`-**64**) & `-**DEATH/ DAY** # `-NUMBER (`-**75**) = (64 + 75) = (`-**139**)!!!~'

ESTELLE'S **BIRTH/DAY** # `-NUMBER (`-**44**) & `-**DEATH/ DAY** # `-NUMBER (`-**63**) = (44 + 63) = (`-**107**)!!!~'

(139 (-) 107) = (`-**32**) = -a PROPHETIC # `-NUMBER!!!~'

(139 + 107) = (`-**246**) / `-*DIVIDED* `-*by* (`-**2**) = (`-**123**) = (23 x 1) = (`-**23**) = -a PROPHETIC # `-NUMBER!!!~'

`-**DIED** at the `-**AGE** of (`-**91**)!!!~'

AMERICAN COMIC SID CAESAR `-**BIRTHDAY** = (**9**/**8**/19/**22**) = (**9** + **8** + 19 + **22**) = (`-**58**)!!!~'

`-**BIRTH/DAY** = (**9**/**8**) = (`-**98**) = "SEVEN `-YEARS `-AWAY from `-AGE of `-DEATH for AMERICAN COMIC SID CAESAR (`-**91**)"!!!~'

"WAS `-**BORN** in (`-**9**) (SEPTEMBER); and, `-**DIED** in (`-**2**) (FEBRUARY)"; and, (**9**/**2**) = (SEPTEMBER 2nd) = (`-**6**)

DAYS AWAY from `-HIS `-**BIRTH/DAY!!!~'** RECIPROCAL (INVERSE/MIRROR) = (**2/9**) = (FEBRUARY 9th) = (`-**3**) DAYS AWAY from `-HIS `-**DEATH/DAY!!!~'** (**6/3**) = "THE `-**REINERS** `-**ABOVE**"!!!~'

(19**22**) = (92 (-) 2 + 1) = (`-**91**) = "AGE of `-DEATH for AMERICAN COMIC SID CAESAR (`-**91**)"!!!~'

AMERICAN COMIC SID CAESAR `-**DEATH/DAY** = (**2**/**12**/20/**14**) = (**2** + **12** + 20 + **14**) = (`-**48**)!!!~'

`-**DEATH/DAY** = (**2/12**) = "FLIP the (`-**2**) OVER to a (`-**7**)" = (**7/12**) = (**ALL-IN-ONE-#-NUMBER**) = (7 + 2) (1) = (`-**91**) = "AGE of `-DEATH for AMERICAN COMIC SID CAESAR (`-**91**)"!!!~'

`-**DEATH/DAY** = (**2/12**) = (2 + 12) = (`-**14**) = `-**DEATH/YEAR** of (`-**14**)!!!~'

(58 (-) 48) = (`-**10**)!!!~'

(58 + 48) = (`-**106**) = (10 x 6) = (`-**60**)!!!~'

AMERICAN COMIC SID CAESAR `-**DIED** (`-**208**) DAYS AWAY from `-**HIS** `-**BIRTHDAY!!!~'** (`-**208**) = (28 + 0) = (`-**28**) = (2 x 8) = (`-**16**) = RECIPROCAL (INVERSE/MIRROR) = (`-**61**) = "FLIP the (`-**6**) OVER to a (`-**9**) = (`-**91**) = "AGE of `-DEATH for AMERICAN COMIC SID CAESAR (`-**91**)"!!!~'

(365 (-) 208) = (`-**157**) = (15 x 7) = (`-**105**)!!!~'

FRAGMENTED `-**BIRTH/DAY** # `-**NUMBER** = (9 + 8 + 1 + 9 + 2 + 2) = (`-**31**) = RECIPROCAL (INVERSE/MIRROR) = (`-**13**) = "A VERY PIVOTAL # `-NUMBER"!!!~'

FRAGMENTED `-**DEATH/DAY** # `-**NUMBER** = (2 + 1 + 2 + 2 + 0 + 1 + 4) = (`-**12**) = RECIPROCAL (INVERSE/MIRROR) = (`-**21**)!!!~'

(31 + 12) = (`-**43**) = RECIPROCAL (INVERSE/MIRROR) = (`-**34**)!!!~'

`-**DIED** at the `-**AGE** of (`-**86**)!!!~'

AMERICAN DANCER & ACTRESS CYD CHARISSE `-**BIRTHDAY** = (**3**/**8**/19/**22**) = (**3** + **8** + 19 + **22**) = (`-**52**)!!!~'

`-**BIRTH/DAY** = (`-**3/8**) = RECIPROCAL (INVERSE/MIRROR) = (`-**8/3**) = (`-**83**) = "**THREE `-YEARS `-AWAY from `-AGE of `-DEATH for AMERICAN DANCER & ACTRESS CYD CHARISSE (`-86)**"!!!~'

"WAS `-**BORN** in (`-**3**) (MARCH); and, `-**DIED** in (`-**6**) (JUNE)"; and, (**3/6**) = (MARCH 6th) = (`-**2**) DAYS AWAY from `-HER `-**BIRTH/DAY**!!!~' RECIPROCAL (INVERSE/MIRROR) = (**6/3**) = (JUNE 3$^{rd}$) = (`-**14**) DAYS AWAY from `-HER `-**DEATH/DAY**!!!~' (**2/14**) = (21 x 4) = (`-**84**) = "**TWO `-YEARS `-AWAY from `-AGE of `-DEATH for AMERICAN DANCER & ACTRESS CYD CHARISSE (`-86)**"!!!~'

(**19**22) = (91 (-) 2 (-) 2) = (`-**87**) = "**ONE `-YEAR `-AWAY from `-AGE of `-DEATH for AMERICAN DANCER & ACTRESS CYD CHARISSE (`-86)**"!!!~'

AMERICAN DANCER & ACTRESS CYD CHARISSE `-**DEATH/DAY** = (**6**/**17**/20/**08**) = (**6** + **17** + 20 + **08**) = (`-**51**)!!!~'

`-**DEATH/DAY** = (**6/17**) = RECIPROCAL (INVERSE/MIRROR) = (**71/6**) = (**ALL-IN-ONE-#-NUMBER**) = (7 + 1) (6) = (`-**86**) = `-**AGE** of `-**DEATH** for AMERICAN DANCER & ACTRESS CYD CHARISSE (`-**86**)”!!!~’

`-**BIRTH/DAY** # `-**NUMBER** (`-**52**); and, `-**DEATH/DAY** # `-**NUMBER** (`-**51**) are `-**JUST** `-**ONLY** `-**OFF** by `-**ONE** (`-**1**) # `-**NUMBER!!!**~’

`-**BIRTH/DAY** = (**3/8**) = (3 x 8) = (`-**24**)!!!~’

`-**DEATH/DAY** = (**6/17**) = (6 x 17) = (`-**102**)!!!~’

(102 + 24) = (`-**126**) = “FLIP the (`-**2**) OVER to a (`-**7**)” = (`-**176**) = (1 + 7) (6) = (`-**86**) = `-**AGE of** `-**DEATH for AMERICAN DANCER & ACTRESS CYD CHARISSE** (`-**86**)”!!!~’

`-**DEATH/DAY** = (**6/17**) = (6 x 17) = (`-**176**) = (1 + 7) (6) = (`-**86**) = `-**AGE of** `-**DEATH for AMERICAN DANCER & ACTRESS CYD CHARISSE** (`-**86**)”!!!~’

`-**DEATH/DAY** = (**6/17**) = (6 + 17) = (`-**23**) = -a PROPHETIC # `-**NUMBER!!!**~’

(52 (-) 51) = (`-**1**)!!!~’

(52 + 51) = (`-**103**) = (10 x 3) = (`-**30**)!!!~’

AMERICAN DANCER & ACTRESS CYD CHARISSE `-**DIED** (`-**101**) DAYS AWAY from `-**HER** `-**BIRTHDAY!!!**~’

(365 (-) 101) = (`-**264**) = (64 x 2) = (`-**128**) = (28 x 1) = (`-**28**) = RECIPROCAL (INVERSE/MIRROR) = (`-**82**) = “FOUR `-**YEARS** `-**AWAY from** `-**AGE of** `-**DEATH for AMERICAN DANCER & ACTRESS CYD CHARISSE** (`-**86**)”!!!~’

FRAGMENTED `-**BIRTH/DAY** # `-**NUMBER** = (3 + 8 + 1 + 9 + 2 + 2) = (`-**25**) = RECIPROCAL (INVERSE/MIRROR) = (`-**52**)!!!~'

FRAGMENTED `-**DEATH/DAY** # `-**NUMBER** = (6 + 1 + 7 + 2 + 0 + 0 + 8) = (`-**24**) = RECIPROCAL (INVERSE/MIRROR) = (`-**42**)!!!~'

(25 + 24) = (`-**49**) = RECIPROCAL (INVERSE/MIRROR) = (`-**94**)!!!~'

(`-**49**) = (49 + 49) = (`-**98**) = RECIPROCAL (INVERSE/MIRROR) = (`-**89**) = "FLIP the (`-**9**) OVER to a (`-**6**)" = (`-**86**) = `-**AGE of `-DEATH for AMERICAN DANCER & ACTRESS CYD CHARISSE (`-86)"!!!~'**

`-**DIED** at the `-**AGE** of (`-**88**)!!!~'

AMERICAN HOST/ACTOR REGIS PHILBIN `-**BIRTHDAY** = (**8/25**/19/**31**) = (**8** + **25** + 19 + **31**) = (`-**83**) = RECIPROCAL (INVERSE/MIRROR) = (`-**38**) = 3(8's) = (`-**888**)!!!~'

`-**BIRTH/DAY** = (**8/25**) = (82 + 5) = (`-**87**) = **"ONE `-YEAR `-AWAY from `-AGE of `-DEATH for AMERICAN HOST/ ACTOR REGIS PHILBIN (`-88)"!!!~'**

`-**MARRIED** to `-**WIFE JOY PHILBIN** from (`-**1970**) for (`-**50**) YEARS!!!~' JOY PHILBIN'S `-BIRTH/DAY # `-NUMBER = (**2/1/19/41**) = (2 + 1 + 19 + 41) = (`-**63**)!!!~' `-SHE was (`-**79**) YEARS of `-AGE at the `-TIME of `-HER `-HUSBAND'S `-DEATH!!!~' (`-**79**) = (7 x 9) = (`-**63**)!!!~'

('-**19**70) = (9 (-) 1) (7 + 0) = `-*EQUALS* = ('-**87**) = "ONE `-YEAR `-AWAY from `-AGE of `-DEATH for AMERICAN HOST/ ACTOR REGIS PHILBIN ('-**88**)"!!!~'

"WAS `-**BORN** in ('-**8**) (AUGUST); and, `-**DIED** in ('-**7**) (JULY)"; and, (**8/7**) = (AUGUST 7th) = ('-**18**) DAYS AWAY from `-HIS `-BIRTH/DAY!!!~' RECIPROCAL (INVERSE/MIRROR) = (**7/8**) = (JULY 8th) = ('-**16**) DAYS AWAY from `-HIS `-**DEATH/ DAY!!!~'** (**18/16**) = (86 + 1 + 1) = ('-**88**) = "AGE of `-DEATH for AMERICAN HOST/ACTOR REGIS PHILBIN ('-**88**)"!!!~'

(1**931**) = (91 (-) 3) x 1) = `-*EQUALS* = ('-**88**) = "AGE of `-DEATH for AMERICAN HOST/ACTOR REGIS PHILBIN ('-**88**)"!!!~'

AMERICAN HOST/ACTOR REGIS PHILBIN `-**DEATH/DAY** = (**7/24**/20/**20**) = (**7** + **24** + 20 + **20**) = ('-**71**)!!!~'

`-**DEATH/DAY** = (**7/24**) = (7 x 24) = ('-**168**) = "The `-**MARK**"!!!~'

`-**DEATH/DAY** = (**7/24**) = (**ALL-IN-ONE-#-NUMBER**) = (7) (2 x 4) = ('-**78**) = RECIPROCAL (INVERSE/MIRROR) = ('-**87**) = "ONE `-YEAR `-AWAY from `-AGE of `-DEATH for AMERICAN HOST/ACTOR REGIS PHILBIN ('-**88**)"!!!~'

(83 (-) 71) = ('-**12**)!!!~'

(83 + 71) = ('-**154**) = (15 x 4) = ('-**60**)!!!~'

AMERICAN HOST/ACTOR REGIS PHILBIN `-**DIED** ('-**32**) DAYS AWAY from `-**HIS** `-**BIRTHDAY!!!~'** ('-**32**) = -a PROPHETIC # `-NUMBER!!!~'

(365 (-) 32) = ('-**333**)!!!~'

FRAGMENTED `-**BIRTH/DAY** # `-**NUMBER** = (8 + 2 + 5 + 1 + 9 + 3 + 1) = (`-**29**) = RECIPROCAL (INVERSE/MIRROR) = (`-**92**) = **"FOUR `-YEARS `-AWAY from `-AGE of `-DEATH for AMERICAN HOST/ACTOR REGIS PHILBIN (`-88)"**!!!~'

/|\ FRAGMENTED `-**DEATH/DAY** # `-**NUMBER** = (7 + 2 + 4 + 2 + 0 + 2 + 0) = (`-**17**) = RECIPROCAL (INVERSE/MIRROR) = (`-**71**) = (17 + 71) = (`-**88**) = **"AGE of `-DEATH for AMERICAN HOST/ACTOR REGIS PHILBIN (`-88)"**!!!~' /|\

(29 + 17) = (`-**46**) = (`-**23**) x (`-**2**) = (`-**232**) = **RECIPROCAL-SEQUENCING-NUMEROLOGY-RSN**!!!~'

`-**DIED** at the `-**AGE** of (`-**74**)!!!~'

AMERICAN EXECUTIVE HERMAN CAIN `-**BIRTHDAY** = (**12/13**/19/**45**) = (**12** + **13** + 19 + **45**) = (`-**89**) = RECIPROCAL (INVERSE/MIRROR) = (`-**98**)!!!~'

`-**BIRTH/DAY** = (**12/13**) = "FLIP the (`-**2**) OVER to a (`-**7**)" = (**17/13**) = (73 + 1 x 1) = (`-**74**) = `-**AGE of `-DEATH for AMERICAN EXECUTIVE HERMAN CAIN (`-74)"**!!!~'

`-**BIRTH/DAY** = (**12/13**) = (23 x 1 x 1) = (`-**23**) = -a PROPHETIC # `-NUMBER!!!~'

`-**MARRIED** to `-**WIFE GLORIA ETCHISON** from (`-**1968**) for (`-**52**) YEARS!!!~'

"WAS `-**BORN** in (`-**12**) (DECEMBER); and, `-**DIED** in (`-**7**) (JULY)"; and, (**12/7**) = (DECEMBER 7th) = (`-**6**) DAYS AWAY from `-HIS `-**BIRTH/DAY**!!!~' RECIPROCAL (INVERSE/MIRROR) = (**7/12**) = (JULY 12th) = (`-**18**) DAYS AWAY from

`-HIS `-**DEATH/DAY!!!**~' (**6/18**) = (68 x 1) = (`-**68**) = "**WAS** `-**MARRIED** in (`-**68**)"!!!~'

(**19**45) = (91 (-) 54) = `-*EQUALS* = (`-**37**) = RECIPROCAL (INVERSE/MIRROR) = (`-**73**) = "**ONE** `-**YEAR** `-**AWAY** from `-**AGE** of `-**DEATH** for **AMERICAN EXECUTIVE HERMAN CAIN** (`-**74**)"!!!~'

AMERICAN EXECUTIVE HERMAN CAIN `-**DEATH/DAY** = (**7**/**30**/20/**20**) = (**7** + **30** + 20 + **20**) = (`-**77**) = "**THREE**`-**YEARS** `-**AWAY** from `-**AGE** of `-**DEATH** for **AMERICAN EXECUTIVE HERMAN CAIN** (`-**74**)"!!!~'

`-**DEATH/DAY** = (**7/30**) = (73 + 0) = (`-**73**) = "**ONE** `-**YEAR** `-**AWAY** from `-**AGE** of `-**DEATH** for **AMERICAN EXECUTIVE HERMAN CAIN** (`-**74**)"!!!~'

`-**DEATH/DAY** = (**7/30**) = (73 + 0) = (`-**73**) = RECIPROCAL (INVERSE/MIRROR) = (`-**37**)!!!~'

(89 (-) 77) = (`-**12**)!!!~'

(89 + 77) = (`-**166**) = (**ALL-IN-ONE-#-NUMBER**) = (1 + 6) (6) = (`-**76**) = "**TWO** `-**YEARS** `-**AWAY** from `-**AGE** of `-**DEATH** for **AMERICAN EXECUTIVE HERMAN CAIN** (`-**74**)"!!!~'

(`-**166**) /|\ `-**ADD** (`-**10**) /|\ `-**MINUS** (`-**2**) = (`-**174**) = (74 x 1) = (`-**74**) = `-**AGE** of `-**DEATH** for **AMERICAN EXECUTIVE HERMAN CAIN** (`-**74**)"!!!~'

AMERICAN EXECUTIVE HERMAN CAIN `-**DIED** (`-**136**) DAYS AWAY from `-**HIS** `-**BIRTHDAY!!!**~' (`-**136**) = (**ALL-IN-ONE-#-NUMBER**) = (6 + 1) /|\ (3 +1) = (`-**74**) = `-**AGE** of

`-DEATH for AMERICAN EXECUTIVE HERMAN CAIN (`-74)"!!!~'

(365 (-) 136) = (`-229) = (22 x 9) = (`-198) = (98 x 1) = (`-98) = RECIPROCAL (INVERSE/MIRROR) = (`-89) = `-BIRTH/DAY # `-NUMBER for AMERICAN EXECUTIVE HERMAN CAIN (`-89)!!!~'

FRAGMENTED `-BIRTH/DAY # `-NUMBER = (1 + 2 + 1 + 3 + 1 + 9 + 4 + 5) = (`-26) = RECIPROCAL (INVERSE/MIRROR) = (`-62)!!!~'

FRAGMENTED `-DEATH/DAY # `-NUMBER = (7 + 3 + 0 + 2 + 0 + 2 + 0) = (`-14) = RECIPROCAL (INVERSE/MIRROR) = (`-41)!!!~'

(26 + 14) = (`-40) = RECIPROCAL (INVERSE/MIRROR) = (`-04)!!!~'

`-DIED at the `-AGE of (`-72)!!!~'

AMERICAN ACTOR JOHN WAYNE `-BIRTHDAY = (5/26/19/07) = (5 + 26 + 19 + 07) = (`-57) = RECIPROCAL (INVERSE/MIRROR) = (`-75) = "THREE `-YEARS `-AWAY from `-AGE of `-DEATH for AMERICAN ACTOR JOHN WAYNE (`-72)"!!!~'

`-BIRTH/DAY = (5/26) = "FLIP the (`-2) OVER to a (`-7)" = (5/76) = (76 (-) 5) = (`-71) = "ONE `-YEAR `-AWAY from `-AGE of `-DEATH for AMERICAN ACTOR JOHN WAYNE (`-72)"!!!~'

`-BIRTH/DAY = (5/26) = (5 x 26) = (`-130) = (13 + 0) = (`-13) = "A VERY PIVOTAL # `-NUMBER"!!!~'

"WAS `-**BORN** in (`-**5**) (MAY); and, `-**DIED** in (`-**6**) (JUNE)"; and, (**5/6**) = (MAY 6th) = (`-**20**) DAYS AWAY from `-HIS `-**BIRTH/ DAY!!!~'** RECIPROCAL (INVERSE/MIRROR) = (**6/5**) = (JUNE 5[th]) = (`-**6**) DAYS AWAY from `-HIS `-**DEATH/DAY!!!~'** (**20/6**) = (20 + 6) = (`-**26**) = "**DAY of `-BIRTH (`-26th)**"!!!~'

`-**BIRTH/YEAR** = (1**90**7) = (90 (-) 17) = `-*EQUALS* = (`-**73**) = "**ONE `-YEAR `-AWAY from `-AGE of `-DEATH for AMERICAN ACTOR JOHN WAYNE (`-72)**"!!!~'

`-**DEATH/YEAR** = (1**9**7**9**) = (1 + 7) (9 + 9) = (8) (18) = (**81 (-) 8**) = `-*EQUALS* = (`-**73**) = "**ONE `-YEAR `-AWAY from `-AGE of `-DEATH for AMERICAN ACTOR JOHN WAYNE (`-72)**"!!!~'

AMERICAN ACTOR JOHN WAYNE `-**DEATH/DAY** = (**6/11**/19/**79**) = (**6** + **11** + 19 + **79**) = (`-**115**)!!!~'

`-**DEATH/DAY** = (**6/11**) = (**ALL-IN-ONE-#-NUMBER**) = (6 + 1) /|\ (1 +1) = (7) (2) = (`-**72**) = `-**AGE of `-DEATH for AMERICAN ACTOR JOHN WAYNE (`-72)**"!!!~'

(115 (-) 57) = (`-**58**)!!!~'

(115 + 57) = (`-**172**) = (72 x 1) = (`-**72**) = `-**AGE of `-DEATH for AMERICAN ACTOR JOHN WAYNE (`-72)**"!!!~'

AMERICAN ACTOR JOHN WAYNE `-**DIED** (`-**16**) DAYS AWAY from `-**HIS `-BIRTHDAY!!!~'** (`-**16**) = RECIPROCAL (INVERSE/MIRROR) = (`-**61**) = (16 + 61) = (`-**77**) = "FLIP the (`-**7**) OVER to a (`-**2**)" = (`-**72**) = `-**AGE of `-DEATH for AMERICAN ACTOR JOHN WAYNE (`-72)**"!!!~'

(365 (-) 16) = (`-**349**) = (49 + 3) = (`-**52**) = "FLIP the (`-**2**) OVER to a (`-**7**)" = (`-**57**) = `-BIRTH/DAY # `-NUMBER for `-AMERICAN ACTOR JOHN WAYNE (`-**57**)!!!~'

FRAGMENTED `-**BIRTH/DAY** # `-**NUMBER** = (5 + 2 + 6 + 1 + 9 + 0 + 7) = (`-**30**) = RECIPROCAL (INVERSE/MIRROR) = (`-**03**)!!!~'

FRAGMENTED `-**DEATH/DAY** # `-**NUMBER** = (6 + 1 + 1 + 1 + 9 + 7 + 9) = (`-**34**) = RECIPROCAL (INVERSE/MIRROR) = (`-**43**)!!!~'

(34 + 43) = (`-**77**) = "FLIP the (`-**7**) OVER to a (`-**2**)" = (`-**72**) = `-AGE of `-DEATH for AMERICAN ACTOR JOHN WAYNE (`-**72**)"!!!~'

(30 + 34) = (`-**64**) = RECIPROCAL (INVERSE/MIRROR) = (`-**46**)!!!~'

(`-19**07**) = `-BIRTH/YEAR!!!~'

(`-19**79**) = `-DEATH/YEAR!!!~'

RECIPROCAL-SEQUENCING-NUMEROLOGY-RSN!!!~'

(`-**64**) = (`-**2**) x (`-**32**) = (`-**232**) = **RECIPROCAL-SEQUENCING-NUMEROLOGY-RSN!!!~'**

`-**DIED** at the `-**AGE** of (`-**59**)!!!~'

AMERICAN ACTOR ROCK HUDSON `-**BIRTHDAY** = (**11**/**17**/19/**25**) = (**11** + **17** + 19 + **25**) = (`-**72**)!!!~'

/|\ `-**BIRTH/DAY** = (**11/17**) = RECIPROCAL (INVERSE/ MIRROR) = (**71/11**) = (71 (-) 11) = (`-**60**) = "ONE `-YEAR `-AWAY from `-AGE of `-DEATH for AMERICAN ACTOR ROCK HUDSON (`-**59**)"!!!~' `-**DIED** in the `-**YEAR** of (`-**60**)!!!~' /|\

"WAS `-**BORN** in (`-**11**) (NOVEMBER); and, `-**DIED** in (`-**10**) (OCTOBER)"; and, (**11/10**) = (NOVEMBER 10th) = (`-**7**) DAYS AWAY from `-HIS `-**BIRTH/DAY**!!!~' RECIPROCAL (INVERSE/ MIRROR) = (**10/11**) = (OCTOBER 11th) = (`-**9**) DAYS AWAY from `-HIS `-**DEATH/DAY**!!!~' (**7/9**) = (7 x 9) = (`-**63**)!!!~'

(**1925**) = (51) + (9 (-) 2) = (51) + (7) = `-*EQUALS* = (`-**58**) = "ONE `-YEAR `-AWAY from `-AGE of `-DEATH for AMERICAN ACTOR ROCK HUDSON (`-**59**)"!!!~'

AMERICAN ACTOR ROCK HUDSON `-**DEATH/DAY** = (**10/2**/19/**85**) = (**10** + **2** + 19 + **85**) = (`-**116**) / `-*DIVIDED* `-*by* (`-**2**) = (`-**58**)!!!~'

(116 (-) 72) = (`-**44**)!!!~'

(116 + 72) = (`-**188**) = (18 x 8) = (`-**144**)!!!~'

AMERICAN ACTOR ROCK HUDSON `-**DIED** (`-**46**) DAYS AWAY from `-HIS `-**BIRTHDAY**!!!~' (`-**46**) = (`-**23**) x (`-**2**) = (`-**232**) = **RECIPROCAL-SEQUENCING-NUMEROLOGY-RSN**!!!~'

(365 (-) 46) = (`-**319**) = (19 x 3) = (`-**57**) = "TWO `-YEARS `-AWAY from `-AGE of `-DEATH for AMERICAN ACTOR ROCK HUDSON (`-**59**)"!!!~'

(365 (-) 46) = (`-**319**) = (31 x 9) = (`-**279**) = (**ALL-IN-ONE-#-NUMBER**) = (7 (-) 2) /|\ (9) = (`-**59**) = `-AGE of `-DEATH for AMERICAN ACTOR ROCK HUDSON (`-**59**)"!!!~'

FRAGMENTED `-**BIRTH/DAY** # `-**NUMBER** = (1 + 1 + 1 + 7 + 1 + 9 + 2 + 5) = (`-**27**) = RECIPROCAL (INVERSE/MIRROR) = (`-**72**) = `-**BIRTH/DAY** # `-**NUMBER** for AMERICAN ACTOR ROCK HUDSON (`-**72**)!!!~'

FRAGMENTED `-**DEATH/DAY** # `-**NUMBER** = (1 + 0 + 2 + 1 + 9 + 8 + 5) = (`-**26**) = RECIPROCAL (INVERSE/MIRROR) = (`-**62**)!!!~'

(27 + 26) = (`-**53**) = RECIPROCAL (INVERSE/MIRROR) = (`-**35**)!!!~'

(27 + 26) = (`-**53**) = "SIX `-YEARS `-AWAY from `-AGE of `-DEATH for AMERICAN ACTOR ROCK HUDSON (`-**59**)"!!!~'

`-**DIED** at the `-**AGE** of (`-**80**)!!!~'

AMERICAN ACTOR MARLON BRANDO `-**BIRTHDAY** = (**4**/**3**/19/**24**) = (**4** + **3** + 19 + **24**) = (`-**50**)!!!~'

"WAS `-**BORN** in (`-**4**) (APRIL); and, `-**DIED** in (`-**7**) (JULY)"; and, (**4**/**7**) = (APRIL 7th) = (`-**4**) DAYS AWAY from `-HIS `-**BIRTH/DAY**!!!~' RECIPROCAL (INVERSE/MIRROR) = (**7**/**4**) = (JULY 4th) = (`-**3**) DAYS AWAY from `-HIS `-**DEATH/DAY**!!!~' (**4**/**3**) = `-**HIS** `-**VERY** `-**OWN** `-**BIRTH/DAY** for AMERICAN ACTOR MARLON BRANDO (**APRIL 3**rd)!!!~'

(1**924**) = (94) (-) 12 = `-*EQUALS* = (`-**82**) = "TWO `-YEARS `-AWAY from `-AGE of `-DEATH for AMERICAN ACTOR MARLON BRANDO (`-**80**)"!!!~'

AMERICAN ACTOR MARLON BRANDO `-**DEATH/DAY**
= (**7**/**1**/20/**04**) = (**7** + **1** + 20 + **04**) = (`-**32**) = -a PROPHETIC #
`-NUMBER!!!~'

(50 (-) 32) = (`-**18**) = RECIPROCAL (INVERSE/MIRROR) =
(`-**81**) = "ONE `-YEAR `-AWAY from `-AGE of `-DEATH for
AMERICAN ACTOR MARLON BRANDO (`-**80**)"!!!~'

(50 + 32) = (`-**82**) = "TWO `-YEARS `-AWAY from `-AGE of
`-DEATH for AMERICAN ACTOR MARLON BRANDO
(`-**80**)"!!!~'

AMERICAN ACTOR MARLON BRANDO `-**DIED** (`-**89**)
DAYS AWAY from `-HIS `-BIRTHDAY!!!~' (`-**89**) = (`-**8**) x (`-**9**)
= (`-**72**)!!!~'

(365 (-) 89) = (`-**276**) = (76 + 2) = (`-**78**) = "TWO `-YEARS `-AWAY
from `-AGE of `-DEATH for AMERICAN ACTOR MARLON
BRANDO (`-**80**)"!!!~'

FRAGMENTED `-**BIRTH/DAY** # `-NUMBER = (4 + 3 + 1 + 9
+ 2 + 4) = (`-**23**) = RECIPROCAL (INVERSE/MIRROR) = (`-
32) = `-**DEATH/DAY** # `-NUMBER for AMERICAN ACTOR
MARLON BRANDO (`-**32**) = -a PROPHETIC # `-NUMBER!!!~'

FRAGMENTED `-**DEATH/DAY** # `-NUMBER = (7 + 1 + 2
+ 0 + 0 + 4) = (`-**14**) = RECIPROCAL (INVERSE/MIRROR) =
(`-**41**)!!!~'

(23 + 14) = (`-**37**) = RECIPROCAL (INVERSE/MIRROR) =
(`-**73**)!!!~'

`-**DIED** at the `-**AGE** of (`-**85**)!!!~'

AMERICAN ACTOR WILFORD BRIMLEY `-**BIRTHDAY** = (**9**/**27**/19/**34**) = (**9** + **27** + 19 + **34**) = (`-**89**) = RECIPROCAL (INVERSE/MIRROR) = (`-**98**) = `-**BORN** in (`-**9**); AND, `-**DIED** in (`-**8**)!!!~'

`-**BIRTH/DAY** = (**9/27**) = (92 (-) 7) = (`-**85**) = `-**AGE** of `-**DEATH** for AMERICAN ACTOR WILFORD BRIMLEY (`-**85**)"!!!~'

"WAS `-**BORN** in (`-**9**) (SEPTEMBER); and, `-**DIED** in (`-**8**) (AUGUST)"; and, (**9/8**) = (SEPTEMBER 8th) = (`-**19**) DAYS AWAY from `-HIS `-**BIRTH/DAY**!!!~' RECIPROCAL (INVERSE/MIRROR) = (**8/9**) = (AUGUST 9th) = (`-**8**) DAYS AWAY from `-HIS `-**DEATH/DAY**!!!~' (**19/8**) = (98 x 1) = (`-**98**) = RECIPROCAL (INVERSE/MIRROR) = (`-**89**) = `-**HIS** `-**VERY** `-**OWN** `-**BIRTH/DAY** # `-**NUMBER** for AMERICAN ACTOR WILFORD BRIMLEY (`-**89**)!!!~'

(**19**34) = (91) (-) (3 + 4) = `-*EQUALS* = (`-**84**) = "ONE `-YEAR `-AWAY from `-AGE of `-DEATH for AMERICAN ACTOR WILFORD BRIMLEY (`-**85**)"!!!~'

AMERICAN ACTOR WILFORD BRIMLEY `-**DEATH/DAY** = (**8**/**1**/20/**20**) = (**8** + **1** + 20 + **20**) = (`-**49**)!!!~'

`-**DEATH/DAY** = (**8/1**) = (`-**81**) = "FOUR `-YEARS `-AWAY from `-AGE of `-DEATH for AMERICAN ACTOR WILFORD BRIMLEY (`-**85**)"!!!~'

(89 (-) 49) = (`-**40**)!!!~'

(89 + 49) = (`-**138**) = RECIPROCAL (INVERSE/MIRROR) = (**831**) = (83 + 1) = (`-**84**) = "ONE `-YEAR `-AWAY from `-AGE

of `-DEATH for AMERICAN ACTOR WILFORD BRIMLEY (`-**85**)"!!!~'

AMERICAN ACTOR WILFORD BRIMLEY `-**DIED** (`-**57**) DAYS AWAY from `-HIS `-BIRTHDAY!!!~' (`-**57**) = (5 x 7) = (`-**35**) = `-HIS `-VERY `-OWN `-FRAGMENTED `-BIRTH/DAY # `-NUMBER (`-**35**)!!!~'

(365 (-) 57) = (`-**308**) = RECIPROCAL (INVERSE/MIRROR) = (`-**803**) = (83 + 0) = (`-**83**) = "TWO `-YEARS `-AWAY from `-AGE of `-DEATH for AMERICAN ACTOR WILFORD BRIMLEY (`-**85**)"!!!~'

FRAGMENTED `-**BIRTH/DAY** # `-NUMBER = (9 + 2 + 7 + 1 + 9 + 3 + 4) = (`-**35**) = RECIPROCAL (INVERSE/MIRROR) = (`-**53**)!!!~'

FRAGMENTED `-**DEATH/DAY** # `-NUMBER = (8 + 1 + 2 + 0 + 2 + 0) = (`-**13**) = "A VERY PIVOTAL # `-NUMBER" = RECIPROCAL (INVERSE/MIRROR) = (`-**31**)!!!~'

(35 + 13) = (`-**48**) = RECIPROCAL (INVERSE/MIRROR) = (`-**84**) = "ONE `-YEAR `-AWAY from `-AGE of `-DEATH for AMERICAN ACTOR WILFORD BRIMLEY (`-**85**)"!!!~'

`-**DIED** at the `-**AGE** of (`-**95**)!!!~'

AMERICAN ACTOR BUDDY EBSEN `-**BIRTHDAY** = (**4**/**2**/19/**08**) = (**4** + **2** + 19 + **08**) = (`-**33**)!!!~'

`-**BIRTH/DAY** = (**4**/**2**) = "FLIP the (`-**2**) OVER to a (`-**7**)" = "MONTH of `-BIRTH (`-**4**); and, MONTH of `-DEATH (`-**7**)!!!~'

/|\ `-**BIRTH/DAY** = (**4/2**) = (`-**42**) = (7 x 6) = (**7/6**) = `-**DEATH/ DAY** for AMERICAN ACTOR BUDDY EBSEN (**JULY 6**[th])!!!~' /|\

"WAS `-**BORN** in (`-**4**) (APRIL); and, `-**DIED** in (`-**7**) (JULY)"; and, (**4/7**) = (APRIL 7th) = (`-**5**) DAYS AWAY from `-HIS `-**BIRTH/ DAY!!!~'** RECIPROCAL (INVERSE/MIRROR) = (**7/4**) = (JULY 4[th]) = (`-**2**) DAYS AWAY from `-HIS `-**DEATH/DAY!!!~'** (**5/2**)!!!~'

(**19**08) = (91) (+) (0 + 8) = `-*EQUALS* = (`-**99**) = "FOUR `-YEARS `-AWAY from `-AGE of `-DEATH for AMERICAN ACTOR BUDDY EBSEN (`-**95**)"!!!~'

AMERICAN ACTOR BUDDY EBSEN `-**DEATH/DAY** = (**7/6**/20/**03**) = (**7** + **6** + 20 + **03**) = (`-**36**) = RECIPROCAL (INVERSE/MIRROR) = (`-**63**) = "FLIP the (`-**6**) OVER to a (`-**9**) = (`-**93**) = "TWO `-YEARS `-AWAY from `-AGE of `-DEATH for AMERICAN ACTOR BUDDY EBSEN (`-**95**)"!!!~'

`-**DEATH/YEAR** = (**20/03**) = (20 + 03) = (`-**23**) = -a PROPHETIC # `-NUMBER!!!~'

(36 (-) 33) = (`-**3**)!!!~'

(36 + 33) = (`-**69**) = RECIPROCAL (INVERSE/MIRROR) = (**96**) = "ONE `-YEAR `-AWAY from `-AGE of `-DEATH for AMERICAN ACTOR BUDDY EBSEN (`-**95**)"!!!~'

/|\ AMERICAN ACTOR BUDDY EBSEN `-**DIED** (`-**95**) DAYS AWAY from `-HIS `-BIRTHDAY!!!~' (`-**95**) = `-HIS `-VERY `-OWN `-AGE of `-DEATH for AMERICAN ACTOR BUDDY EBSEN (`-**95**)!!!~' /|\

(365 (-) 95) = (`-**270**) = (27 + 0) = (`-**27**)!!!~' `-**BORN** in (`-**4**); AND, `-**DIED** in (`-**7**)!!!~' (`-**47**) = RECIPROCAL (INVERSE/ MIRROR) = (`-**74**)!!!~' (74 (-) 47) = (`-**27**)!!!~'

/|\ FRAGMENTED `-**BIRTH/DAY** # `-**NUMBER** = (4 + 2 + 1 + 9 + 0 + 8) = (`-**24**) = RECIPROCAL (INVERSE/MIRROR) = (`-**42**) = (7 x 6) = `-**DEATH/DAY** for AMERICAN ACTOR BUDDY EBSEN (**JULY 6**ᵗʰ)!!!~' /|\

FRAGMENTED `-**DEATH/DAY** # `-**NUMBER** = (7 + 6 + 2 + 0 + 0 + 3) = (`-**18**) = RECIPROCAL (INVERSE/MIRROR) = (`-**81**)!!!~' (18 + 81) = (`-**99**) = "FOUR `-YEARS `-AWAY from `-AGE of `-DEATH for AMERICAN ACTOR BUDDY EBSEN (`-**95**)"!!!~'

(24 + 18) = (`-**42**) = `-**BIRTH/DAY** (`-**42**) & `-**DEATH/DAY** (`-**7/6**) = RECIPROCAL (INVERSE/MIRROR) = (`-**24**) = `-**HIS** `-**VERY** `-**OWN** `-**FRAGMENTED** `-**BIRTH/DAY** # `-**NUMBER** (`-**24**)!!!~'

`-**DIED** at the `-**AGE** of (`-**70**)!!!~'

AMERICAN ACTRESS IRENE RYAN `-**BIRTHDAY** = (**10/17**/19/**02**) = (**10** + **17** + 19 + **02**) = (`-**48**)!!!~'

`-**BIRTH/DAY** = (**10/17**) = RECIPROCAL (INVERSE/ MIRROR) = (**17/10**) = (70 x 1 x 1) = (`-**70**) = `-**AGE of `-DEATH** for AMERICAN ACTRESS IRENE RYAN (`-**70**)"!!!~'

"WAS `-**BORN** in (`-**10**) (OCTOBER); and, `-**DIED** in (`-**4**) (APRIL)"; and, (**10/4**) = (OCTOBER 4ᵗʰ) = (`-**13**) DAYS AWAY from `-HER `-**BIRTH/DAY**!!!~' RECIPROCAL (INVERSE/

MIRROR) = (**4/10**) = (APRIL 10th) = (`-**16**) DAYS AWAY from `-HER `-**DEATH/DAY!!!~'** (**13/16**) = (36 x 1 x 1) = (`-**36**) = RECIPROCAL (INVERSE/MIRROR) = (`-**63**)!!!~' (`-**36**) = `-**DEATH/DAY** # `-**NUMBER** for AMERICAN ACTOR BUDDY EBSEN (`-**36**)!!!~'

(1**902**) = (9 (-) 2) (x) (1) (0) = `-*EQUALS* = (`-**70**) = `-HER `-VERY `-OWN `-AGE of `-DEATH for AMERICAN ACTRESS IRENE RYAN (`-**70**)"!!!~'

AMERICAN ACTRESS IRENE RYAN `-**DEATH/DAY** = (**4**/**26**/19/**73**) = (**4** + **26** + 19 + **73**) = (`-**122**) = (22 + 1) = (`-**23**) = -a PROPHETIC # `-NUMBER!!!~'

`-**DEATH/DAY** = (**4/26**) = RECIPROCAL (INVERSE/MIRROR) = (**62/4**) = (62 + 4) = (`-**66**) = "FOUR `-YEARS `-AWAY from `-AGE of `-DEATH for AMERICAN ACTRESS IRENE RYAN (`-**70**)"!!!~'

`-**DEATH/YEAR** = (`-**73**) = "THREE `-YEARS `-AWAY from `-AGE of `-DEATH for AMERICAN ACTRESS IRENE RYAN (`-**70**)"!!!~'

(122 (-) 48) = (`-**74**) = `-**DIED** this `-**MANY** `-**DAYS** `-**PLUS** a (`-**100**) from `-**BIRTH/DAY!!!~'**

(122 + 48) = (`-**170**) = (70 x 1) = (`-**70**) = `-HER `-VERY `-OWN `-AGE of `-DEATH for AMERICAN ACTRESS IRENE RYAN (`-**70**)"!!!~'

AMERICAN ACTRESS IRENE RYAN `-**DIED** (`-**174**) DAYS AWAY from `-HER `-**BIRTHDAY!!!~'** (`-**174**) = (17 x 4) = (`-**68**) = "The `-**MARK**"!!!~'

(365 (-) 174) = (`-**191**) = (91 (-) 19) = (`-**72**) = "**TWO `-YEARS `-AWAY from `-AGE of `-DEATH for AMERICAN ACTRESS IRENE RYAN (`-70)**"!!!~'

(`-**191**) = **R**ECIPROCAL-**S**EQUENCING-**N**UMEROLOGY-**RSN**!!!~'

FRAGMENTED `-**BIRTH/DAY** # `-NUMBER = (1 + 0 + 1 + 7 + 1 + 9 + 0 + 2) = (`-**21**) = "FLIP the (`-**2**) OVER to a (`-**7**)" = (`-**71**) = "**ONE `-YEAR `-AWAY from `-AGE of `-DEATH for AMERICAN ACTRESS IRENE RYAN (`-70)**"!!!~'

FRAGMENTED `-**BIRTH/DAY** # `-NUMBER = (1 + 0 + 1 + 7 + 1 + 9 + 0 + 2) = (`-**21**) = RECIPROCAL (INVERSE/MIRROR) = (`-**12**) = (21 + 12) = (`-**33**) = `-**BIRTH/DAY** # `-NUMBER for AMERICAN ACTOR BUDDY EBSEN (`-**33**)!!!~'

FRAGMENTED `-**DEATH/DAY** # `-NUMBER = (4 + 2 + 6 + 1 + 9 + 7 + 3) = (`-**32**) = RECIPROCAL (INVERSE/MIRROR) = (`-**23**) = -a PROPHETIC # `-NUMBER!!!~'

(21 + 32) = (`-**53**) = RECIPROCAL (INVERSE/MIRROR) = (`-**35**)!!!~'

`-**DIED** at the `-**AGE** of (`-**82**)!!!~'

AMERICAN ACTRESS DONNA DOUGLAS `-**BIRTHDAY** = (**9/26**/19/**32**) = (**9** + **26** + 19 + **32**) = (`-**86**) = RECIPROCAL (INVERSE/MIRROR) = (`-**68**) = "The `-**MARK**"!!!~'

`-**BIRTH/DAY** = (**9/26**) = (92 (-) 6) = (`-**86**) = "**FOUR `-YEARS `-AWAY from `-AGE of `-DEATH for AMERICAN ACTRESS DONNA DOUGLAS (`-82)**"!!!~'

`-**BORN** in (`-**32**) = -a PROPHETIC # `-NUMBER!!!~'

"WAS `-**BORN** in (`-**9**) (SEPTEMBER); and, `-**DIED** in (`-**1**) (JANUARY)"; and, (**9/1**) = (SEPTEMBER 1st) = (`-**25**) DAYS AWAY from `-HER `-**BIRTH/DAY!!!~'** RECIPROCAL (INVERSE/ MIRROR) = (**1/9**) = (JANUARY 9th) = (`-**8**) DAYS AWAY from `-HER `-**DEATH/DAY!!!~'** (**25/8**) = (25 + 8) = (`-**33**) = `-**BIRTH/ DAY # `-NUMBER for AMERICAN ACTOR BUDDY EBSEN** (`-**33**)!!!~' !!!~'

(1**93**2) = (93) (-) (12) = `-*EQUALS* = (`-**81**) = **"ONE `-YEAR `-AWAY from `-AGE of `-DEATH for AMERICAN ACTRESS DONNA DOUGLAS (`-82)"!!!~'**

AMERICAN ACTRESS DONNA DOUGLAS `-**DEATH/ DAY** = (**1/1**/20/**15**) = (**1** + **1** + 20 + **15**) = (`-**37**) = RECIPROCAL (INVERSE/MIRROR) = (`-**73**)!!!~'

(86 (-) 37) = (`-**49**) = (4 x 9) = (`-**36**) = `-**DEATH/DAY # `-NUMBER for AMERICAN ACTOR BUDDY EBSEN** (`-**36**)!!!~'

(86 + 37) = (`-**123**) = (23 x 1) = (`-**23**) = -a PROPHETIC # `-NUMBER!!!~'

AMERICAN ACTRESS DONNA DOUGLAS `-**DIED** (`-**97**) DAYS AWAY from `-HER `-BIRTHDAY!!!~' (`-**97**) = (9 x 7) = (`-**63**) = RECIPROCAL (INVERSE/MIRROR) = (`-**36**)!!!~'

(365 (-) 97) = (`-**268**) = (68 x 2) = (`-**136**) = RECIPROCAL (INVERSE/MIRROR) = (`-**631**) = (63 x 1) = (`-**63**)!!!~'

FRAGMENTED `-**BIRTH/DAY # `-NUMBER** = (9 + 2 + 6 + 1 + 9 + 3 + 2) = (`-**32**) = RECIPROCAL (INVERSE/MIRROR) = (`-**23**) = -a PROPHETIC # `-NUMBER!!!~'

FRAGMENTED `-**BIRTH/DAY** # `-**NUMBER** = (9 + 2 + 6 + 1 + 9 + 3 + 2) = (`-**32**) = "YEAR of `-BIRTH (`-**32**) for AMERICAN ACTRESS DONNA DOUGLAS"!!!~'

FRAGMENTED `-**DEATH/DAY** # `-**NUMBER** = (1 + 1 + 2 + 0 + 1 + 5) = (`-**10**) = RECIPROCAL (INVERSE/MIRROR) = (`-**01**)!!!~'

(32 + 10) = (`-**42**) = "The `-**MARK**"!!!~' = RECIPROCAL (INVERSE/MIRROR) = (`-**24**)!!!~'

`-**DIED** at the `-**AGE** of (`-**69**)!!!~'

AMERICAN ACTRESS NANCY KULP `-**BIRTHDAY** = (**8/28**/19/**21**) = (**8** + **28** + 19 + **21**) = (`-**76**) = RECIPROCAL (INVERSE/MIRROR) = (`-**67**) = "TWO `-YEARS `-AWAY from `-AGE of `-DEATH for AMERICAN ACTRESS NANCY KULP (`-**69**)"!!!~'

`-**BIRTH/DAY** = (**8/28**) = (82 (-) 8) = (`-**74**) = "FIVE `-YEARS `-AWAY from `-AGE of `-DEATH for AMERICAN ACTRESS NANCY KULP (`-**69**)"!!!~'

`-**BIRTH/DAY** = (**8/28**) = (8 + 28) = (`-**36**) = `-**DEATH/DAY** # `-**NUMBER** for AMERICAN ACTOR BUDDY EBSEN (`-**36**)!!!~'

`-**BIRTH/DAY** = (`-**828**) = **RECIPROCAL-SEQUENCING-NUMEROLOGY-RSN**!!!~'

"WAS `-**BORN** in (`-**8**) (AUGUST); and, `-**DIED** in (`-**2**) (FEBRUARY)"; and, (**8/2**) = (AUGUST 2ⁿᵈ) = (`-**26**) DAYS AWAY from `-HER `-**BIRTH/DAY**!!!~' RECIPROCAL (INVERSE/

MIRROR) = (**2/8**) = (FEBRUARY 8ᵗʰ) = (`-**5**) DAYS AWAY from `-HER `-**DEATH/DAY!!!~'** (**26/5**) = (26 x 5) = (`-**130**) = (13 + 0) = (`-**13**) = "A VERY PIVOTAL # `-NUMBER"!!!~'

(1**921**) = (91) (-) (21) = `-*EQUALS* = (`-**70**) = "ONE `-YEAR `-AWAY from `-AGE of `-DEATH for AMERICAN ACTRESS NANCY KULP (`-**69**)"!!!~' `-**DIED** in the `-**YEAR** `-**OF!!!~'**

AMERICAN ACTRESS NANCY KULP `-**DEATH/DAY** = (**2/3**/19/**91**) = (**2** + **3** + 19 + **91**) = (`-**115**)!!!~'

`-**DEATH/YEAR** = (**19/91**) = (91 (-) 19) = (`-**72**) = "THREE `-YEARS `-AWAY from `-AGE of `-DEATH for AMERICAN ACTRESS NANCY KULP (`-**69**)"!!!~'

`-**DEATH/YEAR** & `-**DEATH/DAY** = (**3/19/91**) = (91 (-) 19 (-) 3) = (`-**69**) = `-AGE of `-DEATH for AMERICAN ACTRESS NANCY KULP (`-**69**)"!!!~'

`-**DEATH/DAY** = (`-**2/3**) = (`-**23**) = -a PROPHETIC # `-NUMBER!!!~'

/|\ `-**DEATH/DAY** # `-**NUMBER** in `-**REVERSE** = (91 (-) 19 (-) 3 (-) 2) = (`-**67**) = RECIPROCAL (INVERSE/MIRROR) = (`-**76**) = `-**BIRTH/DAY** # `-**NUMBER** for AMERICAN ACTRESS NANCY KULP!!!~' /|\

(115 (-) 76) = (`-**39**)!!!~'

(115 + 76) = (`-**191**) = "YEAR of `-DEATH (`-**91**)"; and, = `-EQUALS = **RECIPROCAL-SEQUENCING-NUMEROLOGY-RSN!!!~'**

AMERICAN ACTRESS NANCY KULP `-**DIED** (`-**206**) DAYS AWAY from `-HER `-**BIRTHDAY!!!~'**

(365 (-) 206) = (`-**159**) = (15 x 9) = (`-**135**) = RECIPROCAL (INVERSE/MIRROR) = (`-**531**) = (53 x 1) = (`-**53**)!!!~'

(365 (-) 206) = (`-**159**) = (**ALL-IN-ONE-#-NUMBER**) = (1 + 5) (9) = (`-**69**) = `-**AGE** of `-**DEATH** for **AMERICAN ACTRESS NANCY KULP** (`-**69**)"!!!~'

FRAGMENTED `-**BIRTH/DAY** # `-**NUMBER** = (8 + 2 + 8 + 1 + 9 + 2 + 1) = (`-**31**) = RECIPROCAL (INVERSE/MIRROR) = (`-**13**) = "A VERY PIVOTAL # `-NUMBER"!!!~'

FRAGMENTED `-**DEATH/DAY** # `-**NUMBER** = (2 + 3 + 1 + 9 + 9 + 1) = (`-**25**) = RECIPROCAL (INVERSE/MIRROR) = (`-**52**) = "**AMERICAN ACTOR BUDDY EBSEN** in the `-**MONTH** of `-**DEATH** & `-**BIRTH**"!!!~'

(31 + 25) = (`-**56**) = RECIPROCAL (INVERSE/MIRROR) = (`-**65**) = "**FOUR** `-**YEARS** `-**AWAY** from `-**AGE** of `-**DEATH** for **AMERICAN ACTRESS NANCY KULP** (`-**69**)"!!!~'

AMERICAN ACTRESS NANCY KULP'S `-**AGE** of `-**DEATH** = (`-**69**) = RECIPROCAL (INVERSE/MIRROR) = (`-**96**) = "**ONE** `-**YEAR** `-**AWAY** from `-**AGE** of `-**DEATH** for **AMERICAN ACTOR BUDDY EBSEN** (`-**95**)"!!!~'

`-**BIRTH/YEAR** = (`-1**92**1)!!!~' (`-**92**) = 2(9's) = (`-**99**)!!!~'

`-**DEATH/YEAR** = (`-1**99**1)!!!~'

(`-**19**) = RECIPROCAL (INVERSE/MIRROR) = (`-**91**)!!!~'

`-**DIED** at the `-**AGE** of (`-**65**)!!!~'

AMERICAN ACTOR/COMEDIAN RICHARD PRYOR `-**BIRTHDAY** = (**12/1**/19/**40**) = (**12** + **1** + 19 + **40**) = (`-**72**) = RECIPROCAL (INVERSE/MIRROR) = (`-**27**)!!!~'

`-**BIRTH/DAY** = (`-**121**) = **RECIPROCAL-SEQUENCING-NUMEROLOGY-RSN**!!!~'

`-**BIRTH/DAY** = (`-**121**) = (ALL-IN-ONE-#-NUMBER) = `-**BIRTH**; and, `-**DEATH** in the `-**SAME** `-**MONTH**!!!~'

"WAS `-**BORN** in (`-**12**) (DECEMBER); and, `-**DIED** in (`-**12**) (DECEMBER)"; and, (**12/12**) = (DECEMBER 12th) = (`-**11**) DAYS AWAY from `-HIS `-**BIRTH/DAY**!!!~' RECIPROCAL (INVERSE/MIRROR) = (**12/12**) = (DECEMBER 12[th]) = (`-**2**) DAYS AWAY from `-HIS `-**DEATH/DAY**!!!~' (**11/2**) = `-**BIRTH/DAY** (`-**121**) (SWIPE (`-**1**)) = (`-**112**) / `-*DIVIDED* `-*by* (`-**2**) = (`-**56**) = RECIPROCAL (INVERSE/MIRROR) = (`-**65**) = `-**HIS** `-**VERY** `-**OWN** `-**AGE** of `-**DEATH** for AMERICAN ACTOR/COMEDIAN RICHARD PRYOR (`-**65**)!!!~'

(**19**40) = (40) + (19) = `-*EQUALS* = (`-**59**) = "FLIP the (`-**9**) OVER to a (`-**6**)" = (`-**56**) = RECIPROCAL (INVERSE/MIRROR) = (`-**65**) = `-**HIS** `-**VERY** `-**OWN** `-**AGE** of `-**DEATH** for AMERICAN ACTOR/COMEDIAN RICHARD PRYOR (`-**65**)!!!~'

AMERICAN ACTOR/COMEDIAN RICHARD PRYOR `-**DEATH/DAY** = (**12/10**/20/**05**) = (**12** + **10** + 20 + **05**) = (`-**47**)!!!~'

`-**BIRTH/DAY** = (`-**121**)!!!~'

`-**DEATH/DAY** = (`-**121**(0))!!!~' "JUST `-**ADD** a `-**ZERO** (`-**0**)"!!!~'

(121 + 121) = (`-**242**) = **RECIPROCAL-SEQUENCING-NUMEROLOGY-RSN**!!!~'

(72 (-) 47) = (`-**25**)!!!~'

(72 + 47) = (`-**119**) = (11 x 9) = (`-**99**) = RECIPROCAL (INVERSE/MIRROR) = (`-**66**) = "**ONE** `-**YEAR** `-**AWAY** from `-**AGE** of `-**DEATH** for **AMERICAN ACTOR/COMEDIAN RICHARD PRYOR** (`-**65**)"!!!~'

AMERICAN ACTOR/COMEDIAN RICHARD PRYOR `-**DIED** (`-**9**) DAYS AWAY from `-**HIS** `-**BIRTHDAY**!!!~'

(365 (-) 9) = (`-**356**) = (56 x 3) = (`-**168**) = "The `-**MARK**"!!!~'

FRAGMENTED `-**BIRTH/DAY** # `-**NUMBER** = (1 + 2 + 1 + 1 + 9 + 4 + 0) = (`-**18**) = RECIPROCAL (INVERSE/MIRROR) = (`-**81**)!!!~' (81 (-) 18) = (`-**63**) = "**TWO** `-**YEARS** `-**AWAY** from `-**AGE** of `-**DEATH** for **AMERICAN ACTOR/COMEDIAN RICHARD PRYOR** (`-**65**)"!!!~'

FRAGMENTED `-**DEATH/DAY** # `-**NUMBER** = (1 + 2 + 1 + 0 + 2 + 0 + 0 + 5) = (`-**11**)!!!~'

(18 + 11) = (`-**29**) = RECIPROCAL (INVERSE/MIRROR) = (`-**92**)!!!~'

(92 (-) 29) = (`-**63**) = "**TWO** `-**YEARS** `-**AWAY** from `-**AGE** of `-**DEATH** for **AMERICAN ACTOR/COMEDIAN RICHARD PRYOR** (`-**65**)"!!!~'

`-**DIED** at the `-**AGE** of (`-**33**)!!!~'

AMERICAN ACTOR/COMEDIAN JOHN BELUSHI `-**BIRTHDAY** = (**1**/**24**/19/**49**) = (**1** + **24** + 19 + **49**) = (`-**93**) = RECIPROCAL (INVERSE/MIRROR) = (`-**39**) = "SIX `-YEARS `-AWAY from `-AGE of `-DEATH for AMERICAN ACTOR/ COMEDIAN JOHN BELUSHI (`-**33**)"!!!~'

`-**BIRTH/DAY** = (`-**124**) = (**ALL-IN-ONE-#-NUMBER**) = (1 + 2) (4) = (`-**34**) = "ONE `-YEAR `-AWAY from `-AGE of `-DEATH for AMERICAN ACTOR/COMEDIAN JOHN BELUSHI (`-**33**)"!!!~'

`-**BIRTH/YEAR** = (**19/49**) = (19 + 49) = (`-**68**) = "The `-**MARK**"!!!~'

"WAS `-**BORN** in (`-**1**) (JANUARY); and, `-**DIED** in (`-**3**) (MARCH)"; and, (**1/3**) = (JANUARY 3rd) = (`-**21**) DAYS AWAY from `-HIS `-**BIRTH/DAY!!!**~' RECIPROCAL (INVERSE/MIRROR) = (**3/1**) = (MARCH 1$^{st}$) = (`-**4**) DAYS AWAY from `-HIS `-**DEATH/ DAY!!!**~' (**21/4**) = `-**BIRTH/DAY** (`-**124**) (SWIPE (`-**1**)) = (`-**214**) = (ALL-IN-ONE-#-NUMBER) = (2 + 1) (4) = (`-**34**) = "ONE `-YEAR `-AWAY from `-AGE of `-DEATH for AMERICAN ACTOR/COMEDIAN JOHN BELUSHI (`-**33**)"!!!~'

(**19**49) = (49) (-) (19) = `-*EQUALS* = (`-**30**) = "THREE `-YEARS `-AWAY from `-AGE of `-DEATH for AMERICAN ACTOR/ COMEDIAN JOHN BELUSHI (`-**33**)"!!!~'

AMERICAN ACTOR/COMEDIAN JOHN BELUSHI `-**DEATH/DAY** = (**3**/**5**/19/**82**) = (**3** + **5** + 19 + **82**) = (`-**109**)!!!~'

`-**DEATH/DAY** = (**3/5**) = (`-**35**) = "TWO `-YEARS `-AWAY from `-AGE of `-DEATH for AMERICAN ACTOR/COMEDIAN JOHN BELUSHI (`-**33**)"!!!~'

`-BIRTH/DAY # `-NUMBER in `-REVERSE = (49 (-) 19 (-) 24 (-) 1) = (`-5)!!!~'

`-DEATH/DAY # `-NUMBER in `-REVERSE = (82 (-) 19 (-) 5 (-) 3) = (`-55)!!!~'

(`-5) /|\ (`-55) = 3(5's) = (3/5) = "DAY of `-DEATH (MARCH 5th)"!!!~'

(109 (-) 93) = (`-16)!!!~'

(109 + 93) = (`-202)!!!~'

(202 + 16) = (`-218) = (18 x 2) = (`-36) = "THREE `-YEARS `-AWAY from `-AGE of `-DEATH for AMERICAN ACTOR/ COMEDIAN JOHN BELUSHI (`-33)"!!!~'

AMERICAN ACTOR/COMEDIAN JOHN BELUSHI `-DIED (`-40) DAYS AWAY from `-HIS `-BIRTHDAY!!!~'

(365 (-) 40) = (`-325) = (`-32.5) = (ROUNDED `-UP) = (`-33) = `-AGE of `-DEATH for AMERICAN ACTOR/COMEDIAN JOHN BELUSHI (`-33)"!!!~'

/|\ FRAGMENTED `-BIRTH/DAY # `-NUMBER = (1 + 2 + 4 + 1 + 9 + 4 + 9) = (`-30) = RECIPROCAL (INVERSE/MIRROR) = (`-03)!!!~' (30 + 03) = (`-33) = `-AGE of `-DEATH for AMERICAN ACTOR/COMEDIAN JOHN BELUSHI (`-33)"!!!~' /|\

FRAGMENTED `-DEATH/DAY # `-NUMBER = (3 + 5 + 1 + 9 + 8 + 2) = (`-28) = RECIPROCAL (INVERSE/MIRROR) = (`-82) = "DIED in (`-82) for AMERICAN ACTOR/COMEDIAN JOHN BELUSHI (`-82)!!!~'

(30 + 28) = (`-**58**) = RECIPROCAL (INVERSE/MIRROR) = (`-**85**)!!!~'

`-**DIED** at the `-**AGE** of (`-**43**)!!!~'

CANADIAN ACTOR/COMEDIAN JOHN CANDY `-**BIRTHDAY** = (**10/31**/19/**50**) = (**10** + **31** + 19 + **50**) = (`-**110**)!!!~'

`-**BIRTH/DAY** = (`-**10/31**) = (10 + 31) = (`-**41**) = "TWO `-YEARS `-AWAY from `-AGE of `-DEATH for CANADIAN ACTOR/ COMEDIAN JOHN CANDY (`-**43**)"!!!~'

"WAS `-**BORN** in (`-**10**) (OCTOBER); and, `-**DIED** in (`-**3**) (MARCH)"; and, (**10/3**) = (OCTOBER 3rd) = (`-**28**) DAYS AWAY from `-HIS `-**BIRTH/DAY**!!!~' RECIPROCAL (INVERSE/ MIRROR) = (**3/10**) = (MARCH 10th) = (`-**6**) DAYS AWAY from `-HIS `-**DEATH/DAY**!!!~' (**28/6**) = (28 + 6) = (**34**) = RECIPROCAL (INVERSE/MIRROR) = (`-**43**) = `-**AGE** of `-**DEATH** for CANADIAN ACTOR/COMEDIAN JOHN CANDY (`-**43**)"!!!~'

(1**950**) = (9 (-) 5) (1 + 0) = `-*EQUALS* = (`-**41**) = "TWO `-YEARS `-AWAY from `-AGE of `-DEATH for CANADIAN ACTOR/ COMEDIAN JOHN CANDY (`-**43**)"!!!~'

CANADIAN ACTOR/COMEDIAN JOHN CANDY `-**DEATH/ DAY** = (**3/4**/19/**94**) = (**3** + **4** + 19 + **94**) = (`-**120**)!!!~'

/|\ `-**DEATH/DAY** = (**3/4**) = (`-**34**) = RECIPROCAL (INVERSE/ MIRROR) = (`-**43**) = `-**AGE of `-DEATH for CANADIAN ACTOR/COMEDIAN JOHN CANDY (`-**43**)"!!!~' /|\

`-**DEATH/DAY** # `-**NUMBER in** `-**REVERSE** = (94 (-) 19 (-) 4 (-) 3) = (`-**68**) = "The `-**MARK**"!!!~'

(120 (-) 110) = (`-**10**)!!!~'

(120 + 110) = (`-**230**) = (23 + 0) = (`-**23**) = -a PROPHETIC # `-NUMBER!!!~'

(230 + 10) = (`-**240**) = (24 + 0) = (`-**24**) = RECIPROCAL (INVERSE/MIRROR) = (`-**42**) = "**ONE `-YEAR `-AWAY from `-AGE of `-DEATH for CANADIAN ACTOR/COMEDIAN JOHN CANDY (`-43)**"!!!~'

CANADIAN ACTOR/COMEDIAN JOHN CANDY `-**DIED** (`-**124**) DAYS AWAY from `-**HIS** `-**BIRTHDAY!!!~'** `-**BIRTH/ DAY** (`-**1/24**) for AMERICAN ACTOR/COMEDIAN JOHN BELUSHI (**JANUARY 24**[th])!!!~' **DIED** a `-**DAY** in the `-**MONTH** /|\ `-**PREVIOUS** /|\ to **JOHN BELUSHI** (3/4) /|\ (3/5)!!!~'

/|** (365 (-) 124) = (`-**241**) = (41 + 2) = (`-43**) = `-**AGE of `-DEATH for CANADIAN ACTOR/COMEDIAN JOHN CANDY (`-43)**"!!!~' **/|**

FRAGMENTED `-**BIRTH/DAY** # `-**NUMBER** = (1 + 0 + 3 + 1 + 1 + 9 + 5 + 0) = (`-**20**) = RECIPROCAL (INVERSE/MIRROR) = (`-**02**)!!!~'

FRAGMENTED `-**DEATH/DAY** # `-**NUMBER** = (3 + 4 + 1 + 9 + 9 + 4) = (`-**30**) = RECIPROCAL (INVERSE/MIRROR) = (`-**03**)!!!~'

(**20** + **30**) = (`-**50**) = RECIPROCAL (INVERSE/MIRROR) = (`-**05**)!!!~'

(50 + 05) = (`-**55**) = (`-**23**) + (`-**32**) = -a PROPHETIC # `-NUMBER!!!~'

`-**BIRTH/YEAR** = (`-**1950**) = (50 (-) 19) = (`-**31**) = RECIPROCAL (INVERSE/MIRROR) = (`-**13**) = "A VERY PIVOTAL # `-NUMBER"!!!~'

`-**DEATH/YEAR** = (`-**1994**) = (19 + 94) = (`-**113**) = (13 x 1) = (`-**13**) = "A VERY PIVOTAL # `-NUMBER"!!!~'

`-**DIED** at the `-**AGE** of (`-**33**)!!!~'

AMERICAN ACTOR/COMEDIAN CHRIS FARLEY `-**BIRTHDAY** = (**2**/**15**/19/**64**) = (**2** + **15** + 19 + **64**) = (`-**100**) = "SWIVEL POINT"!!!~'

`-**BIRTH/DAY** = (**2/15**) = (2 x 15) = (`-**30**) = "THREE `-YEARS `-AWAY from `-AGE of `-DEATH for AMERICAN ACTOR/COMEDIAN CHRIS FARLEY (`-**33**)"!!!~'

"WAS `-**BORN** in (`-**2**) (FEBRUARY); and, `-**DIED** in (`-**12**) (DECEMBER)"; and, (**2/12**) = (FEBRUARY 12th) = (`-**3**) DAYS AWAY from `-HIS `-**BIRTH/DAY**!!!~' RECIPROCAL (INVERSE/MIRROR) = (**12/2**) = (DECEMBER 2[nd]) = (`-**16**) DAYS AWAY from `-HIS `-**DEATH/DAY**!!!~' (**3/16**) = (36 x 1) = (`-**36**) = "THREE `-YEARS `-AWAY from `-AGE of `-DEATH for AMERICAN ACTOR/COMEDIAN CHRIS FARLEY (`-**33**)"!!!~'

(19**64**) = (9 (-) 6) (-) (1 (-) 4) = `-*EQUALS* = (`-**33**) = `-AGE of `-DEATH for AMERICAN ACTOR/COMEDIAN CHRIS FARLEY (`-**33**)"!!!~'

AMERICAN ACTOR/COMEDIAN CHRIS FARLEY `-**DEATH/DAY** = (**12**/**18**/19/**97**) = (**12** + **18** + 19 + **97**) = (`-**146**)!!!~'

`-**DEATH/DAY** = (**12/18**) = (12 + 18) = (`-**30**) = "**THREE `-YEARS `-AWAY from `-AGE of `-DEATH for AMERICAN ACTOR/ COMEDIAN CHRIS FARLEY (`-33)**"!!!~'

(146 (-) 100) = (`-**46**)!!!~'

(146 + 100) = (`-**246**)!!!~'

(246 + 46) = (`-**292**) = **RECIPROCAL-SEQUENCING-NUMEROLOGY-RSN**!!!~'

AMERICAN ACTOR/COMEDIAN CHRIS FARLEY `-**DIED** (`-**59**) DAYS AWAY from `-**HIS `-BIRTHDAY**!!!~'

(365 (-) 59) = (`-**306**) = (36 + 0) = (`-**36**) = "**THREE `-YEARS `-AWAY from `-AGE of `-DEATH for AMERICAN ACTOR/ COMEDIAN CHRIS FARLEY (`-33)**"!!!~'

(365 (-) 59) = (`-**306**) = (36 + 0) = (`-**36**) = RECIPROCAL (INVERSE/MIRROR) = (`-63) = (9 x 7) = (`-**97**) = `-**DIED** in (`-**97**)!!!~'

FRAGMENTED `-**BIRTH/DAY** # `-**NUMBER** = (2 + 1 + 5 + 1 + 9 + 6 + 4) = (`-**28**) = RECIPROCAL (INVERSE/MIRROR) = (`-**82**)!!!~'

FRAGMENTED `-**DEATH/DAY** # `-**NUMBER** = (1 + 2 + 1 + 8 + 1 + 9 + 9 + 7) = (`-**38**) = RECIPROCAL (INVERSE/MIRROR) = (`-**83**)!!!~'

(28 + 38) = (`-**66**) / `-*DIVIDED by* (`-**2**) = (`-**33**) = `-**AGE of `-DEATH for AMERICAN ACTOR/COMEDIAN CHRIS FARLEY (`-33)**"!!!~'

`-**DIED** at the `-**AGE** of (`-**42**)!!!~'

AMERICAN COMEDIAN GILDA RADNER `-**BIRTHDAY** = (**6/28**/19/**46**) = (**6** + **28** + 19 + **46**) = (`-**99**) = RECIPROCAL (INVERSE/MIRROR) = (`-**66**)!!!~'

`-**BIRTH/DAY** = (**6/28**) = (6 x 28) = (`-**168**) = "The `-**MARK**"!!!~'

"WAS `-**BORN** in (`-**6**) (JUNE); and, `-**DIED** in (`-**5**) (MAY)"; and, (**6/5**) = (19 + 46) = (`-**65**) = `-**BIRTH/YEAR** = (JUNE 5th) = (`-**23**) DAYS AWAY from `-HER `-**BIRTH/DAY**!!!~' RECIPROCAL (INVERSE/MIRROR) = (**5/6**) = (MAY 6$^{th}$) = (`-**14**) DAYS AWAY from `-HER `-**DEATH/DAY**!!!~' (**23/14**) = (23 x 14) = (`-**322**) = (**ALL-IN-ONE-#-NUMBER**) = (2 + 2) (-3) = (`-**43**) = "**ONE** `-**YEAR** `-**AWAY from** `-**AGE** of `-**DEATH** for AMERICAN COMEDIAN GILDA RADNER (`-**42**)"!!!~'

(**19**46) = (91) (-) (46) = `-*EQUALS* = (`-**45**) = "**THREE** `-**YEARS** `-**AWAY from** `-**AGE** of `-**DEATH** for AMERICAN COMEDIAN GILDA RADNER (`-**42**)"!!!~'

AMERICAN COMEDIAN GILDA RADNER `-**DEATH/DAY** = (**5/20**/19/**89**) = (**5** + **20** + 19 + **89**) = (`-**133**) = (33 + 1) = (`-**34**) = `-FRAGMENTED `-**DEATH/DAY** # `-**NUMBER** (`-**34**)!!!~'

`-**DEATH/DAY** = (**5/20**) = (52 + 0) = (`-**52**) = "**TEN** `-**YEARS** `-**AWAY from** `-**AGE** of `-**DEATH** for AMERICAN COMEDIAN GILDA RADNER (`-**42**)"!!!~'

AMERICAN COMEDIAN GILDA RADNER `-**DEATH/DAY** = (**5/20**/19/**89**) = (**5** + **20** + 19 + **89**) = (`-**133**) = (13 x 3) = (`-**39**) = "**DIED** this `-**MANY** `-**DAYS** `-**AWAY from** `-**HER** `-**BIRTH/ DAY** (`-**39**)!!!~'

`-DEATH/DAY` # `-NUMBER` in `-REVERSE` = (89 (-) 19 (-) 20 (-) 5) = (`-45`) = "THREE `-YEARS` `-AWAY` from `-AGE` of `-DEATH` for AMERICAN COMEDIAN GILDA RADNER (`-42`)"!!!~'

(133 (-) 99) = (`-34`) = `-FRAGMENTED` `-DEATH/DAY` # `-NUMBER` (`-34`)!!!~'

(133 + 99) = (`-232`) = RECIPROCAL-SEQUENCING-NUMEROLOGY-RSN!!!~'

(232 + 34) = (`-266`) = (66 x 2) = (`-132`) = (32 x 1) = (`-32`) = -a PROPHETIC # `-NUMBER`!!!~'

AMERICAN COMEDIAN GILDA RADNER `-DIED` (`-39`) DAYS AWAY from `-HER` `-BIRTHDAY`!!!~'

(365 (-) 39) = (`-326`) = (32 + 6) = (`-38`) = "FOUR `-YEARS` `-AWAY` from `-AGE` of `-DEATH` for AMERICAN COMEDIAN GILDA RADNER (`-42`)"!!!~'

FRAGMENTED `-BIRTH/DAY` # `-NUMBER` = (6 + 2 + 8 + 1 + 9 + 4 + 6) = (`-36`) = RECIPROCAL (INVERSE/MIRROR) = (`-63`)!!!~'

/|\ `-BIRTH/DAY` = (`6/28`) = (6 + 28) = (`-34`) = `-FRAGMENTED` `-DEATH/DAY` # `-NUMBER` (`-34`)!!!~' /|\

FRAGMENTED `-DEATH/DAY` # `-NUMBER` = (5 + 2 + 0 + 1 + 9 + 8 + 9) = (`-34`) = RECIPROCAL (INVERSE/MIRROR) = (`-43`) = "ONE `-YEAR` `-AWAY` from `-AGE` of `-DEATH` for AMERICAN COMEDIAN GILDA RADNER (`-42`)"!!!~'

$(36 + 34) = (`-70) =$ "FLIP the $(`-7)$ OVER to a $(`-2) = (`-20) =$ "**DAY of `-DEATH** for AMERICAN COMEDIAN GILDA RADNER $(`-20th)$"!!!~'

$(36 + 34) = (`-70) = (89 (-) 19) = (19/89) =$ "**DEATH/YEAR** for AMERICAN COMEDIAN GILDA RADNER $(`-1989)$"!!!~'

`-**DIED** at the `-**AGE** of $(`-38)$!!!~'

/|\ AMERICAN COMEDIAN SAM KINISON `-**BIRTHDAY** = $(12/8/19/53) = (12 + 8 + 19 + 53) = (`-92) =$ `-**BIRTH/DAY #** `-**NUMBER** = $(`-92)$; AND, then `-**HE** `-**DIED** in $(`-92)$!!!~' /|\

`-**BIRTH/DAY** = $(12/8) =$ (**ALL-IN-ONE-#-NUMBER**) = $(1 + 2)$ $(8) = (`-38) =$ `-**AGE of `-DEATH** for AMERICAN COMEDIAN SAM KINISON $(`-38)$"!!!~'

`-**BIRTH/YEAR** = $(`-53) =$ RECIPROCAL (INVERSE/MIRROR) = $(`-35) =$ "**THREE `-YEARS `-AWAY** from `-AGE of `-DEATH for AMERICAN COMEDIAN SAM KINISON $(`-38)$"!!!~'

"WAS `-**BORN** in $(`-12)$ (DECEMBER); and, `-**DIED** in $(`-4)$ (APRIL)"; and, $(12/4) =$ (DECEMBER $4^{th}) = (`-4)$ DAYS AWAY from `-HIS `-**BIRTH/DAY**!!!~' RECIPROCAL (INVERSE/ MIRROR) = $(4/12) =$ (APRIL $12^{th}) = (`-2)$ DAYS AWAY from `-HIS `-**DEATH/DAY**!!!~' $(4/2) = (4 x 2) = (`-8) =$ "**DAY of `-BIRTH** (`-8th) for AMERICAN COMEDIAN SAM KINISON"!!!~'

$(1953) = (53) (-) (19) =$ `-*EQUALS* = $(`-34) =$ "**FOUR `-YEARS `-AWAY** from `-AGE of `-DEATH for AMERICAN COMEDIAN SAM KINISON $(`-38)$"!!!~'

AMERICAN COMEDIAN SAM KINISON `-**DEATH/DAY** = (**4**/**10**/19/**92**) = (**4** + **10** + 19 + **92**) = (`-**125**) = (**ALL-IN-ONE-#-NUMBER**) = (1 + 2) (5) = (`-**35**) = "**THREE** `-**YEARS** `-**AWAY** from `-**AGE** of `-**DEATH** for **AMERICAN COMEDIAN SAM KINISON** (`-**38**)"!!!~'

`-**DEATH/DAY** = (**4/10**) = (4 x 10) = (`-**40**) = "**TWO** `-**YEARS** `-**AWAY** from `-**AGE** of `-**DEATH** for **AMERICAN COMEDIAN SAM KINISON** (`-**38**)"!!!~'

`-**DEATH/DAY** = (**4/10**) = (41 + 0) = (`-**41**) = "**THREE** `-**YEARS** `-**AWAY** from `-**AGE** of `-**DEATH** for **AMERICAN COMEDIAN SAM KINISON** (`-**38**)"!!!~'

(125 (-) 92) = (`-**33**)!!!~'

(125 + 92) = (`-**217**) = (2 x 17) = (`-**34**) = "**FOUR** `-**YEARS** `-**AWAY** from `-**AGE** of `-**DEATH** for **AMERICAN COMEDIAN SAM KINISON** (`-**38**)"!!!~'

(125 + 92) = (`-**217**) = (21 x 7) = (`-**147**) = (**ALL-IN-ONE-#-NUMBER**) = (4 (-) 1) (7) = (`-**37**) = "**ONE** `-**YEAR** `-**AWAY** from `-**AGE** of `-**DEATH** for **AMERICAN COMEDIAN SAM KINISON** (`-**38**)"!!!~'

AMERICAN COMEDIAN SAM KINISON `-**DIED** (`-**123**) DAYS AWAY from `-**HIS** `-**BIRTHDAY**!!!~' (`-**123**) = (23 x 1) = (`-**23**) = -a PROPHETIC # `-NUMBER!!!~'

(365 (-) 123) = (`-**242**) = (42 (-) 2) = (`-**40**) = "**TWO** `-**YEARS** `-**AWAY** from `-**AGE** of `-**DEATH** for **AMERICAN COMEDIAN SAM KINISON** (`-**38**)"!!!~'

(365 (-) 123) = (`-**242**) = **RECIPROCAL-SEQUENCING-NUMEROLOGY-RSN!!!~'**

/|\ FRAGMENTED `-**BIRTH/DAY** # `-**NUMBER** = (1 + 2 + 8 + 1 + 9 + 5 + 3) = (`-**29**) = RECIPROCAL (INVERSE/MIRROR) = (`-**92**) = `-**BIRTH/DAY** # `-**NUMBER** for **AMERICAN COMEDIAN SAM KINISON** (`-**92**)!!!~' /|\

/|\ FRAGMENTED `-**BIRTH/DAY** # `-**NUMBER** = (1 + 2 + 8 + 1 + 9 + 5 + 3) = (`-**29**) = RECIPROCAL (INVERSE/MIRROR) = (`-**92**) = `-**DEATH/YEAR** of **AMERICAN COMEDIAN SAM KINISON** = (`-**92**)!!!~' /|\

(92 (-) 29) = (`-**63**) = RECIPROCAL (INVERSE/MIRROR) = (`-**36**) = "**TWO `-YEARS `-AWAY from `-AGE of `-DEATH for AMERICAN COMEDIAN SAM KINISON** (`-**38**)"!!!~'

FRAGMENTED `-**DEATH/DAY** # `-**NUMBER** = (4 + 1 + 0 + 1 + 9 + **9** + **2**) = (`-**26**) = RECIPROCAL (INVERSE/MIRROR) = (`-**62**)!!!~'

(62 (-) 26) = (`-**36**) = "**TWO `-YEARS `-AWAY from `-AGE of `-DEATH for AMERICAN COMEDIAN SAM KINISON** (`-**38**)"!!!~'

(29 + 26) = (`-**55**) = (`-**23**) + (`-**32**) = -a PROPHETIC # `-NUMBER!!!~'

`-**DIED** at the `-**AGE** of (`-**50**)!!!~'

AMERICAN ACTOR/COMEDIAN BERNIE MAC `-**BIRTHDAY** = (**10/5**/19/**57**) = (**10** + **5** + 19 + **57**) = (`-**91**) = RECIPROCAL (INVERSE/MIRROR) = (`-**19**)!!!~'

/|\ (91 (-) 19) = (`-**72**) = (8 x 9) = (**8/9**) = `-**DEATH/DAY** for AMERICAN ACTOR/COMEDIAN BERNIE MAC (`-**AUGUST 9ᵗʰ**)"!!!~'

`-**BIRTH/DAY** = (**10/5**) = (10 x 5) = (`-**50**) = `-**AGE** of `-**DEATH** for AMERICAN ACTOR/COMEDIAN BERNIE MAC (`-**50**)"!!!~' /|\

"WAS `-**BORN** in (`-**10**) (OCTOBER); and, `-**DIED** in (`-**8**) (AUGUST)"; and, (**10/8**) = (OCTOBER 8ᵗʰ) = (`-**3**) DAYS AWAY from `-HIS `-**BIRTH/DAY**!!!~' RECIPROCAL (INVERSE/ MIRROR) = (**8/10**) = (AUGUST 10ᵗʰ) = (`-**1**) DAY AWAY from `-HIS `-**DEATH/DAY**!!!~' (**3/1**) = (**31**) = RECIPROCAL (INVERSE/ MIRROR) = (`-**13**) = "A VERY PIVOTAL # `-NUMBER"!!!~'

(19**57**) = (75) (-) (19) = `-*EQUALS* = (`-**56**) = "SIX `-YEARS `-AWAY from `-AGE of `-DEATH for AMERICAN ACTOR/ COMEDIAN BERNIE MAC (`-**50**)"!!!~'

AMERICAN ACTOR/COMEDIAN BERNIE MAC `-**DEATH/ DAY** = (**8/9**/20/**08**) = (**8** + **9** + 20 + **08**) = (`-**45**) = "FIVE `-YEARS `-AWAY from `-AGE of `-DEATH for AMERICAN ACTOR/ COMEDIAN BERNIE MAC (`-**50**)"!!!~'

`-**DEATH/DAY** = (**8/9**) = (8 x 9) = (`-**72**) = "**LOOK** to `-**BIRTH/ DAY** # `-**NUMBER** `-**ABOVE** = (91 (-) 19) = (`-**72**) = (8 x 9) = `-**DEATH/DAY**"!!!~'

(91 (-) 45) = (`-**46**) = (`-**23**) x (`-**2**) = (`-**232**) = **RECIPROCAL-SEQUENCING-NUMEROLOGY-RSN**!!!~'

(91 + 45) = (`-**136**) = (36 x 1) = (`-**36**) = RECIPROCAL (INVERSE/ MIRROR) = (`-**63**)!!!~'

/|\ AMERICAN ACTOR/COMEDIAN BERNIE MAC `-**DIED** (`-**57**) DAYS AWAY from `-HIS `-**BIRTHDAY!!!**~' (`-**57**) = AMERICAN ACTOR/COMEDIAN BERNIE MAC was `-**BORN** in (`-**57**)!!!~' /|\

(365 (-) 57) = (`-**308**) = (38 + 0) = (`-**38**) = (**19** + **19**) = (`-RECIPROCAL~'/INVERSE/MIRROR) /|\ `-**BIRTH/DAY #** `-**NUMBER** (`-**91**)"!!!~'

FRAGMENTED `-**BIRTH/DAY #** `-**NUMBER** = (1 + 0 + 5 + 1 + 9 + 5 + 7) = (`-**28**) = RECIPROCAL (INVERSE/MIRROR) = (`-**82**)!!!~'

(82 (-) 28) = (`-**54**) = **"FOUR `-YEARS `-AWAY from `-AGE of `-DEATH for** AMERICAN ACTOR/COMEDIAN BERNIE MAC (`-**50**)"!!!~'

FRAGMENTED `-**BIRTH/DAY #** `-**NUMBER** = (1 + 0 + 5 + 1 + 9 + 5 + 7) = (`-**28**) = **"JUST `-ADD `-TWO `-ZERO'S** (`-**00**)" = **"DIED in** (`-**2008**)!!!~'

FRAGMENTED `-**DEATH/DAY #** `-**NUMBER** = (8 + 9 + **2** + 0 + 0 + **8**) = (`-**27**) = RECIPROCAL (INVERSE/MIRROR) = (`-**72**) = (8 x 9) = (**8/9**) = `-**DEATH/DAY for** AMERICAN ACTOR/ COMEDIAN BERNIE MAC (AUGUST 9th)!!!~'

(28 + 27) = (`-**55**) = (`-**23**) + (`-**32**) = -a PROPHETIC # `-NUMBER!!!~'

(28 + 27) = (`-**55**) = **"FIVE `-YEARS `-AWAY from `-AGE of `-DEATH for** AMERICAN ACTOR/COMEDIAN BERNIE MAC (`-**50**)"!!!~'

`-**DIED** at the `-**AGE** of (`-**68**) = "The `-**MARK**"!!!~'

AMERICAN ACTOR/COMEDIAN REDD FOXX `-**BIRTHDAY** = (**12/9**/19/**22**) = (**12** + **9** + 19 + **22**) = (`-**62**) = "FLIP the (`-**2**) OVER to a (`-**7**)" = (`-**67**) = "**ONE `-YEAR `-AWAY from `-AGE of `-DEATH for AMERICAN ACTOR/COMEDIAN REDD FOXX (`-68)**"!!!~'

`-**BIRTH/DAY** = (**12/9**) = "FLIP the (`-**2**) OVER to a (`-**7**)" = (**17/9**) = "FLIP the (`-**9**) OVER to a (`-**6**)" = (**17/6**) = RECIPROCAL (INVERSE/MIRROR) = (**6/71**) = (**ALL-IN-ONE-#-NUMBER**) = (6) (7 + 1) = (`-**68**) = `-**AGE of `-DEATH for AMERICAN ACTOR/COMEDIAN REDD FOXX (`-68)**"!!!~'

`-**BIRTH/YEAR** = (**19/22**) = (91 (-) 22) = (`-**69**) = "**ONE `-YEAR `-AWAY from `-AGE of `-DEATH for AMERICAN ACTOR/COMEDIAN REDD FOXX (`-68)**"!!!~'

`-**BIRTH/DAY** = (**12/9**) = `-**BIRTH/YEAR** = (**192**/2) = "**SWIPE 1**"!!!~'

(`-**12**) = RECIPROCAL (INVERSE/MIRROR) = (`-**21**)!!!~'

`-**BIRTH/DAY** = (**12/9**) = (21 x 9) = (`-**189**) = RECIPROCAL (INVERSE/MIRROR) = (`-**981**) = (98 x 1) = (`-**98**) = "FLIP the (`-**9**) OVER to a (`-**6**)" = (`-**68**) = `-**AGE of `-DEATH for AMERICAN ACTOR/COMEDIAN REDD FOXX (`-68)**"!!!~'

"WAS `-**BORN** in (`-**12**) (DECEMBER); and, `-**DIED** in (`-**10**) (OCTOBER)"; and, (**12/10**) = (DECEMBER 10th) = (`-**1**) DAY AWAY from `-HIS `-**BIRTH/DAY**!!!~' RECIPROCAL (INVERSE/MIRROR) = (**10/12**) = (OCTOBER 12th) = (`-**1**) DAY AWAY from `-HIS `-**DEATH/DAY**!!!~' (**1/1**) = (`-**11**) = "**DAY of `-DEATH (`-11**th)"!!!~'

(19**22**) = (91) (-) (22) = `-*EQUALS* = (`-**69**) = "ONE `-YEAR `-AWAY from `-AGE of `-DEATH for AMERICAN ACTOR/ COMEDIAN REDD FOXX (`-**68**)"!!!~' `-**DIED** in the `-**YEAR OF** (`-**69**)!!!~'

AMERICAN ACTOR/COMEDIAN REDD FOXX `-**DEATH/ DAY** = (**10/11**/19/**91**) = (**10** + **11** + 19 + **91**) = (`-**131**) = (13 x1) = (`-**13**) = "A VERY PIVOTAL # `-NUMBER"!!!~'

`-**DEATH/YEAR** = (**19/91**) = (91 (-) 19) = (`-**72**) = "FOUR `-YEARS `-AWAY from `-AGE of `-DEATH for AMERICAN ACTOR/ COMEDIAN REDD FOXX (`-**68**)"!!!~'

`-**AGE** of `-**DEATH** for ACTOR/COMEDIAN REDD FOXX = (`-**68**) = "FLIP the (`-**6**) OVER to a (`-**9**)" = (`-**98**) = (9 x 8) = (`-**72**) = (19 (-) 91)!!!~'

(131 (-) 62) = (`-**69**) = "ONE `-YEAR `-AWAY from `-AGE of `-DEATH for AMERICAN ACTOR/COMEDIAN REDD FOXX (`-**68**)"!!!~'

(131 + 62) = (`-**193**) = (93 x 1) = (`-**93**) = RECIPROCAL (INVERSE/ MIRROR) = (`-**39**)!!!~'

AMERICAN ACTOR/COMEDIAN REDD FOXX `-**DIED** (`-**59**) DAYS AWAY from `-**HIS** `-**BIRTHDAY**!!!~' (`-**59**) = `-**SUBTRACT ONE #** `-**NUMBER**; and, then `-**ADD the** `-**OTHER #** `-**NUMBER** = (`-**68**) = `-AGE of `-DEATH for AMERICAN ACTOR/COMEDIAN REDD FOXX (`-**68**)"!!!~'

(365 (-) 59) = (`-**306**) = (36 + 0) = (`-**36**) = RECIPROCAL (INVERSE/MIRROR) = (`-**63**) = "FIVE `-YEARS `-AWAY from `-AGE of `-DEATH for AMERICAN ACTOR/COMEDIAN REDD FOXX (`-**68**)"!!!~'

FRAGMENTED `-**BIRTH/DAY** # `-**NUMBER** = (1 + 2 + 9 + 1 + 9 + 2 + 2) = (`-**26**) = RECIPROCAL (INVERSE/MIRROR) = (`-**62**) = "**SIX `-YEARS `-AWAY from `-AGE of `-DEATH for AMERICAN ACTOR/COMEDIAN REDD FOXX (`-68)**"!!!~'

FRAGMENTED `-**DEATH/DAY** # `-**NUMBER** = (1 + 0 + 1 + 1 + 1 + 9 + 9 + 1) = (`-**23**) = RECIPROCAL (INVERSE/MIRROR) = (`-**32**) = -a PROPHETIC # `-NUMBER!!!~'

(26 + 23) = (`-**49**)!!!~'

`-**BIRTH/DAY** = (**12/9**) /|\ `-**DEATH/DAY** = (**10/11**)

(12 + 9 + 10 + 11) = (`-**42**) = "**The `-MARK**"!!!~'

`-**DEATH/YEAR** = (`-**19/91**)

(`-**19**) = RECIPROCAL (INVERSE/MIRROR) = (`-**91**)!!!~'

`-**DIED** at the `-**AGE** of (`-**71**)!!!~'

AMERICAN COMEDIAN GEORGE CARLIN `-**BIRTHDAY** = (**5/12**/19/**37**) = (**5** + **12** + 19 + **37**) = (`-**73**) = RECIPROCAL (INVERSE/MIRROR) = (`-**37**) = `-**BIRTH/YEAR** for AMERICAN COMEDIAN GEORGE CARLIN (`-**37**)!!!~'

/|\ `-**BIRTH/DAY** = (**5/12**) = (5 + 12) = (`-**17**) = RECIPROCAL (INVERSE/MIRROR) = (`-**71**) = `-**AGE of `-DEATH for AMERICAN COMEDIAN GEORGE CARLIN (`-71)**"!!!~' /|\

AMERICAN COMEDIAN GEORGE CARLIN `-**BIRTHDAY** = (**5/12**/19/**37**) = (**5** + **12** + 19 + **37**) = (`-**73**) = "**TWO `-YEARS**

`-AWAY from `-AGE of `-DEATH for AMERICAN COMEDIAN GEORGE CARLIN (`-71)"!!!~'

"WAS `-**BORN** in (`-**5**) (MAY); and, `-**DIED** in (`-**6**) (JUNE)"; and, (**5/6**) = (MAY 6th) = (`-**6**) DAYS AWAY from `-HIS `-**BIRTH/DAY!!!~'** RECIPROCAL (INVERSE/MIRROR) = (**6/5**) = (JUNE 5[th]) = (`-**17**) DAY AWAY from `-HIS `-**DEATH/DAY!!!~'** (**6/17**) = (6 + 17) = (`-**23**) = -a PROPHETIC # `-NUMBER!!!~'

(1**937**) = (93) (-) (17) = `-*EQUALS* = (`-**76**) = "FIVE `-YEARS `-AWAY from `-AGE of `-DEATH for AMERICAN COMEDIAN GEORGE CARLIN (`-71)"!!!~'

AMERICAN COMEDIAN GEORGE CARLIN `-**DEATH/DAY** = (**6/22**/20/**08**) = (**6** + **22** + 20 + **08**) = (`-**56**)!!!~'

`-**DEATH/DAY** = (**6/22**) = (6 x 22) = (`-**132**) = (32 x 1) = (`-**32**) = -a PROPHETIC # `-NUMBER!!!~'

`-**DEATH/DAY** = (**6/22**) = (6 + 22) = (`-**28**) = "JUST `-**ADD** `-**TWO** `-**ZERO'S** (`-**00**)" = "**DIED** in (`-**2008**)!!!~'

/|\ (73 (-) 56) = (`-**17**) = RECIPROCAL (INVERSE/MIRROR) = (`-**71**) = `-AGE of `-DEATH for AMERICAN COMEDIAN GEORGE CARLIN (`-71)"!!!~'

(73 + 56) = (`-**129**) = RECIPROCAL (INVERSE/MIRROR) = (`-**921**) = (**ALL-IN-ONE-#-NUMBER**) = (9 (-) 2) (1) = (`-**71**) = `-AGE of `-DEATH for AMERICAN COMEDIAN GEORGE CARLIN (`-71)"!!!~' /|\

AMERICAN COMEDIAN GEORGE CARLIN `-**DIED** (`-**41**) DAYS AWAY from `-**HIS** `-**BIRTHDAY!!!~'**

(365 (-) 41) = (`-**324**) = "FLIP the (`-**2**) OVER to a (`-**7**)" = (`-**374**) = (**ALL-IN-ONE-#-NUMBER**) = (7) (4 (-) 3) = (`-**71**) = `-**AGE** of `-**DEATH** for **AMERICAN COMEDIAN GEORGE CARLIN** (`-**71**)"!!!~'

FRAGMENTED `-**BIRTH/DAY** # `-**NUMBER** = (5 + 1 + 2 + 1 + 9 + 3 + 7) = (`-**28**) = RECIPROCAL (INVERSE/MIRROR) = (`-**82**)!!!~'

FRAGMENTED `-**BIRTH/DAY** # `-**NUMBER** = (5 + 1 + 2 + 1 + 9 + 3 + 7) = (`-**28**) = "JUST `-**ADD** `-**TWO** `-**ZERO'S** (`-**00**)" = "**DIED** in (`-**2008**)!!!~'

FRAGMENTED `-**DEATH/DAY** # `-**NUMBER** = (6 + 2 + 2 + **2** + 0 + 0 + **8**) = (`-**20**) = RECIPROCAL (INVERSE/MIRROR) = (`-**02**)!!!~' (20 + 02) = (`-**22**) = "**DAY** of `-**DEATH** (**22**nd) **OF THE** `-**MONTH**"!!!~'

(28 + 20) = (`-**48**) = RECIPROCAL (INVERSE/MIRROR) = (`-**84**)!!!~'

`-**DIED** at the `-**AGE** of (`-**81**)!!!~'

/|\ AMERICAN COMEDIAN JOAN RIVERS `-**BIRTHDAY** = (**6/8**/19/**33**) = (**6** + **8** + 19 + **33**) = (`-**66**) = RECIPROCAL (INVERSE/MIRROR) = (`-**99**) = (9 x 9) = (`-**81**) = `-**AGE** of `-**DEATH** for **AMERICAN COMEDIAN JOAN RIVERS** (`-**81**)"!!!~' /|\

`-**BIRTH/DAY** = (**6/8**) = (`-**68**) = "The `-**MARK**"!!!~'

`-**BIRTH/DAY** = (**6/8**) = (`-**68**) = RECIPROCAL (INVERSE/ MIRROR) = (`-**86**) = "**FIVE** `-**YEARS** `-**AWAY** from `-**AGE**

of `-DEATH for AMERICAN COMEDIAN JOAN RIVERS (`-81)"!!!~'

"WAS `-**BORN** in (`-**6**) (JUNE); and, `-**DIED** in (`-**9**) (SEPTEMBER)"; `-**ONE** `-**DAY** `-**AWAY** from `-**BIRTH/DAY** (`-**6/8**) and, (**6/9**) = (JUNE 9th) = (`-**1**) DAY AWAY from `-HER `-**BIRTH/DAY**!!!~' RECIPROCAL (INVERSE/MIRROR) = (**9/6**) = (SEPTEMBER 6th) = `-**TWO** `-**DAYS** `-**AWAY from** `-**DEATH/ DAY** (`-**9/4**) = (`-**2**) DAYS AWAY from `-HER `-**DEATH/DAY**!!!~' (**1/2**) = `-**AGE of** `-**DEATH** (`-**81**) (-) (**12**) = (`-**69**) = `-**BORN**; and, `-**DIED** `-**IN**!!!~'

(**19**33) = (9 (-) 1) (3 (-) 3) = `-*EQUALS* = (`-**80**) = "**ONE** `-**YEAR** `-**AWAY from** `-**AGE of** `-**DEATH for AMERICAN COMEDIAN JOAN RIVERS** (`-**81**)"!!!~'

AMERICAN COMEDIAN JOAN RIVERS `-**DEATH/DAY** = (**9/4**/20/**14**) = (**9** + **4** + 20 + **14**) = (`-**47**)!!!~'

(66 (-) 47) = (`-**19**)!!!~'

(66 + 47) = (`-**113**) = (13 x 1) = (`-**13**) = "A VERY PIVOTAL # `-NUMBER"!!!~'

(113 + 19) = (`-**132**) = (32 x 1) = (`-**32**) = -a PROPHETIC # `-NUMBER!!!~'

AMERICAN COMEDIAN JOAN RIVERS `-**DIED** (`-**88**) DAYS AWAY from `-**HER** `-**BIRTHDAY**!!!~' (`-**88**) = (8 x 8) = (`-**64**) = (`-**2**) x (`-**32**) = (`-**232**) = **RECIPROCAL-SEQUENCING-NUMEROLOGY-RSN**!!!~'

(365 (-) 88) = (`-**277**) = (77 + 2) = (`-**79**) = **"TWO `-YEARS `-AWAY from `-AGE of `-DEATH for AMERICAN COMEDIAN JOAN RIVERS (`-81)"!!!~'**

FRAGMENTED `-**BIRTH/DAY** # `-NUMBER = (6 + 8 + 1 + 9 + 3 + 3) = (`-**30**) = RECIPROCAL (INVERSE/MIRROR) = (`-**03**)!!!~'

FRAGMENTED `-**DEATH/DAY** # `-NUMBER = (9 + 4 + 2 + 0 + 1 + 4) = (`-**20**) = RECIPROCAL (INVERSE/MIRROR) = (`-**02**)!!!~'

(**3**0 + **2**0) = (`-**50**) = RECIPROCAL (INVERSE/MIRROR) = (`-**05**)!!!~'

(50 + 05) = (`-**55**) = (`-**23**) + (`-**32**) = -a PROPHETIC # `-NUMBER!!!~'

`-**DIED** at the `-**AGE** of (`-**63**)!!!~'

AMERICAN ACTOR/COMEDIAN ROBIN WILLIAMS `-**BIRTHDAY** = (**7**/**21**/19/**51**) = (**7** + **21** + 19 + **51**) = (`-**98**) = RECIPROCAL (INVERSE/MIRROR) = (`-**89**)!!!~'

`-**BIRTH/DAY** = (**7/21**) = (**ALL-IN-ONE-#-NUMBER**) = (7 (-) 1) (2 + 1) = (`-**63**) = `-**AGE of `-DEATH for AMERICAN ACTOR/ COMEDIAN ROBIN WILLIAMS (`-63)"!!!~'**

"WAS `-**BORN** in (`-**7**) (JULY); and, `-**DIED** in (`-**8**) (AUGUST)"; and, (**7/8**) = (JULY 8th) = (`-**13**) DAYS AWAY from `-HIS `-**BIRTH/ DAY!!!~'** RECIPROCAL (INVERSE/MIRROR) = (**8/7**) = (AUGUST 7[th]) = (`-**4**) DAYS AWAY from `-HIS `-**DEATH/**

DAY!!!~' (**13/4**) = (34 x 1) = (`-**34**)!!!~' (34 + 34) = (`-**68**) = "The `-**MARK**"!!!~'

(**19**51) = (5 + 1) (9 (-) 1) = `-*EQUALS* = (`-**68**) = "FIVE `-YEARS `-AWAY from `-AGE of `-DEATH for AMERICAN ACTOR/ COMEDIAN ROBIN WILLIAMS (`-**63**)"!!!~'

AMERICAN ACTOR/COMEDIAN ROBIN WILLIAMS `-**DEATH/DAY** = (**8/11**/20/**14**) = (**8** + **11** + 20 + **14**) = (`-**53**)!!!~'

`-**DEATH/DAY** = (**8/11**) = (8 x 11) = (`-**88**) = "AMERICAN COMEDIAN JOAN RIVERS `-**DIED** this `-**MANY** `-**DAYS** `-**AWAY** from `-HER `-**BIRTH/DAY**"!!!~'

(98 (-) 53) = (`-**45**)!!!~'

(98 + 53) = (`-**151**) = (ALL-IN-ONE-#-NUMBER) = (1 + 5) (1) = (`-**61**) = "TWO `-YEARS `-AWAY from `-AGE of `-DEATH for AMERICAN ACTOR/COMEDIAN ROBIN WILLIAMS (`-**63**)"!!!~'

(151 + 45) = (`-**196**) = (96 + 1) = (`-**97**) = (9 x 7) = (`-**63**) = `-AGE of `-DEATH for AMERICAN ACTOR/COMEDIAN ROBIN WILLIAMS (`-**63**)"!!!~'

AMERICAN ACTOR/COMEDIAN ROBIN WILLIAMS `-**DIED** (`-**21**) DAYS AWAY from `-HIS `-**BIRTHDAY**!!!~' (`-**21**) = "**DAY** of `-**BIRTH** (`-**21**ˢᵗ)"!!!~'

(21 + 21) = (`-**42**) = "The `-**MARK**"!!!~'

(365 (-) 21) = (`-**344**) = (44 x 3) = (`-**132**) = (32 x 1) = (`-**32**) = -a PROPHETIC # `-NUMBER!!!~'

(365 (-) 21) = (`-**344**) = (34 x 4) = (`-**136**) = (36 x 1) = (`-**36**) = RECIPROCAL (INVERSE/MIRROR) = (`-**63**) = `-**AGE of `-DEATH for AMERICAN ACTOR/COMEDIAN ROBIN WILLIAMS (`-63**)"!!!~'

FRAGMENTED `-**BIRTH/DAY** # `-**NUMBER** = (7 + 2 + 1 + 1 + 9 + 5 + 1) = (`-**26**) = RECIPROCAL (INVERSE/MIRROR) = (`-**62**) = "ONE `-YEAR `-AWAY from `-AGE of `-DEATH for AMERICAN ACTOR/COMEDIAN ROBIN WILLIAMS (`-**63**)"!!!~'

FRAGMENTED `-**DEATH/DAY** # `-**NUMBER** = (**8** + **1** + **1** + 2 + 0 + 1 + 4) = (`-**17**) = RECIPROCAL (INVERSE/MIRROR) = (`-**71**)!!!~'

(71 + 17) = (`-**88**) = (8 x 11) = (**8/11**) = `-**DEATH/DAY** for AMERICAN ACTOR/COMEDIAN ROBIN WILLIAMS (`-**AUGUST 11**th)!!!~'

(**26** + **17**) = (`-**43**) = RECIPROCAL (INVERSE/MIRROR) = (`-**34**) = "SEE `-ABOVE"!!!~' `-**DEATH/YEAR** = (**20/14**) = (20 + 14) = (`-**34**)!!!~'

`-**BIRTH/DAY** = (**7/21**) = (7 + 21) = (`-**28**)!!!~'

`-**DEATH/YEAR** = (**20/14**) = (2 x 14) = (`-**28**)!!!~'

`-**DIED** at the `-**AGE** of (`-**49**)!!!~'

AMERICAN/CANADIAN ACTOR/COMEDIAN PHIL HARTMAN `-**BIRTHDAY** = (**9/24**/19/**48**) = (**9** + **24** + 19 + **48**) = (`-**100**) = "SWIVEL POINT"!!!~'

`-**BIRTH/YEAR** = (`-**48**) = "ONE `-YEAR `-AWAY from `-AGE of `-DEATH for AMERICAN/CANADIAN ACTOR/COMEDIAN PHIL HARTMAN (`-**49**)"!!!~'

`-**BIRTH/DAY** = (**9/24**) = (**ALL-IN-ONE-#-NUMBER**) = (92 (-) 24) = (`-**68**) = "The `-**MARK**"!!!~'

`-**BIRTH/DAY** = (**9/24**) = (**ALL-IN-ONE-#-NUMBER**) = (9) (2 x 4) = (`-**98**) = `-**DEATH/YEAR** = (`-**98**) / `-*DIVIDED* `-*by* (`-**2**) = (`-**49**) = `-AGE of `-DEATH for AMERICAN/CANADIAN ACTOR/COMEDIAN PHIL HARTMAN (`-**49**)"!!!~'

`-**BIRTH/DAY** = (**9/24**) = (9 x 24) = (`-**216**) = (2 x 16) = (`-**32**) = -a PROPHETIC # `-NUMBER!!!~'

"WAS `-**BORN** in (`-**9**) (SEPTEMBER); and, `-**DIED** in (`-**5**) (MAY)"; and, (**9/5**) = (SEPTEMBER 5th) = (`-**19**) DAYS AWAY from `-HIS `-**BIRTH/DAY!!!~'** RECIPROCAL (INVERSE/ MIRROR) = (**5/9**) = (MAY 9th) = (`-**19**) DAYS AWAY from `-HIS `-**DEATH/DAY!!!~'** (**19/19**) = `-**DIED** (`-**119**) `-**DAYS** `-**AWAY** from `-**BIRTH/DAY!!!~'**

"The `-**MARK**" = (`-**68**) (-) `-*MINUS* (-) `-AGE of `-DEATH (`-**49**) = (`-**19**)!!!~'

(**19**48) = (91) (-) (48) = `-*EQUALS* = (`-**43**) = "SIX `-YEARS `-AWAY from `-AGE of `-DEATH for AMERICAN/CANADIAN ACTOR/COMEDIAN PHIL HARTMAN (`-**49**)"!!!~'

AMERICAN/CANADIAN ACTOR/COMEDIAN PHIL HARTMAN `-**DEATH/DAY** = (**5/28**/19/**98**) = (**5** + **28** + 19 + **98**) = (`-**150**)!!!~'

`-**DEATH/YEAR** = (`-**98**) / `-DIVIDED by (`-**2**) = (`-**49**) = `-AGE of `-DEATH for AMERICAN/CANADIAN ACTOR/ COMEDIAN PHIL HARTMAN (`-**49**)"!!!~'

`-**DEATH/DAY** # `-**NUMBER** in `-**REVERSE** = (98 (-) 19 (-) 28 (-) 5) = (`-**46**) = "FLIP the (`-**6**) OVER to a (`-**9**)" = (`-**49**) = `-AGE of `-DEATH for AMERICAN/CANADIAN ACTOR/ COMEDIAN PHIL HARTMAN (`-**49**)"!!!~'

(150 (-) 100) = (`-**50**) = "ONE `-YEAR `-AWAY from `-AGE of `-DEATH for AMERICAN/CANADIAN ACTOR/COMEDIAN PHIL HARTMAN (`-**49**)"!!!~'

(150 + 100) = (`-**250**) = (50 (-) 2) = (`-**48**) = "ONE `-YEAR `-AWAY from `-AGE of `-DEATH for AMERICAN/CANADIAN ACTOR/COMEDIAN PHIL HARTMAN (`-**49**)"!!!~'

AMERICAN/CANADIAN ACTOR/COMEDIAN PHIL HARTMAN `-**DIED** (`-**119**) DAYS AWAY from `-HIS `-BIRTHDAY!!!~' (`-**119**) = (11 x 9) = (`-**99**) / `-*DIVIDED* `-*by* (`-**2**) = (`-**49.5**) = `-AGE of `-DEATH for AMERICAN/CANADIAN ACTOR/COMEDIAN PHIL HARTMAN (`-**49**)"!!!~'

(365 (-) 119) = (`-**246**) = (46 + 2) = (`-**48**) = "ONE `-YEAR `-AWAY from `-AGE of `-DEATH for AMERICAN/CANADIAN ACTOR/COMEDIAN PHIL HARTMAN (`-**49**)"!!!~'

FRAGMENTED `-**BIRTH/DAY** # `-**NUMBER** = (9 + 2 + 4 + 1 + 9 + 4 + 8) = (`-**37**) = RECIPROCAL (INVERSE/MIRROR) = (`-**73**)!!!~'

FRAGMENTED `-**DEATH/DAY** # `-**NUMBER** = (5 + 2 + 8 + 1 + 9 + 9 + 8) = (`-**42**) = "The `-**MARK**" = RECIPROCAL (INVERSE/MIRROR) = (`-**24**)!!!~'

$(37 + 42) = (`-79) =$ RECIPROCAL (INVERSE/MIRROR) $= (`-97)$!!!~'

$(37 + 42) = (`-79) = (98 (-) 19) = `-DEATH/YEAR = (`-19/98)$!!!~'

`-BIRTH/DAY $= (9/24) = (9 + 24) = (`-33)$!!!~'

`-DEATH/DAY $= (5/28) = (5 + 28) = (`-33)$!!!~'

`-BIRTH/DAY $=$ `-DEATH/DAY!!!~'

$(`-33) + (`-33) = (`-66) =$ RECIPROCAL (INVERSE/MIRROR) $= (`-99)$!!!~'

$(`-99) (-) (`-66) = (`-33)$!!!~'

`-DIED at the `-AGE of $(`-40)$!!!~'

SINGER/SONGWRITER JOHN LENNON `-BIRTHDAY $= (10/9/19/40) = (10 + 9 + 19 + 40) = (`-78) =$ RECIPROCAL (INVERSE/MIRROR) $= (`-87)$!!!~'

/|\ `-BIRTH/YEAR $= (40) =$ `-DIED at the `-AGE of $(`-40)$ for SINGER/SONGWRITER JOHN LENNON $(`-40)$"!!!~' /|\

"WAS `-BORN in $(`-10)$ (OCTOBER); and, `-DIED in $(`-12)$ (DECEMBER)"; and, $(10/12) =$ (OCTOBER 12th) $= (`-3)$ DAYS AWAY from `-HIS `-BIRTH/DAY!!!~' RECIPROCAL (INVERSE/MIRROR) $= (12/10) =$ (DECEMBER 10th) $= (`-2)$ DAYS AWAY from `-HIS `-DEATH/DAY!!!~' $(3/2) = (`-32) =$ -a PROPHETIC # `-NUMBER!!!~'

(1**94**0) = (9 (-) 4) (X) (10) = `-*EQUALS* = (`-**50**) = "**TEN** `-**YEARS** `-**AWAY from** `-**AGE of** `-**DEATH for SINGER/SONGWRITER JOHN LENNON** (`-**40**)"!!!~'

(1**94**0) = (9 + 4) (+) (10) = (13) (+) (10) = `-*EQUALS* = (`-**23**) = -a PROPHETIC # `-NUMBER!!!~'

SINGER/SONGWRITER JOHN LENNON `-**DEATH/DAY** = (**12**/**8**/19/**80**) = (**12** + **8** + 19 + **80**) = (`-**119**)!!!~'

`-**DEATH/DAY** # `-**NUMBER** in `-**REVERSE** = (80 (-) 19 (-) 8 (-) 12) = (`-**41**) = "**ONE** `-**YEAR** `-**AWAY from** `-**AGE of** `-**DEATH for SINGER/SONGWRITER JOHN LENNON** (`-**40**)"!!!~'

(119 (-) 78) = (`-**41**) = "**ONE** `-**YEAR** `-**AWAY from** `-**AGE of** `-**DEATH for SINGER/SONGWRITER JOHN LENNON** (`-**40**)"!!!~'

(119 + 78) = (`-**197**) = (19 x 7) = (`-**133**) = (33 (-) 1) = (`-**32**) = -a PROPHETIC # `-NUMBER!!!~'

(119 + 78) = (`-**197**) = (19 x 7) = (`-**133**) = (13 x 3) = (`-**39**) = "**ONE** `-**YEAR** `-**AWAY from** `-**AGE of** `-**DEATH for SINGER/ SONGWRITER JOHN LENNON** (`-**40**)"!!!~'

SINGER/SONGWRITER JOHN LENNON `-**DIED** (`-**60**) DAYS AWAY from `-**HIS** `-**BIRTHDAY**!!!~'

`-**DEATH/YEAR** = (`-**19/80**) = (80 (-) 19) = (`-**61**)!!!~'

(365 (-) 60) = (`-**305**) = (35 + 0) = (`-**35**) = "**FIVE** `-**YEARS** `-**AWAY from** `-**AGE of** `-**DEATH for SINGER/SONGWRITER JOHN LENNON** (`-**40**)"!!!~'

FRAGMENTED `-**BIRTH/DAY** # `-**NUMBER** = (1 + 0 + 9 + 1 + 9 + 4 + 0) = (`-**24**) = RECIPROCAL (INVERSE/MIRROR) = (`-**42**) = "The `-**MARK**"!!!~'

FRAGMENTED `-**DEATH/DAY** # `-**NUMBER** = (1 + 2 + 8 + 1 + 9 + 8 + 0) = (`-**29**) = RECIPROCAL (INVERSE/MIRROR) = (`-**92**)!!!~'

(24 + 29) = (`-**53**) = RECIPROCAL (INVERSE/MIRROR) = (`-**35**) = "**FIVE `-YEARS `-AWAY from `-AGE of `-DEATH for SINGER/SONGWRITER JOHN LENNON (`-40)"**!!!~'

`-**BIRTH/DAY** = (**10/9**)!!!~'

`-**DEATH/DAY** = (**12/8**)!!!~'

(10 + 9 + 12 + 8) = (`-**39**) = "**ONE `-YEAR `-AWAY from `-AGE of `-DEATH for SINGER/SONGWRITER JOHN LENNON (`-40)"**!!!~'

`-**DIED** at the `-**AGE** of (`-**58**)!!!~'

SINGER/SONGWRITER GEORGE HARRISON `-**BIRTHDAY** = (**2/25**/19/**43**) = (2 + **25** + 19 + **43**) = (`-**89**) = RECIPROCAL (INVERSE/MIRROR) = (`-**98**)!!!~'

(`-**89**) (-) `-**AGE** of `-**DEATH** (`-**58**) = (`-**31**) = RECIPROCAL (INVERSE/MIRROR) = (`-**13**) = "A VERY PIVOTAL # `-NUMBER"!!!~'

`-**BIRTH/DAY** = (**2/25**) = RECIPROCAL (INVERSE/MIRROR) = (**52/2**) = (**ALL-IN-ONE-#-NUMBER**) = (5) (2 x 2) = (`-**54**) =

"FOUR `-YEARS `-AWAY from `-AGE of `-DEATH for SINGER/ SONGWRITER GEORGE HARRISON (`-58)"!!!~'

`-**BIRTH/YEAR** = (`-**19/43**) = (19 + 43) = (`-**62**) = **"FOUR `-YEARS `-AWAY from `-AGE of `-DEATH for SINGER/SONGWRITER GEORGE HARRISON (`-58)"!!!~'**

"WAS `-**BORN** in (`-**2**) (FEBRUARY); and, `-**DIED** in (`-**11**) (NOVEMBER)"; and, (**2/11**) = (FEBRUARY 11th) = (`-**14**) DAYS AWAY from `-HIS `-**BIRTH/DAY**!!!~' RECIPROCAL (INVERSE/ MIRROR) = (**11/2**) = (NOVEMBER 2nd) = (`-**27**) DAYS AWAY from `-HIS `-**DEATH/DAY**!!!~' (**14/27**) = (`-**27**) = RECIPROCAL (INVERSE/MIRROR) = (`-**72**) = (72 (-) 14) = (`-**58**) = `-**AGE of `-DEATH for SINGER/SONGWRITER GEORGE HARRISON (`-58)"!!!~'**

(1**9**4**3**) = (9 (-) 4) (1 + 3) = `-*EQUALS* = (`-**54**) = **"FOUR `-YEARS `-AWAY from `-AGE of `-DEATH for SINGER/SONGWRITER GEORGE HARRISON (`-58)"!!!~'**

SINGER/SONGWRITER GEORGE HARRISON `-**DEATH/ DAY** = (**11/29**/20/**01**) = (**11** + **29** + 20 + **01**) = (`-**61**) = **"THREE `-YEARS `-AWAY from `-AGE of `-DEATH for SINGER/ SONGWRITER GEORGE HARRISON (`-58)"!!!~'**

`-FROM `-**DEATH/DAY** in `-**REVERSE** = (92 (-) 20 (-) 1 (-) 11) = (`-**60**) = **"TWO `-YEARS `-AWAY from `-AGE of `-DEATH for SINGER/SONGWRITER GEORGE HARRISON (`-58)"!!!~'**

(89 (-) 61) = (`-**28**)!!!~'

(89 + 61) = (`-**150**) = (50 + 1) = (`-**51**) = **"SEVEN `-YEARS `-AWAY from `-AGE of `-DEATH for SINGER/SONGWRITER GEORGE HARRISON (`-58)"!!!~'**

(150 + 28) = (`-**178**) = (78 x 1) = (`-**78**) = `-BIRTH/DAY # `-NUMBER of SINGER/SONGWRITER JOHN LENNON (`-**78**)!!!~'

SINGER/SONGWRITER GEORGE HARRISON `-**DIED** (`-**88**) DAYS AWAY from `-HIS `-**BIRTHDAY**!!!~' (`-**88**) = `-HIS `-VERY `-OWN `-**BIRTH/DAY** # `-**NUMBER** was (`-**89**)!!!~'

(365 (-) 88) = (`-**277**) = (77 x 2) = (`-**154**) = (15 x 4) = (`-**60**) = "TWO `-YEARS `-AWAY from `-AGE of `-DEATH for SINGER/ SONGWRITER GEORGE HARRISON (`-**58**)"!!!~'

(365 (-) 88) = (`-**277**) = (27 x 7) = (`-**189**) = (89 x 1) = (`-**89**) = `-**BIRTH/DAY** # `-**NUMBER** for SINGER/SONGWRITER GEORGE HARRISON (`-**89**)"!!!~'

/|\ FRAGMENTED `-**BIRTH/DAY** # `-**NUMBER** = (2 + 2 + 5 + 1 + 9 + 4 + 3) = (`-**26**) = RECIPROCAL (INVERSE/MIRROR) = (`-**62**)!!!~'

(`-**26**) + (`-**62**) = (`-**88**) = "**DIED** this `-**MANY** `-**DAYS** from `-HIS `-VERY `-OWN `-**BIRTH/DAY**"!!!~' /|\

FRAGMENTED `-**DEATH/DAY** # `-**NUMBER** = (1 + 1 + 2 + 9 + 2 + 0 + 0 + 1) = (`-**16**) = RECIPROCAL (INVERSE/MIRROR) = (`-**61**) = "**HIS** `-VERY `-OWN `-**DEATH/DAY** # `-**NUMBER** (`-**61**)"!!!~'

(26 + 16) = (`-**42**) = "The `-**MARK**"!!!~' = RECIPROCAL (INVERSE/MIRROR) = (`-**24**)!!!~'

GEORGE HARRISON `-**BIRTH/DAY** = (**2/25**)!!!~'

GEORGE HARRISON `-**DEATH/DAY** = (**11/29**) = (11 + 29) = (`-**40**) = `-**AGE** of `-**DEATH** for **SINGER/SONGWRITER** JOHN LENNON (`-**40**)"!!!~'

(2 + 25 + 11 + 29) = (`-**67**) = RECIPROCAL (INVERSE/MIRROR) = (`-**76**)!!!~'

(67 + 76) = (`-**143**) = (43 x 1) = (`-**43**) = "WAS `-**BORN** in (`-**43**)"!!!~'

(`-**43**) + (`-**43**) = (`-**86**) = RECIPROCAL (INVERSE/MIRROR) = (`-**68**) = "The `-**MARK**"!!!~'

SINGER/SONGWRITER GEORGE HARRISON `-**AGE** of `-**DEATH** (`-**58**) = (5 x 8) = (`-**40**) = `-**AGE** of `-**DEATH** for **SINGER/SONGWRITER** JOHN LENNON (`-**40**)"!!!~'

`-**DIED** at the `-**AGE** of (`-**66**)!!!~'

SINGER/SONGWRITER DAVEY JONES `-**BIRTHDAY** = (**12/30**/19/**45**) = (**12** + **30** + 19 + **45**) = (`-**106**) = RECIPROCAL (INVERSE/MIRROR) = (`-**601**) = (60 + 1) = (`-**61**) = "**DIED** this `-**MANY** `-**DAYS** `-**AWAY** from `-**BIRTH/DAY**"!!!~'

`-**BIRTH/DAY** = (**12/30**) = (23 x 1 + 0) = (`-**23**) = -a PROPHETIC # `-NUMBER!!!~'

`-**BIRTH/YEAR** = (**19/45**) = (19 + 45) = (`-**64**) = "TWO `-**YEARS** `-**AWAY** from `-**AGE** of `-**DEATH** for SINGER/SONGWRITER DAVEY JONES (`-**66**)"!!!~'

"WAS `-**BORN** in (`-**12**) (DECEMBER); and, `-**DIED** in (`-**2**) (FEBRUARY)"; and, (**12/2**) = (DECEMBER 2ⁿᵈ) = (`-**28**) DAYS AWAY from `-HIS `-**BIRTH/DAY**!!!~' RECIPROCAL (INVERSE/

MIRROR) = (**2/12**) = (FEBRUARY 12th) = (`-**17**) DAYS AWAY from `-HIS `-**DEATH/DAY!!!~'** (**28/17**) = (28 + 17) = (`-**45**) = "**YEAR of `-BIRTH** (`-**45**)"!!!~'

(1**94**5) = (5 + 1) (9 (-) 4) = `-*EQUALS* = (`-**65**) = "**ONE `-YEAR `-AWAY from `-AGE of `-DEATH for SINGER/SONGWRITER DAVEY JONES** (`-**66**)"!!!~'

SINGER/SONGWRITER DAVEY JONES `-**DEATH/DAY** = (**2/29**/20/**12**) = (**2** + **29** + 20 + **12**) = (`-**63**) = "**THREE `-YEARS `-AWAY from `-AGE of `-DEATH for SINGER/SONGWRITER DAVEY JONES** (`-**66**)"!!!~'

`-**AGE of `-DEATH** = (`-**66**) = (6 x 6) = (`-**36**) = RECIPROCAL (INVERSE/MIRROR) = (`-**63**) = `-**DEATH/DAY # `-NUMBER for SINGER/SONGWRITER DAVEY JONES** (`-**63**)!!!~'

`-**DEATH/DAY** = (**2/29**) = (29 x 2) = (`-**58**) = `-**AGE of `-DEATH for SINGER/SONGWRITER GEORGE HARRISON** (`-**58**)"!!!~'

`-**DEATH/DAY** in `-**REVERSE** = (92 (-) 20 (-) 12 (-) 2) = (`-**58**) = `-**AGE of `-DEATH for SINGER/SONGWRITER GEORGE HARRISON** (`-**58**)"!!!~'

`-**DEATH/DAY** = (**2/29**) = (29 + 2) = (`-**31**) = RECIPROCAL (INVERSE/MIRROR) = (`-**13**) = "A VERY PIVOTAL # `-NUMBER"!!!~'

`-**DEATH/YEAR** = (**20/12**) = (20 + 12) = (`-**32**) = -a PROPHETIC # `-NUMBER!!!~'

(106 (-) 63) = (`-**43**) = "SEE `-BELOW"!!!~'

(106 + 63) = (`-**169**) = (69 (-) 1) = (`-**68**) = "The `-**MARK**"!!!~' = "TWO `-YEARS `-AWAY from `-AGE of `-DEATH for SINGER/ SONGWRITER DAVEY JONES (`-**66**)"!!!~'

(169 (-) 43) = (`-**126**) = (26 x 1) = (`-**26**) = 2(6's) = (`-**66**) = `-AGE of `-DEATH for SINGER/SONGWRITER DAVEY JONES (`-**66**)"!!!~'

SINGER/SONGWRITER DAVEY JONES `-**DIED** (`-**61**) DAYS AWAY from `-HIS `-BIRTHDAY!!!~' (`-**61**) = SINGER/ SONGWRITER JOHN LENNON `-**DIED** (`-**60**) DAYS AWAY from `-HIS `-BIRTH/DAY!!!~'

`-**DEATH/YEAR** of `-SINGER/SONGWRITER JOHN LENNON = (`-**19/80**) = (80 (-) 19) = (`-**61**)!!!~'

(366 (-) 61) = (`-**305**) = (35 + 0) = (`-**35**) = "FIVE `-YEARS `-AWAY from `-AGE of `-DEATH for SINGER/SONGWRITER JOHN LENNON (`-**40**)"!!!~'

FRAGMENTED `-**BIRTH/DAY** # `-NUMBER = (1 + 2 + 3 + 0 + 1 + 9 + 4 + 5) = (`-**25**) = RECIPROCAL (INVERSE/MIRROR) = (`-**52**)!!!~'

(25 + 52) = (`-**77**) = SINGER/SONGWRITER PETER TORK `-**DIED** at the `-**AGE** of (`-**77**)!!!~'

FRAGMENTED `-**DEATH/DAY** # `-NUMBER = (2 + 2 + 9 + 2 + 0 + 1 + 2) = (`-**18**) = RECIPROCAL (INVERSE/MIRROR) = (`-**81**)!!!~'

(81 (-) 18) = (`-**63**) = `-**DEATH/DAY** # `-**NUMBER** for SINGER/ SONGWRITER DAVEY JONES (`-**63**)!!!~'

(25 + 18) = (`-**43**) = RECIPROCAL (INVERSE/MIRROR) = (`-**34**)!!!~'

(43 + 34) = (`-**77**) = **SINGER/SONGWRITER PETER TORK `-DIED at the `-AGE of** (`-**77**)!!!~'

`-**AGE of** `-**DEATH** for DAVEY JONES (`-**66**) + `-**AGE of** `-**DEATH** for PETER TORK (`-**77**) = (**66/77**) = (66 + 77) = (`-**143**)!!!~'

(43 + 43) = (`-**86**) = RECIPROCAL (INVERSE/MIRROR) = (`-**68**) = "The `-**MARK**"!!!~'

`-**DIED** at the `-**AGE** of (`-**77**)!!!~'

SINGER/SONGWRITER PETER TORK `-**BIRTHDAY** = (**2/13**/19/**42**) = (**2** + **13** + 19 + **42**) = (`-**76**) = **"ONE `-YEAR `-AWAY from `-AGE of `-DEATH for SINGER/SONGWRITER PETER TORK** (`-**77**)"!!!~'

`-**BIRTH/DAY # `-NUMBER** = (`-**76**) = RECIPROCAL (INVERSE/MIRROR) = (`-**67**) = (**66/77**) = **"AGES of `-DEATH for DAVEY JONES & PETER TORK"**!!!~'

`-**BIRTH/DAY** = (**2/13**) = (2 x 13) = (`-**26**) = RECIPROCAL (INVERSE/MIRROR) = (`-**62**) = **"HIS `-VERY `-OWN `-DEATH/DAY # `-NUMBER** (`-**62**)"!!!~'

`-**BIRTH/DAY** = (**2/13**) = (23 x 1) = (`-**23**) = -a PROPHETIC # `-NUMBER!!!~'

`-**BIRTH/YEAR** = (**19/42**) = (19 + 42) = (`-**61**) = "SINGER/ SONGWRITER DAVEY JONES `-**DIED** this `-**MANY** `-**DAYS** `-**AWAY** from `-**HIS** `-**BIRTH/DAY** (`-**61**)"!!!~'

"WAS `-**BORN** in (`-**2**) (FEBRUARY); and, `-**DIED** in (`-**2**) (FEBRUARY)"; and, (**2/2**) = (FEBRUARY 2nd) = (`-**11**) DAYS AWAY from `-**HIS** `-**BIRTH/DAY**!!!~' RECIPROCAL (INVERSE/ MIRROR) = (**2/2**) = (FEBRUARY 2nd) = (`-**19**) DAYS AWAY from `-**HIS** `-**DEATH/DAY**!!!~' (**11/19**) = (`-**19**) = RECIPROCAL (INVERSE/MIRROR) = (`-**91**) = (91 (-) 11) = (`-**80**) = "THREE `-**YEARS** `-**AWAY** from `-**AGE** of `-**DEATH** for SINGER/ SONGWRITER PETER TORK (`-**77**)"!!!~'

(1**94**2) = (92) (-) (14) = `-*EQUALS* = (`-**78**) = "ONE `-**YEAR** `-**AWAY** from `-**AGE** of `-**DEATH** for SINGER/SONGWRITER PETER TORK (`-**77**)"!!!~'

SINGER/SONGWRITER PETER TORK `-**DEATH/DAY** = (**2/21**/20/**19**) = (**2** + **21** + 20 + **19**) = (`-**62**)!!!~' SINGER/ SONGWRITER DAVEY JONES' `-**DEATH/DAY** # `-**NUMBER** = `-**EQUALED** = (`-**63**)!!!~'

`-**DEATH/DAY** = (**2/21**) = "FLIP the (`-**2**) OVER to a (`-**7**)" = (**7/71**) = (77 x 1) = (`-**77**) = `-**AGE** of `-**DEATH** for SINGER/ SONGWRITER PETER TORK (`-**77**)"!!!~'

PETER TORK `-**BIRTH/DAY** # `-**NUMBER** = (`-**76**) = RECIPROCAL (INVERSE/MIRROR) = (`-**67**) = "FLIP the (`-**7**) OVER to a (`-**2**) = (`-**62**) = PETER TORK `-**DEATH/DAY** # `-**NUMBER**!!!~'

`-**DEATH/DAY** = (**2/21**) = (21 + 2) = (`-**23**) = -a PROPHETIC # `-**NUMBER**!!!~'

`-**DEATH/DAY** = (**2/21**) = (21 x 2) = (`-**42**) = "The `-**MARK**"!!!~'

`-**DEATH/YEAR** = (**20/19**) = (20 + 19) = (`-**39**) x (`-**2**) = (`-**78**) = "ONE `-YEAR `-AWAY from `-AGE of `-DEATH for SINGER/ SONGWRITER PETER TORK (`-**77**)"!!!~'

(76 (-) 62) = (`-**14**)!!!~'

(76 + 62) = (`-**138**) = (38 + 1) = (`-**39**) x (`-**2**) = (`-**78**) = "ONE `-YEAR `-AWAY from `-AGE of `-DEATH for SINGER/SONGWRITER PETER TORK (`-**77**)"!!!~'

(138 (-) 14) = (`-**124**) = (24 x 1) = (`-**24**) = RECIPROCAL (INVERSE/MIRROR) = (`-**42**) = `-**BIRTH/YEAR** (`-**42**) of SINGER/SONGWRITER PETER TORK (`-**42**)"!!!~'

SINGER/SONGWRITER PETER TORK `-**DIED** (`-**8**) DAYS AWAY from `-HIS `-BIRTHDAY!!!~'

(365 (-) 8) = (`-**357**) = (57 x 3) = (`-**171**) = (**ALL-IN-ONE-#-NUMBER**) = (1 + 1) (7) = (`-**27**) = 2(7's) = (`-**77**) = `-AGE of `-DEATH for SINGER/SONGWRITER PETER TORK (`-**77**)"!!!~'

/|\ FRAGMENTED `-**BIRTH/DAY** # `-**NUMBER** = (2 + 1 + 3 + 1 + 9 + 4 + 2) = (`-**22**) = "FLIP the (`-**2**) OVER to a (`-**7**) = (`-**77**) = `-AGE of `-DEATH for SINGER/SONGWRITER PETER TORK (`-**77**)"!!!~' /|\

/|\ FRAGMENTED `-**DEATH/DAY** # `-**NUMBER** = (2 + 2 + 1 + 2 + 0 + 1 + 9) = (`-**17**) = RECIPROCAL (INVERSE/MIRROR) = (`-**71**) = (**17/71**) = (77 x 1 x 1) = (`-**77**) = `-AGE of `-DEATH for SINGER/SONGWRITER PETER TORK (`-**77**)"!!!~' /|\

(22 + 17) = (`-**39**) x (`-**2**) = (`-**78**) = "ONE `-YEAR `-AWAY from `-AGE of `-DEATH for SINGER/SONGWRITER PETER TORK (`-**77**)"!!!~'

`-**AGE** of `-DEATH for DAVEY JONES (`-**66**) + `-**AGE** of `-DEATH for PETER TORK (`-**77**) = (**66/77**) = (66 + 77) = (`-**143**) = "SEE `-ABOVE & `-BELOW"!!!~'

PETER TORK `-**BIRTH/DAY** = (`-**13**) /|\ PETER TORK `-**DEATH/DAY** = (`-**21**)!!!~'

(13 + 21) = (`-**34**) = RECIPROCAL (INVERSE/MIRROR) = (`-**43**)!!!~'

(43 + 43) = (`-**86**) = RECIPROCAL (INVERSE/MIRROR) = (`-**68**) = "The `-**MARK**"!!!~'

PETER TORK `-**AGE** of `-**DEATH** = (`-**77**) = (7 x 7) = (`-**49**) = (4 x 9) = (`-**36**) = RECIPROCAL (INVERSE/MIRROR) = (`-**63**) = `-**DEATH/DAY** # `-**NUMBER** for SINGER/SONGWRITER DAVEY JONES (`-**63**)!!!~'

`-**DIED** at the `-**AGE** of (`-**27**)!!!~'

SINGER/SONGWRITER JIMI HENDRIX `-**BIRTHDAY** = (**11/27**/19/**42**) = (**11** + **27** + 19 + **42**) = (`-**99**) = RECIPROCAL (INVERSE/MIRROR) = (`-**66**)!!!~'

`-**BIRTH/DAY** = (**11/27**) = (27 x 1 x 1) = (`-**27**) = `-**AGE** of `-**DEATH** (`-**27**) for SINGER/SONGWRITER JIMI HENDRIX (`-**27**)"!!!~'

`-**DAY** of `-**BIRTH** = (`-**27**th) = `-**DIED** at the `-**AGE** of (`-**27**) **for SINGER/SONGWRITER JIMI HENDRIX** (`-**27**)"!!!~'

/|\ FRAGMENTED `-**BIRTH/DAY** # `-**NUMBER** = (1 + 1 + 2 + 7 + 1 + 9 + 4 + 2) = (`-**27**) = `-**AGE of `-DEATH for SINGER/ SONGWRITER JIMI HENDRIX** (`-**27**)"!!!~' /|\

`-**BIRTH/YEAR** = (`-**19/42**) = (42 (-) 19) = (`-**23**) = -a PROPHETIC # `-NUMBER!!!~'

"WAS `-**BORN** in (`-**11**) (NOVEMBER); and, `-**DIED** in (`-**9**) (SEPTEMBER)"; and, (**11/9**) = (NOVEMBER 9th) = (`-**18**) DAYS AWAY from `-HIS `-**BIRTH/DAY!!!~'** RECIPROCAL (INVERSE/ MIRROR) = (**9/11**) = (SEPTEMBER 11th) = (`-**7**) DAYS AWAY from `-HIS `-**DEATH/DAY!!!~'** (**18/7**) = (18 x 7) = (`-**126**) = (26 + 1) = (`-**27**) = `-**AGE of `-DEATH for SINGER/SONGWRITER JIMI HENDRIX** (`-**27**)"!!!~'

(**19**42) = (4 (-) 2) (1 (-) 9) = `-*EQUALS* = (`-**28**) = **"ONE `-YEAR `-AWAY from `-AGE of `-DEATH for SINGER/SONGWRITER JIMI HENDRIX** (`-**27**)"!!!~'

SINGER/SONGWRITER JIMI HENDRIX `-**DEATH/DAY** = (**9/18**/19/**70**) = (**9** + **18** + 19 + **70**) = (`-**116**) = (**ALL-IN-ONE- #-NUMBER**) = (1 + 1) (6) = (`-**26**) = **"ONE `-YEAR `-AWAY from `-AGE of `-DEATH for SINGER/SONGWRITER JIMI HENDRIX** (`-**27**)"!!!~'

/|\ `-**DEATH/DAY** = (**9/18**) = (9 + 18) = (`-**27**) = `-**DAY** of `-**BIRTH** (`-**27**th); and, `-**AGE of `-DEATH for SINGER/SONGWRITER JIMI HENDRIX** (`-**27**)"!!!~'

'-MARTIAL '-ARTIST & '-ACTOR '-BRUCE '-LEE was '-**BORN** on a (`-27$^{th}$); and, '-**DIED** on (**7/20**) = (20 + 7) = (`-27)!!!~' /|\

'-**DEATH/DAY** = (**9/18**) = (9 x 18) = (`-**162**) = RECIPROCAL (INVERSE/MIRROR) = (`-**261**) = (26 + 1) = (`-**27**) = '-AGE of '-DEATH for SINGER/SONGWRITER JIMI HENDRIX (`-**27**)"!!!~'

'-**DEATH/DAY** # '-**NUMBER** in '-**REVERSE** = (70 (-) 19 (-) 18 (-) 9) = (`-**24**) = "THREE '-YEARS '-AWAY from '-AGE of '-DEATH for SINGER/SONGWRITER JIMI HENDRIX (`-**27**)"!!!~'

(116 (-) 99) = (`-**17**) = "TEN '-YEARS '-AWAY from '-AGE of '-DEATH for SINGER/SONGWRITER JIMI HENDRIX (`-**27**)"!!!~'

(116 + 99) = (`-**215**) = (21 + 5) = (`-**26**) = "ONE '-YEAR '-AWAY from '-AGE of '-DEATH for SINGER/SONGWRITER JIMI HENDRIX (`-**27**)"!!!~'

(215 + 17) = (`-**232**) = **RECIPROCAL-SEQUENCING-NUMEROLOGY-RSN**!!!~'

SINGER/SONGWRITER JIMI HENDRIX '-**DIED** (`-**70**) DAYS AWAY from '-**HIS** '-**BIRTHDAY**!!!~' (`-**70**) = '-**DIED** in the '-**YEAR** of (`-**70**)!!!~'

/|\ '-**DEATH/YEAR** = (`-**19/70**) = (19 + 70) = (`-**89**) = (8 x 9) = (`-**72**) = RECIPROCAL (INVERSE/MIRROR) = (`-**27**) = '-AGE of '-DEATH for SINGER/SONGWRITER JIMI HENDRIX (`-**27**)"!!!~' /|\

(365 (-) 70) = (`-**295**) = (29 x 5) = (`-**145**) = (14 x 5) = (`-**70**) = "**DIED** this `-MANY `-DAYS `-AWAY from `-**BIRTH/DAY**; and, *in fact is the* `-**DEATH/YEAR** of (`-**70**) for SINGER/SONGWRITER JIMI HENDRIX"!!!~'

/|\ FRAGMENTED `-**BIRTH/DAY** # `-**NUMBER** = (1 + 1 + 2 + 7 + 1 + 9 + 4 + 2) = (`-**27**) = `-**AGE** of `-**DEATH** for SINGER/ SONGWRITER JIMI HENDRIX (`-**27**)"!!!~' /|\

FRAGMENTED `-**BIRTH/DAY** # `-**NUMBER** = (1 + 1 + 2 + 7 + 1 + 9 + 4 + 2) = (`-**27**) = RECIPROCAL (INVERSE/MIRROR) = (`-**72**)!!!~'

FRAGMENTED `-**DEATH/DAY** # `-**NUMBER** = (9 + 1 + 8 + 1 + 9 + 7 + 0) = (`-**35**) = RECIPROCAL (INVERSE/MIRROR) = (`-**53**)!!!~'

(27 + 35) = (`-**62**) = RECIPROCAL (INVERSE/MIRROR) = (`-**26**) = "**ONE** `-YEAR `-AWAY from `-AGE of `-DEATH for SINGER/ SONGWRITER JIMI HENDRIX (`-**27**)"!!!~'

`-**DIED** at the `-**AGE** of (`-**76**)!!!~'

SINGER/SONGWRITER ARETHA FRANKLIN `-**BIRTHDAY** = (**3/25**/19/**42**) = (**3** + **25** + 19 + **42**) = (`-**89**) = RECIPROCAL (INVERSE/MIRROR) = (`-**98**)!!!~'

`-**BIRTH/DAY** # `-**NUMBER** = (`-**89**) = (8 x 9) = (`-**72**)!!!~'

`-BIRTH/DAY = (**3/25**) = (3 x 25) = (`-**75**) = "**ONE** `-YEAR `-AWAY from `-AGE of `-DEATH for SINGER/SONGWRITER ARETHA FRANKLIN (`-**76**)"!!!~'

131

`-**BIRTH/DAY** = (**3/25**) = (3 + 25) = (`-**28**) = "FLIP the (`-**2**) OVER to a (`-**7**)" = (`-**78**) = "**TWO** `-**YEARS** `-**AWAY from** `-**AGE of** `-**DEATH for SINGER/SONGWRITER ARETHA FRANKLIN** (`-**76**)"!!!~'

`-**BIRTH/YEAR** = (`-**19/42**) = (42 (-) 19) = (`-**23**) = -a PROPHETIC # `-NUMBER!!!~'

"WAS `-**BORN** in (`-**3**) (MARCH); and, `-**DIED** in (`-**8**) (AUGUST)"; and, (**3/8**) = (`-**38** x **2**) = (`-**76**) = "**AGE of** `-**DEATH**" = (MARCH 8[th]) = (`-**17**) DAYS AWAY from `-HER `-**BIRTH/DAY**!!!~' RECIPROCAL (INVERSE/MIRROR) = (**8/3**) = (AUGUST 3rd) = (`-**13**) DAYS AWAY from `-HER `-**DEATH/DAY**!!!~' (**17/13**) = (17 x 13) = (`-**221**) = "FLIP the (`-**2**) OVER to a (`-**7**)" = (`-**771**) = (77 (-) 1) = (`-**76**) = `-**AGE of** `-**DEATH for SINGER/SONGWRITER ARETHA FRANKLIN** (`-**76**)"!!!~'

(1**9**4**2**) = (92) (14) = `-*EQUALS* = (`-**78**) = "**TWO** `-**YEARS** `-**AWAY from** `-**AGE of** `-**DEATH for SINGER/SONGWRITER ARETHA FRANKLIN** (`-**76**)"!!!~'

SINGER/SONGWRITER ARETHA FRANKLIN `-**DEATH/DAY** = (**8/16**/20/**18**) = (**8** + **16** + 20 + **18**) = (`-**62**) = RECIPROCAL (INVERSE/MIRROR) = (`-**26**) = "FLIP the (`-**2**) OVER to a (`-**7**)" = (`-**76**) = `-**AGE of** `-**DEATH for SINGER/SONGWRITER ARETHA FRANKLIN** (`-**76**)"!!!~'

`-**DEATH/DAY** = (**8/16**) = (**ALL-IN-ONE-#-NUMBER**) = (8 (-) 1) (6) = (`-**76**) = `-**AGE of** `-**DEATH for SINGER/SONGWRITER ARETHA FRANKLIN** (`-**76**)"!!!~'

`-**DEATH/DAY** = (**8/16**) = (86 x 1) = (`-**86**) = RECIPROCAL (INVERSE/MIRROR) = (`-**68**) = "**The** `-**MARK**"!!!~'

`-**DEATH/DAY** = (**8/16**) = (8 + 16) = (`-**24**) = "FLIP the (`-**2**) OVER to a (`-**7**)" = (`-**74**) = "**TWO `-YEARS `-AWAY from `-AGE of `-DEATH for SINGER/SONGWRITER ARETHA FRANKLIN (`-76)**"!!!~'

`-**DEATH/YEAR** = (`-**20/18**) = (20 + 18) = (`-**38**) x `-*TIMES* (`-**2**) = (`-**76**) = `-**AGE of `-DEATH for SINGER/SONGWRITER ARETHA FRANKLIN (`-76)**"!!!~'

(89 (-) 62) = (`-**27**) = `-**AGE of `-DEATH for SINGER/ SONGWRITER JIMI HENDRIX (`-27)**"!!!~'

(89 (-) 62) = (`-**27**) = "FLIP the (`-**2**) OVER to a (`-**7**)" = (`-**77**) = "**ONE `-YEAR `-AWAY from `-AGE of `-DEATH for SINGER/ SONGWRITER ARETHA FRANKLIN (`-76)**"!!!~'

(89 + 62) = (`-**151**) = **RECIPROCAL-SEQUENCING-NUMEROLOGY-RSN**!!!~'

(151 + 27) = (`-**178**) = (78 (-) 1) = (`-**77**) = "**ONE `-YEAR `-AWAY from `-AGE of `-DEATH for SINGER/SONGWRITER ARETHA FRANKLIN (`-76)**"!!!~'

SINGER/SONGWRITER ARETHA FRANKLIN `-**DIED** (`-**144**) DAYS AWAY from `-**HER `-BIRTHDAY**!!!~'

(365 (-) 144) = (`-**221**) = "FLIP the (`-**2**) OVER to a (`-**7**)" = (`-**771**) = (77 (-) 1) = (`-**76**) = `-**AGE of `-DEATH for SINGER/ SONGWRITER ARETHA FRANKLIN (`-76)**"!!!~'

/|\ FRAGMENTED `-**BIRTH/DAY** # `-**NUMBER** = (3 + 2 + 5 + 1 + 9 + 4 + 2) = (`-**26**) = "FLIP the (`-**2**) OVER to a (`-**7**)" = (`-**76**) = `-**AGE of `-DEATH for SINGER/SONGWRITER ARETHA FRANKLIN (`-76)**"!!!~' /|\

FRAGMENTED `-**BIRTH/DAY** # `-**NUMBER** = (3 + 2 + 5 + 1 + 9 + 4 + 2) = (`-**26**) = RECIPROCAL (INVERSE/MIRROR) = (`-**62**) = `-**HER** `-**VERY** `-**OWN** `-**DEATH/DAY** # `-**NUMBER** (`-**62**)!!!~'

FRAGMENTED `-**DEATH/DAY** # `-**NUMBER** = (8 + 1 + 6 + 2 + 0 + 1 + 8) = (`-**26**) = RECIPROCAL (INVERSE/MIRROR) = (`-**62**) = *"SEE `-ABOVE"*!!!~'

FRAGMENTED `-**BIRTH/DAY** # `-**NUMBER** (`-**26**) = `-*EQUALS* = FRAGMENTED `-**DEATH/DAY** # `-**NUMBER** (`-**26**)!!!~'

(26 + 26) = (`-**52**) = RECIPROCAL (INVERSE/MIRROR) = (`-**25**) = "FLIP the (`-**2**) OVER to a (`-**7**)" = (`-**75**) = **"ONE `-YEAR `-AWAY from `-AGE of `-DEATH for SINGER/SONGWRITER ARETHA FRANKLIN (`-76)"**!!!~'

ARETHA FRANKLIN `-AGE of `-DEATH = (`-**76**) = (7 x 6) = (`-**42**) = **"The `-MARK"**!!!~' = **"YEAR of `-BIRTH (`-42)"**!!!~'

`-**DIED** at the `-**AGE** of (`-**22**)!!!~'

SINGER/SONGWRITER BUDDY HOLLY `-**BIRTHDAY** = (**9/7**/19/**36**) = (**9** + **7** + 19 + **36**) = (`-**71**) = RECIPROCAL (INVERSE/MIRROR) = (`-**17**) = **"RITCHIE VALENS `-DIED at the `-AGE of (`-17)"**!!!~'

`-**BIRTH/DAY** = (**9/7**) = (9 x 7) = (`-**63**) = RECIPROCAL (INVERSE/MIRROR) = (`-**36**) = **"WAS `-BORN in (`-36)"**!!!~'

(`-36) + (`-36) = (`-72) = "FLIP the (`-7) OVER to a (`-2)" = (`-22) = `-AGE of `-DEATH for SINGER/SONGWRITER BUDDY HOLLY (`-22)"!!!~'

`-SEPTEMBER (`-30) DAYS = (`-30) (-) (`-7) = (`-23) = -a PROPHETIC # `-NUMBER!!!~'

`-BIRTH/YEAR = (`-1936) = (36 (-) 19) = (`-17) = RECIPROCAL (INVERSE/MIRROR) = (`-71) = `-BIRTH/DAY # `-NUMBER of SINGER/SONGWRITER BUDDY HOLLY!!!~'

`-BIRTH/YEAR = (`-36) = RECIPROCAL (INVERSE/MIRROR) = (`-63)!!!~'

(`-63) (-) (`-36) = (`-27) = "FLIP the (`-7) OVER to a (`-2)" = (`-22) = `-AGE of `-DEATH for SINGER/SONGWRITER BUDDY HOLLY (`-22)"!!!~'

"WAS `-BORN in (`-9) (SEPTEMBER); and, `-DIED in (`-2) (FEBRUARY)"; and, (9/2) = (SEPTEMBER 2nd) = (`-5) DAYS AWAY from `-HIS `-BIRTH/DAY!!!~' RECIPROCAL (INVERSE/ MIRROR) = (2/9) = (FEBRUARY 9th) = (`-6) DAYS AWAY from `-HIS `-DEATH/DAY!!!~' (5/6) = (5 + 6) = (`-11) x `-TIMES (`-2) = (`-22) = `-AGE of `-DEATH for SINGER/SONGWRITER BUDDY HOLLY (`-22)"!!!~'

(1936) = (3 (-) 1) (9 (-) 6) = `-EQUALS = (`-23) = "ONE `-YEAR `-AWAY from `-AGE of `-DEATH for SINGER/SONGWRITER BUDDY HOLLY (`-22)"!!!~'

SINGER/SONGWRITER BUDDY HOLLY `-DEATH/DAY = (2/3/19/59) = (2 + 3 + 19 + 59) = (`-83) = RECIPROCAL (INVERSE/ MIRROR) = (`-38) = "THE `-DEATH # `-NUMBERS"!!!~'

`-**DEATH/DAY** = (`-**2/3**) = (`-**23**) = "ONE `-YEAR `-AWAY from `-AGE of `-DEATH for SINGER/SONGWRITER BUDDY HOLLY (`-**22**)"!!!~'

`-**DEATH/DAY** = (`-**2/3**) = (`-**23**) = -a PROPHETIC # `-NUMBER!!!~'

`-**DEATH/DAY** # `-**NUMBER** in `-**REVERSE** = (59 (-) 19 (-) 3 (-) 2) = (`-**35**)!!!~'

(83 (-) 71) = (`-**12**)!!!~'

(83 + 71) = (`-**154**) = (54 x 1) = (`-**54**) / `-*DIVIDED* `-*by* (`-**2**) = (`-**27**) = "FLIP the (`-**7**) OVER to a (`-**2**)" = (`-**22**) = `-AGE of `-DEATH for SINGER/SONGWRITER BUDDY HOLLY (`-**22**)"!!!~'

(154 + 12) = (`-**166**) = "THE `-SAME # `-NUMBER (`-**166**) for BUDDY HOLLY, RITCHIE VALENS; and, "THE BIG BOPPER" (`-**166**)"!!!~'

(`-**166**) = (`-**16.6**) = ROUNDED UP = (`-**17**) = `-AGE of `-DEATH for SINGER/SONGWRITER RITCHIE VALENS (`-**17**)"!!!~'

(`-**166**) = (16 + 6) = (`-**22**) = `-AGE of `-DEATH for SINGER/ SONGWRITER BUDDY HOLLY (`-**22**)"!!!~'

SINGER/SONGWRITER BUDDY HOLLY `-**DIED** (`-**149**) DAYS AWAY from `-HIS `-**BIRTHDAY!!!**~' (`-**149**) = (14 + 9) = (`-**23**) = -a PROPHETIC # `-NUMBER = "ONE `-YEAR `-AWAY from `-AGE of `-DEATH for SINGER/SONGWRITER BUDDY HOLLY (`-**22**)"!!!~'

(365 (-) 149) = (`-**216**) = (**21.6**) = ROUNDED UP = (`-**22**) = `-AGE of `-DEATH for SINGER/SONGWRITER BUDDY HOLLY (`-**22**)"!!!~'

(365 (-) 149) = (`-**216**) = (16 x 2) = (`-**32**) = -a PROPHETIC # `-NUMBER!!!~'

/|\ FRAGMENTED `-**BIRTH/DAY** # `-**NUMBER** = (9 + 7 + 1 + 9 + 3 + 6) = (`-**35**) = `-**DEATH/DAY** # `-**NUMBER** in `-**REVERSE** for `-**SINGER/SONGWRITER BUDDY HOLLY** (`-**35**)!!!~' /|\

FRAGMENTED `-**BIRTH/DAY** # `-**NUMBER** = (9 + 7 + 1 + 9 + 3 + 6) = (`-**35**) = RECIPROCAL (INVERSE/MIRROR) = (`-**53**)!!!~'

FRAGMENTED `-**DEATH/DAY** # `-**NUMBER** = (2 + 3 + 1 + 9 + 5 + 9) = (`-**29**) = RECIPROCAL (INVERSE/MIRROR) = (`-**92**) = "FLIP the (`-**2**) OVER to a (`-**7**)" = (`-**97**) = `-**BIRTH/DAY** for **SINGER/SONGWRITER `-BUDDY HOLLY (SEPTEMBER 7**[th])!!!~'

(35 + 29) = (`-**64**) = RECIPROCAL (INVERSE/ MIRROR) = (`-**46**) = (23 x 2) = (`-**232**) = **RECIPROCAL-SEQUENCING-NUMEROLOGY-RSN**!!!~'

`-**BIRTH/DAY** = (**9/7**)!!!~'

`-**DEATH/DAY** = (**2/3**)!!!~'

(9 + 7 + 2 + 3) = (`-**21**) = **"ONE `-YEAR `-AWAY from `-AGE of `-DEATH for SINGER/SONGWRITER BUDDY HOLLY** (`-**22**)"!!!~'

`-**DIED** at the `-**AGE** of (`-**17**)!!!~'

SINGER/SONGWRITER RITCHIE VALENS `-**BIRTHDAY** = (**5/13**/19/**41**) = (**5** + **13** + 19 + **41**) = (`-**78**) = RECIPROCAL (INVERSE/MIRROR) = (`-**87**)!!!~'

`-**BIRTH/DAY** = (**5/13**) = (5 + 13) = (`-**18**) = "ONE `-YEAR `-AWAY from `-AGE of `-DEATH for SINGER/SONGWRITER RITCHIE VALENS (`-**17**)"!!!~'

`-**BIRTH/DAY** # `-**NUMBER** = (`-**78**) = (7 + 8) = (`-**15**) = "TWO `-YEARS `-AWAY from `-AGE of `-DEATH for SINGER/SONGWRITER RITCHIE VALENS (`-**17**)"!!!~'

`-**BIRTH/YEAR** = (`-**1941**) = (41 (-) 19) = (`-**22**) = `-AGE of `-DEATH for SINGER/SONGWRITER BUDDY HOLLY (`-**22**)"!!!~'

"WAS `-**BORN** in (`-**5**) (MAY); and, `-**DIED** in (`-**2**) (FEBRUARY)"; and, (**5/2**) = (MAY 2ⁿᵈ) = (`-**11**) DAYS AWAY from `-HIS `-**BIRTH/DAY**!!!~' RECIPROCAL (INVERSE/MIRROR) = (**2/5**) = (FEBRUARY 5ᵗʰ) = (`-**2**) DAYS AWAY from `-HIS `-**DEATH/DAY**!!!~' (**11/2**) = "FLIP the (`-**2**) OVER to a (`-**7**)" = (`-**117**) = (17 x 1) = (`-**17**) = `-AGE of `-DEATH for SINGER/SONGWRITER RITCHIE VALENS (`-**17**)"!!!~'

(**11/2**) = (`-**11**) x (`-**2**) = (`-**22**) = `-AGE of `-DEATH for SINGER/SONGWRITER BUDDY HOLLY (`-**22**)"!!!~'

(**19**4**1**) = (4 + 1) (9 x 1) = `-*EQUALS* = (`-**59**) = `-YEAR of `-DEATH for SINGER/SONGWRITER RITCHIE VALENS (`-**1959**)"!!!~'

SINGER/SONGWRITER RITCHIE VALENS `-**DEATH/DAY** = (**2/3**/19/**59**) = (**2** + **3** + 19 + **59**) = (`-**83**) = RECIPROCAL (INVERSE/MIRROR) = (`-**38**) = "THE `-DEATH # `-NUMBERS"!!!~'

`-**DEATH/DAY** = (`-**2/3**) = (`-**23**) = -a PROPHETIC # `-NUMBER!!!~'

`-**DEATH/DAY** # `-**NUMBER** in `-**REVERSE** = (59 (-) 19 (-) 3 (-) 2) = (`-**35**)!!!~'

(83 (-) 78) = (`-**5**)!!!~'

(83 + 78) = (`-**161**) = (16 + 1) = (`-**17**) = `-**AGE** of `-**DEATH** for **SINGER/SONGWRITER RITCHIE VALENS** (`-**17**)"!!!~'

(161 + 5) = (`-**166**) = "**THE** `-**SAME** # `-**NUMBER** (`-**166**) for **BUDDY HOLLY, RITCHIE VALENS; and, "THE BIG BOPPER**" (`-**166**)"!!!~'

(`-**166**) = (`-**16.6**) = ROUNDED UP = (`-**17**) = `-**AGE** of `-**DEATH** for **SINGER/SONGWRITER RITCHIE VALENS** (`-**17**)"!!!~'

(`-**166**) = (16 + 6) = (`-**22**) = `-**AGE** of `-**DEATH** for **SINGER/ SONGWRITER BUDDY HOLLY** (`-**22**)"!!!~'

SINGER/SONGWRITER RITCHIE VALENS `-**DIED** (`-**99**) DAYS AWAY from `-**HIS** `-**BIRTHDAY!!!**~' (`-**99**) = RECIPROCAL (INVERSE/MIRROR) = (`-**66**)!!!~'

(365 (-) 99) = (`-**266**) = (26 (-) 6) = (`-**20**) = "**THREE** `-**YEARS** `-**AWAY** from `-**AGE** of `-**DEATH** for **SINGER/SONGWRITER RITCHIE VALENS** (`-**17**)"!!!~'

(365 (-) 99) = (`-**266**) = (26 + 6) = (`-**32**) = -a PROPHETIC # `-**NUMBER!!!**~'

(365 (-) 99) = (`-**266**) = (66 x 2) = (`-**132**) = (32 x 1) = (`-**32**) = -a PROPHETIC # `-**NUMBER!!!**~'

FRAGMENTED `-**BIRTH/DAY** # `-**NUMBER** = (5 + 1 + 3 + 1 + 9 + 4 + 1) = (`-**24**) = RECIPROCAL (INVERSE/MIRROR) = (`-**42**)!!!~'

(`-42) (-) (`-24) = (`-18) = "ONE `-YEAR `-AWAY from `-AGE of `-DEATH for SINGER/SONGWRITER RITCHIE VALENS (`-17)"!!!~'

FRAGMENTED `-**DEATH/DAY** # `-NUMBER = (2 + 3 + 1 + 9 + 5 + 9) = (`-**29**) = RECIPROCAL (INVERSE/MIRROR) = (`-**92**)!!!~'

(29 + 92) = (`-**121**) = (21 + 1) = (`-**22**) = `-AGE of `-DEATH for SINGER/SONGWRITER BUDDY HOLLY (`-**22**)"!!!~'

(24 + 29) = (`-**53**) = RECIPROCAL (INVERSE/MIRROR) = (`-**35**) = `-**DEATH/DAY** # `-**NUMBER** in `-**REVERSE** for `-SINGER/SONGWRITER RITCHIE VALENS (`-**35**)!!!~'

`-**BIRTH/DAY** = (**5/13**) = (53 x 1) = (`-**53**)!!!~'

`-**DEATH/DAY** = (**2/3**)!!!~'

(5 + 13 + 2 + 3) = (`-**23**) = -a PROPHETIC # `-NUMBER!!!~'

`-**DIED** at the `-**AGE** of (`-**28**)!!!~'

SINGER/SONGWRITER "THE BIG BOPPER" `-**BIRTHDAY** = (**10/24**/19/**30**) = (**10** + **24** + 19 + **30**) = (`-**83**) = RECIPROCAL (INVERSE/MIRROR) = (`-**38**) = "THE `-DEATH # `-NUMBERS"!!!~'

`-**BIRTH/DAY** # `-**NUMBER** = (`-**83**) = `-*EQUALS* = `-HIS `-**VERY** `-**OWN** `-**DEATH/DAY** # `-**NUMBER** (`-**83**)!!!~'

`-**BIRTH/DAY** = (**10/24**) = (24 (-) 10) = (`-**14**) x (`-**2**) = (`-**28**) = `-**AGE** of `-**DEATH** for SINGER/SONGWRITER "THE BIG BOPPER" (`-**28**)"!!!~'

`-**BIRTH/YEAR** = (`-**1930**) = (19 + 30) = (`-**49**) = (4 x 9) = (`-**36**) = "YEAR of `-BIRTH for SINGER/SONGWRITER BUDDY HOLLY (`-**1936**)"!!!~'

`-**BIRTH/YEAR** = (`-**30**) = "TWO `-YEARS `-AWAY from `-**AGE** of `-**DEATH** for SINGER/SONGWRITER "THE BIG BOPPER" (`-**28**)"!!!~'

"WAS `-**BORN** in (`-**10**) (OCTOBER); and, `-**DIED** in (`-**2**) (FEBRUARY)"; and, (**10/2**) = (OCTOBER 2nd) = (`-**22**) DAYS AWAY from `-HIS `-**BIRTH/DAY!!!~'** RECIPROCAL (INVERSE/ MIRROR) = (**2/10**) = (FEBRUARY $10^{th}$) = (`-**7**) DAYS AWAY from `-HIS `-**DEATH/DAY!!!~'** (**22/7**) = (22 + 7) = (`-**29**) = "ONE `-YEAR `-AWAY from `-AGE of `-DEATH for SINGER/ SONGWRITER "THE BIG BOPPER" (`-**28**)"!!!~'

(**19**30) = (3 (-) 1) (9 + 0) = `-*EQUALS* = (`-**29**) = "ONE `-YEAR `-AWAY from `-AGE of `-DEATH for SINGER/SONGWRITER "THE BIG BOPPER" (`-**28**)"!!!~'

SINGER/SONGWRITER "THE BIG BOPPER" `-**DEATH/DAY** = (**2/3**/19/**59**) = (**2** + **3** + 19 + **59**) = (`-**83**) = RECIPROCAL (INVERSE/ MIRROR) = (`-**38**) = "THE `-DEATH # `-NUMBERS"!!!~'

`-**DEATH/DAY** = (`-**2/3**) = (`-**23**) = -a PROPHETIC # `-NUMBER!!!~'

`-**DEATH/DAY** # `-**NUMBER** in `-**REVERSE** = (59 (-) 19 (-) 3 (-) 2) = (`-**35**)!!!~'

(83 (-) 83) = (`-**0**)!!!~'

(83 + 83) = (`-**166**) = `-**BOTH**; `-BIRTH/DAY # `-NUMBER (`-**83**); and, `-DEATH/DAY # `-NUMBER (`-**83**); `-**ADDED** `-**UP** `-**TOGETHER**!!!~'

(`-**166**) = (`-**16.6**) = ROUNDED UP = (`-**17**) = `-AGE of `-DEATH for SINGER/SONGWRITER RITCHIE VALENS (`-**17**)"!!!~'

(`-**166**) = (16 + 6) = (`-**22**) = `-AGE of `-DEATH for SINGER/ SONGWRITER BUDDY HOLLY (`-**22**)"!!!~'

(166 + 0) = (`-**166**) = "THE `-SAME # `-NUMBER (`-**166**) for BUDDY HOLLY, RITCHIE VALENS; and, "THE BIG BOPPER" (`-**166**)"!!!~'

SINGER/SONGWRITER "THE BIG BOPPER" `-**DIED** (`-**102**) DAYS AWAY from `-HIS `-BIRTHDAY!!!~' (`-**102**) = RECIPROCAL (INVERSE/MIRROR) = (`-**201**)!!!~'

(102 + 201) = (`-**303**) = **RECIPROCAL-SEQUENCING-NUMEROLOGY-RSN**!!!~'

(365 (-) 102) = (`-**263**) = (63 x 2) = (`-**126**) = (26 + 1) = (`-**27**) = "ONE `-YEAR `-AWAY from `-AGE of `-DEATH for SINGER/ SONGWRITER "THE BIG BOPPER" (`-**28**)"!!!~'

(365 (-) 102) = (`-**263**) = (26 x 3) = (`-**78**) = `-**BIRTH/DAY #** `-**NUMBER** of SINGER/SONGWRITER RITCHIE VALENS (`-**78**)!!!~'

FRAGMENTED `-**BIRTH/DAY #** `-**NUMBER** = (1 + 0 + 2 + 4 + 1 + 9 + 3 + 0) = (`-**20**) = RECIPROCAL (INVERSE/MIRROR) = (`-**02**)!!!~'

(`-**20**) + (`-**02**) = (`-**22**) = `-AGE of `-DEATH for SINGER/ SONGWRITER BUDDY HOLLY (`-**22**)"!!!~'

FRAGMENTED `-**DEATH/DAY** # `-NUMBER = (2 + 3 + 1 + 9 + 5 + 9) = (`-**29**) = "ONE `-YEAR `-AWAY from `-AGE of `-DEATH for SINGER/SONGWRITER "THE BIG BOPPER" (`-**28**)"!!!~'

FRAGMENTED `-**DEATH/DAY** # `-NUMBER = (2 + 3 + 1 + 9 + 5 + 9) = (`-**29**) = RECIPROCAL (INVERSE/MIRROR) = (`-**92**)!!!~'

(92 (-) 29) = (`-**63**) = RECIPROCAL (INVERSE/MIRROR) = (`-**36**) = (4 x 9) = (`-**49**)!!!~'

(20 + 29) = (`-**49**) = (19 + 30) = (`-**19/30**) = "**YEAR** of `-BIRTH for SINGER/SONGWRITER "THE BIG BOPPER" (`-**1930**)"!!!~'

`-*BUDDY HOLLY* `-BIRTH/DAY # `-NUMBER (`-**71**) (**+**) `-*RITCHIE VALENS* `-BIRTH/DAY # `-NUMBER (`-**78**) = (`-**149**) = (49 x 1) = (`-**49**)!!!~'

`-**BIRTH/DAY** = (**10/24**)!!!~'

`-**DEATH/DAY** = (**2/3**)!!!~'

(10 + 24 + 2 + 3) = (`-**39**) = (3 x 9) = (`-**27**) = "ONE `-YEAR `-AWAY from `-AGE of `-DEATH for SINGER/SONGWRITER "THE BIG BOPPER" (`-**28**)"!!!~'

`-*BUDDY HOLLY* `-**AGE** of `-**DEATH** (`-**22**) (**+**) `-*RITCHIE VALENS* `-**AGE** of `-**DEATH** (`-**17**) = (`-**39**)!!!~'

(`-**39**) + (`-**39**) = (`-**78**) = `-**BIRTH/DAY** # `-**NUMBER** of SINGER/ SONGWRITER RITCHIE VALENS (`-**78**)!!!~'

`-**DIED** at the `-**AGE** of (`-**55**)!!!~'

SINGER/SONGWRITER TAMMY WYNETTE `-**BIRTHDAY** = (**5/5**/19/**42**) = (**5** + **5** + 19 + **42**) = (`-**71**) = RECIPROCAL (INVERSE/MIRROR) = (`-**17**)!!!~'

(71 (-) 17) = (`-**54**) = "ONE `-YEAR `-AWAY from `-AGE of `-DEATH for SINGER/SONGWRITER TAMMY WYNETTE (`-**55**)"!!!~'

`-**BIRTH/DAY** = (`-**5/5**) = (`-**55**) = `-**AGE** of `-**DEATH** for SINGER/SONGWRITER TAMMY WYNETTE (`-**55**)!!!~'

`-**BIRTH/YEAR** = (`-**1942**) = (42 (-) 19) = (`-**23**) = -a PROPHETIC # `-NUMBER!!!~'

`-**AGE** of `-**DEATH** = (`-**55**) = (`-**23**) + (`-**32**)!!!~'

"WAS `-**BORN** in (`-**5**) (MAY); and, `-**DIED** in (`-**4**) (APRIL)"; and, (**5/4**) = (MAY 4th) = (`-**1**) DAY AWAY from `-HER `-**BIRTH/ DAY**!!!~' RECIPROCAL (INVERSE/MIRROR) = (**4/5**) = (APRIL 5th) = (`-**1**) DAY AWAY from `-HER `-**DEATH/DAY**!!!~' (**1/1**) = (`-**11**) x (`-**5**) = (`-**55**) = `-**AGE** of `-**DEATH** for SINGER/ SONGWRITER TAMMY WYNETTE (`-**55**)"!!!~'

(19**4**2) = (9 (-) 4) (1 + 2) = `-*EQUALS* = (`-**53**) = "TWO `-YEARS `-AWAY from `-AGE of `-DEATH for SINGER/SONGWRITER TAMMY WYNETTE (`-**55**)"!!!~'

SINGER/SONGWRITER TAMMY WYNETTE `-**DEATH/ DAY** = (**4**/**6**/19/**98**) = (**4** + **6** + 19 + **98**) = (`-**127**) = "FLIP the (`-**7**) OVER to a (`-**2**)" = (`-**122**) = (22 + 1) = (`-**23**) = -a PROPHETIC # `-NUMBER!!!~'

`-**DEATH/DAY** = (`-**4/6**) = `-**SUBTRACT** from ONE # `-**NUMBER**; and, then `-**ADD** to the `-**OTHER** # `-**NUMBER** = (`-**55**) = `-**AGE** of `-DEATH for SINGER/SONGWRITER TAMMY WYNETTE (`-**55**)"!!!~'

`-**DEATH/DAY** = (`-**4/6**) = (`-**46**) = (`-**23**) x (`-**2**) = (`-**232**) = RECIPROCAL-**S**EQUENCING-**N**UMEROLOGY-**RSN**!!!~'

(`-**127**) = (71 x 2) = (`-**142**) = (42 x 1) = (`-**42**) = "The `-**MARK**"!!!~'

`-**DEATH/DAY** # `-**NUMBER** in `-**REVERSE** = (98 (-) 19 (-) 6 (-) 4) = (`-**69**) = (6 x 9) = (`-**54**) = "ONE `-YEAR `-AWAY from `-AGE of `-DEATH for SINGER/SONGWRITER TAMMY WYNETTE (`-**55**)"!!!~'

(127 (-) 71) = (`-**56**) = "ONE `-YEAR `-AWAY from `-AGE of `-DEATH for SINGER/SONGWRITER TAMMY WYNETTE (`-**55**)"!!!~'

(127 + 71) = (`-**197**) = (19 x 7) = (`-**133**) = (33 (-) 1) = (`-**32**) = -a PROPHETIC # `-NUMBER!!!~'

(197 + 57) = (`-**253**) = (53 + 2) = (`-**55**) = `-**AGE** of `-DEATH for SINGER/SONGWRITER TAMMY WYNETTE (`-**55**)"!!!~'

SINGER/SONGWRITER TAMMY WYNETTE `-**DIED** (`-**29**) DAYS AWAY from `-**HER** `-**BIRTHDAY**!!!~' (`-**29**) = "FLIP the (`-**2**) OVER to a (`-**7**)" = (`-**79**) = `-**DEATH/YEAR** (`-**1998**) = (98 (-) 19) = (`-**79**)!!!~'

`-**DEATH/YEAR** = (`-**19/98**) = (19 + 98) = (`-**117**) = RECIPROCAL (INVERSE/MIRROR) = (`-**711**) = (71 x 1) = (`-**71**) = `-**BIRTH/ DAY** # `-**NUMBER** for SINGER/SONGWRITER TAMMY WYNETTE (`-**71**)!!!~'

(365 (-) 29) = (`-**336**) = (33 x 6) = (`-**198**) = (98 x 1) = (`-**98**) = `-**DEATH/YEAR** for SINGER/SONGWRITER TAMMY WYNETTE (`-**1998**)"!!!~'

FRAGMENTED `-**BIRTH/DAY** # `-**NUMBER** = (5 + 5 + 1 + 9 + 4 + 2) = (`-**26**) = RECIPROCAL (INVERSE/MIRROR) = (`-**62**)!!!~'

FRAGMENTED `-**DEATH/DAY** # `-**NUMBER** = (4 + 6 + 1 + 9 + 9 + 8) = (`-**37**) = RECIPROCAL (INVERSE/MIRROR) = (`-**73**)!!!~'

(26 + 37) = (`-**63**) = RECIPROCAL (INVERSE/MIRROR) = (`-**36**)"!!!~'

`-**DIED** at the `-**AGE** of (`-**57**)!!!~'

SINGER/SONGWRITER PRINCE `-**BIRTHDAY** = (**6**/**7**/19/**58**) = (**6** + **7** + 19 + **58**) = (`-**90**) = RECIPROCAL (INVERSE/MIRROR) = (`-**09**)!!!~'

`-**BIRTH/DAY** = (`-**6/7**) = (6 x 7) = (`-**42**) = "The `-**MARK**"!!!~'

`-**BIRTH/YEAR** = (**58**) = `-**DIED** at the `-**AGE** of (`-**57**) for SINGER/SONGWRITER PRINCE (`-**57**)"!!!~' `-**DIED** in the `-**YEAR** `-**OF**!!!~'

`-**BIRTH/YEAR** = (**58**) = (5 + 8) = (`-**13**) = "A VERY PIVOTAL # `-NUMBER"!!!~'

"WAS `-**BORN** in (`-**6**) (JUNE); and, `-**DIED** in (`-**4**) (APRIL)"; and, (**6/4**) = (JUNE 4th) = (`-**3**) DAYS AWAY from `-HIS `-**BIRTH/ DAY**!!!~' RECIPROCAL (INVERSE/MIRROR) = (**4/6**) = (APRIL 6$^{th}$) = (`-**15**) DAYS AWAY from `-HIS `-**DEATH/DAY**!!!~' (**3/15**) = (3 x 15) = (`-**45**) = RECIPROCAL (INVERSE/MIRROR) = (`-**54**) = "THREE `-YEARS `-AWAY from `-AGE of `-DEATH for SINGER/SONGWRITER PRINCE (`-**57**)"!!!~'

(1**95**8) = (9 (-) 5) (1 (-) 8) = `-*EQUALS* = (`-**47**) = "**DIED** this `-**MANY** `-**DAYS** `-**AWAY** from `-**BIRTH/DAY** for SINGER/ SONGWRITER PRINCE (`-**47**)"!!!~'

(**19**5**8**) = (1 + 5) (9 + 8) = `-*EQUALS* = (`-**617**) = (67 x 1) = (`-**67**) = `-**BIRTH/DAY** for SINGER/SONGWRITER PRINCE (`-**JUNE 7**th)"!!!~'

SINGER/SONGWRITER PRINCE `-**DEATH/DAY** = (**4/21**/20/**16**) = (**4** + **21** + 20 + **16**) = (`-**61**) = RECIPROCAL (INVERSE/MIRROR) = (`-**16**) = `-**DEATH/YEAR** for SINGER/ SONGWRITER PRINCE!!!~'

(`-**61**) = "FOUR `-YEARS `-AWAY from `-AGE of `-DEATH for SINGER/SONGWRITER PRINCE (`-**57**)"!!!~'

`-**DEATH/DAY** = (**4/21**) = (4 + 21) = (`-**25**) = RECIPROCAL (INVERSE/MIRROR) = (`-**52**) = "FLIP the (`-**2**) OVER to a (`-**7**)" = (`-**57**) = `-**AGE of `-DEATH for SINGER/SONGWRITER PRINCE (`-**57**)"!!!~'

(90 (-) 61) = (`-**29**) x (`-**2**) = (`-**58**) = `-**BIRTH/YEAR** of SINGER/ SONGWRITER PRINCE (`-**1958**)"!!!~'

(90 + 61) = (`-**151**) = (51 + 1) = (`-**52**) = "FLIP the (`-**2**) OVER to a (`-**7**)" = `-AGE of `-DEATH for SINGER/SONGWRITER PRINCE (`-**57**)"!!!~'

(151 (-) 29) = (`-**122**) = (22 + 1) = (`-**23**) = -a PROPHETIC # `-NUMBER!!!~'

SINGER/SONGWRITER PRINCE `-**DIED** (`-**47**) DAYS AWAY from `-**HIS** `-**BIRTHDAY!!!**~'

(365 (-) 47) = (`-**318**) = (18 x 3) = (`-**54**) = "THREE `-YEARS `-AWAY from `-AGE of `-DEATH for SINGER/SONGWRITER PRINCE (`-**57**)"!!!~'

(365 (-) 47) = (`-**318**) = (`-**31.8**) = ROUNDED UP = (`-**32**) = -a PROPHETIC # `-NUMBER!!!~'

FRAGMENTED `-**BIRTH/DAY** # `-**NUMBER** = (6 + 7 + 1 + 9 + 5 + 8) = (`-**36**) = RECIPROCAL (INVERSE/MIRROR) = (`-**63**) = "SIX `-YEARS `-AWAY from `-AGE of `-DEATH for SINGER/SONGWRITER PRINCE (`-**57**)"!!!~'

FRAGMENTED `-**DEATH/DAY** # `-**NUMBER** = (4 + 2 + 1 + 2 + 0 + 1 + 6) = (`-**16**) = `-**DEATH/YEAR** for SINGER/SONGWRITER PRINCE (`-**16**)!!!~'

FRAGMENTED `-**DEATH/DAY** # `-**NUMBER** = (4 + 2 + 1 + 2 + 0 + 1 + 6) = (`-**16**) = RECIPROCAL (INVERSE/MIRROR) = (`-**61**) = `-**DEATH/DAY** # `-**NUMBER** for SINGER/SONGWRITER PRINCE (`-**61**)!!!~'

(36 + 16) = (`-**52**) = "FLIP the (`-**2**) OVER to a (`-**7**)" = `-AGE of `-DEATH for SINGER/SONGWRITER PRINCE (`-**57**)"!!!~'

`-**DIED** at the `-**AGE** of (`-**50**)!!!~'

SINGER/SONGWRITER MICHAEL JACKSON `-**BIRTHDAY** = (**8**/**29**/19/**58**) = (**8** + **29** + 19 + **58**) = (`-**114**) = RECIPROCAL (INVERSE/MIRROR) = (`-**411**) = (41 + 1) = (`-**42**) = "The `-**MARK**"!!!~'

`-**BIRTH/DAY** = (**8/29**) = (82 (-) 29) = (`-**53**) = "THREE `-YEARS `-AWAY from `-AGE of `-DEATH for SINGER/SONGWRITER MICHAEL JACKSON (`-**50**)"!!!~'

`-**BIRTH/YEAR** = (**58**) = `-**BIRTH/DAY** (`-**29**th) x (`-**2**)!!!~'

`-**BIRTH/YEAR** = (**58**) = (5 + 8) = (`-**13**) = "A VERY PIVOTAL # `-NUMBER"!!!~'

"WAS `-**BORN** in (`-**8**) (AUGUST); and, `-**DIED** in (`-**6**) (JUNE)"; and, (**8/6**) = "The `-**MARK**"!!!~' = (AUGUST 6th) = (`-**23**) DAYS AWAY from `-HIS `-**BIRTH/DAY**!!!~' RECIPROCAL (INVERSE/MIRROR) = (**6/8**) = (JUNE 8th) = (`-**17**) DAYS AWAY from `-HIS `-**DEATH/DAY**!!!~' (**23/17**) = (32 + 17) = (`-**49**) = "ONE `-YEAR `-AWAY from `-AGE of `-DEATH for SINGER/SONGWRITER MICHAEL JACKSON (`-**50**)"!!!~'

(`-**23**) = RECIPROCAL (INVERSE/MIRROR) = (`-**32**)!!!~'

(19**58**) = (9 (-) 5) (1 (-) 8) = `-*EQUALS* = (`-**47**) = "THREE `-YEARS `-AWAY from `-AGE of `-DEATH for SINGER/SONGWRITER MICHAEL JACKSON (`-**50**)"!!!~'

SINGER/SONGWRITER MICHAEL JACKSON `-**DEATH/ DAY** = (**6/25**/20/**09**) = (**6** + **25** + 20 + **09**) = (`-**60**) = RECIPROCAL (INVERSE/MIRROR) = (`-**06**) = "FLIP the (`-**6**) OVER to a (`-**9**)" = (`-**09**) = `-**DEATH/YEAR** for SINGER/SONGWRITER MICHAEL JACKSON!!!~'

`-SINGER/SONGWRITER PRINCE had a `-DEATH/DAY #
`-NUMBER of (`-61)!!!~'

`-DAY of `-DEATH = (`-25th) x `-TIMES (`-2) = (`-50) = `-AGE of
`-DEATH for SINGER/SONGWRITER MICHAEL JACKSON
(`-50)"!!!~'

`-DAY of `-DEATH = (`-25th) = RECIPROCAL (INVERSE/
MIRROR) = (`-52) = "TWO `-YEARS `-AWAY from `-AGE of
`-DEATH for SINGER/SONGWRITER MICHAEL JACKSON
(`-50)"!!!~'

`-DEATH/DAY = (`-6/25) = (6 + 25) = (`-31) = RECIPROCAL
(INVERSE/MIRROR) = (`-13) = "A VERY PIVOTAL #
`-NUMBER"!!!~'

(114 (-) 60) = (`-54) = "FOUR `-YEARS `-AWAY from `-AGE of
`-DEATH for SINGER/SONGWRITER MICHAEL JACKSON
(`-50)"!!!~'

(114 (-) 60) = (`-54) = `-MOTHER KATHERINE ESTHER
JACKSON was `-BORN on (`-5/4) = (MAY 4th)!!!~'

(114 + 60) = (`-174) = (17 x 4) = (`-68) = "The `-MARK"!!!~'

(114 + 60) = (`-174) = (74 + 1) = (`-75) = "FLIP the (`-7) OVER to
a (`-2)" = (`-25)!!!~'

(75 (-) 25) = (`-50) = `-AGE of `-DEATH for SINGER/
SONGWRITER MICHAEL JACKSON (`-50)"!!!~'

SINGER/SONGWRITER MICHAEL JACKSON `-DIED (`-65)
DAYS AWAY from `-HIS `-BIRTHDAY!!!~' (`-65) = `-DEATH/
DAY = (`-625)!!!~'

(365 (-) 65) = (`-**300**)!!!~'

FRAGMENTED `-**BIRTH/DAY** # `-**NUMBER** = (8 + 2 + 9 + 1 + 9 + 5 + 8) = (`-**42**) = "The `-**MARK**"!!!~' = RECIPROCAL (INVERSE/MIRROR) = (`-**24**)!!!~'

FRAGMENTED `-**BIRTH/DAY** # `-**NUMBER** = (`-**42**) = `-***EQUALS*** = RECIPROCAL (INVERSE/MIRROR) = (`-**24**) = FRAGMENTED `-**DEATH/DAY** # `-**NUMBER**!!!~'

FRAGMENTED `-**DEATH/DAY** # `-**NUMBER** = (6 + 2 + 5 + 2 + 0 + 0 + 9) = (`-**24**) = RECIPROCAL (INVERSE/MIRROR) = (`-**42**) = "The `-**MARK**"!!!~'

(42 + 24) = (`-**66**)!!!~'

MICHAEL JACKSON `-**BIRTH/DAY** = (**8/29**)!!!~'

MICHAEL JACKSON `-**DEATH/DAY** = (**6/25**)!!!~'

(8 + 29 + 6 + 25) = (`-**68**) = "The `-**MARK**"!!!~'

SINGER/SONGWRITER MICHAEL JACKSON `-**BIRTH/DAY** = (`-**29**[th]) = `-**DEATH/YEAR** = (`-**20/09**) = (20 + 09) = (`-**29**)!!!~'

(29 + 29) = (`-**58**) = "**YEAR of `-BIRTH (`-*1958*)**"!!!~'

`-**DIED** at the `-**AGE** of (`-**48**)!!!~'

SINGER/SONGWRITER   WHITNEY   HOUSTON `-**BIRTHDAY** = (**8/9**/19/**63**) = (**8** + **9** + 19 + **63**) = (`-**99**) = RECIPROCAL (INVERSE/MIRROR) = (`-**66**)!!!~'

`-**BIRTH/DAY** = (**8/9**) = "FLIP the (`-**9**) OVER to a (`-**6**)" = (**8/6**) = (8 x 6) = (`-**48**) = `-**AGE** of `-**DEATH** for **SINGER/ SONGWRITER WHITNEY HOUSTON** (`-**48**)"!!!~'

(`-**99/66**) = `-**AGE** of `-**DEATH** (`-**48**) x `-*TIMES* (`-**2**) = (`-**96**)!!!~'

`-**AGE** of `-**DEATH** = (`-**48**) = (4 x 8) = (`-**32**) = -a PROPHETIC # `-NUMBER!!!~'

"WAS `-**BORN** in (`-**8**) (AUGUST); and, `-**DIED** in (`-**2**) (FEBRUARY)"; and, (**8/2**) = (AUGUST 2nd) = (`-**7**) DAYS AWAY from `-HER `-**BIRTH/DAY**!!!~' RECIPROCAL (INVERSE/ MIRROR) = (**2/8**) = (FEBRUARY 8$^{th}$) = (`-**3**) DAYS AWAY from `-HER `-**DEATH/DAY**!!!~' (**7/3**) = (7 x 3) = (`-**21**) = (21 x 1) = (`-**2/11**) = `-**DEATH/DAY**!!!~'

(19**63**) = (1 + 3) (9 (-) 6) = `-*EQUALS* = (`-**43**) = "FIVE `-YEARS `-AWAY from `-AGE of `-DEATH for SINGER/SONGWRITER WHITNEY HOUSTON (`-**48**)"!!!~'

SINGER/SONGWRITER WHITNEY HOUSTON `-**DEATH/ DAY** = (**2/11**/20/**12**) = (**2** + **11** + 20 + **12**) = (`-**45**)!!!~'

`-**DEATH/DAY** = (`-**2/11**) = (2 + 11) = (`-**13**) = "A VERY PIVOTAL # `-NUMBER"!!!~'

`-**DEATH/YEAR** = (`-**2012**) = (20 + 12) = (`-**32**) = -a PROPHETIC # `-NUMBER!!!~'

(99 (-) 45) = (`-**54**) = RECIPROCAL (INVERSE/MIRROR) = (`-**45**) = `-**DEATH/DAY** # `-**NUMBER** for SINGER/SONGWRITER WHITNEY HOUSTON (`-**45**)" = "THREE `-YEARS `-AWAY from `-AGE of `-DEATH for SINGER/SONGWRITER WHITNEY HOUSTON (`-**48**)"!!!~'

(99 (-) 45) = (`-**54**) = "**SIX `-YEARS `-AWAY from `-AGE of `-DEATH for SINGER/SONGWRITER WHITNEY HOUSTON (`-48)**"!!!~'

(99 + 45) = (`-**144**) = (44 + 1) = (`-**45**) = "**THREE `-YEARS `-AWAY from `-AGE of `-DEATH for SINGER/SONGWRITER WHITNEY HOUSTON (`-48)**"!!!~'

(99 + 45) = (`-**144**) = (44 + 1) = (`-**45**) = `-**DEATH/DAY # `-NUMBER for SINGER/SONGWRITER WHITNEY HOUSTON (`-45)**"!!!~'

(144 + 54) = (`-**198**) = (98 + 1) = (`-**99**) = `-**BIRTH/DAY # `-NUMBER for SINGER/SONGWRITER WHITNEY HOUSTON (`-99)**"!!!~'

SINGER/SONGWRITER WHITNEY HOUSTON `-**DIED** (`-**180**) DAYS AWAY from `-**HER `-BIRTHDAY!!!~'**

(366 (-) 180) = (`-**186**) = (86 x 1) = (`-**86**) = RECIPROCAL (INVERSE/MIRROR) = (`-**68**) = "**The `-MARK**"!!!~'

(366 (-) 180) = (`-**186**) = (86 x 1) = (`-**86**) = "FLIP the (`-**6**) OVER to a (`-**9**)" = (`-**89**) = `-**BIRTH/DAY for SINGER/SONGWRITER WHITNEY HOUSTON (AUGUST 9th)**"!!!~'

FRAGMENTED `-**BIRTH/DAY # `-NUMBER** = (8 + 9 + 1 + 9 + 6 + 3) = (`-**36**) = RECIPROCAL (INVERSE/MIRROR) = (`-**63**) = `-**BIRTH/YEAR for SINGER/SONGWRITER WHITNEY HOUSTON (`-1963)**"!!!~'

FRAGMENTED `-**DEATH/DAY # `-NUMBER** = (2 + 1 + 1 + 2 + 0 + 1 + 2) = (`-**9**)!!!~'

(36 + 9) = (`-**45**) = RECIPROCAL (INVERSE/MIRROR) = (`-**54**)"!!!~'

(36 + 9) = (`-**45**) = "THREE `-YEARS `-AWAY from `-AGE of `-DEATH for SINGER/SONGWRITER WHITNEY HOUSTON (`-**48**)"!!!~'

(36 + 9) = (`-**45**) = `-**DEATH/DAY** # `-**NUMBER** for SINGER/ SONGWRITER WHITNEY HOUSTON (`-**45**)"!!!~'

`-**DIED** at the `-**AGE** of (`-**27**)!!!~'

SINGER/SONGWRITER KURT COBAIN `-**BIRTHDAY** = (**2**/**20**/19/**67**) = (**2** + **20** + 19 + **67**) = (`-**108**) = RECIPROCAL (INVERSE/MIRROR) = (`-**801**)!!!~'

`-**BIRTH/DAY** = (**2/20**) = (2 + 20) = (`-**22**) = "FLIP the (`-**2**) OVER to a (`-**7**)" = (`-**27**) = `-**DIED** at the `-**AGE** of (`-**27**) for SINGER/ SONGWRITER KURT COBAIN (`-**27**)"!!!~'

`-**BIRTH/YEAR** = (`-**19/67**) = (19 + 67) = (`-**86**) = RECIPROCAL (INVERSE/MIRROR) = (`-**68**) = "The `-**MARK**"!!!~'

`-**BIRTH/YEAR** = (`-**67**) = (6 + 7) = (`-**13**) = "A VERY PIVOTAL # `-NUMBER"!!!~'

`-**BIRTH/YEAR** = (`-**67**) = (6 x 7) = (`-**42**) = "The `-**MARK**"!!!~'

"WAS `-**BORN** in (`-**2**) (FEBRUARY); and, `-**DIED** in (`-**4**) (APRIL)"; and, (**2/4**) = (FEBRUARY 4th) = (`-**16**) DAYS AWAY from `-HIS `-**BIRTH/DAY**!!!~' RECIPROCAL (INVERSE/MIRROR) = (**4/2**) = (APRIL 2nd) = (`-**3**) DAYS AWAY from `-HIS `-**DEATH/ DAY**!!!~' (**16/3**) = RECIPROCAL (INVERSE/MIRROR) =

(**3/16**) = (**ALL-IN-ONE-#-NUMBER**) = (3 (-) 1) (6) = (`-**26**) = "ONE `-YEAR `-AWAY from `-AGE of `-DEATH for SINGER/ SONGWRITER KURT COBAIN (`-**27**)"!!!~'

(1**967**) = (9 (-) 7) (1 + 6) = `-*EQUALS* = (`-**27**) = `-AGE of `-DEATH for SINGER/SONGWRITER KURT COBAIN (`-**27**)"!!!~'

SINGER/SONGWRITER KURT COBAIN `-**DEATH/DAY** = (**4/5**/19/**94**) = (**4** + **5** + 19 + **94**) = (`-**122**) = (22 + 1) = (`-**23**) = -a PROPHETIC # `-NUMBER!!!~'

`-**DEATH/DAY** = (**4/5**) = (`-**45**) = RECIPROCAL (INVERSE/ MIRROR) = (`-**54**) = `-**AGE of** `-**DEATH** (`-**27**) x `-*TIMES* (`-**2**) = (`-**54**)!!!~'

`-**DEATH/DAY** = (**4/5**) = (4 x 5) = (`-**20**) = "SEVEN `-YEARS `-AWAY from `-AGE of `-DEATH for SINGER/SONGWRITER KURT COBAIN (`-**27**)"!!!~'

`-**MARTIAL** `-**ARTIST** & `-**ACTOR** `-**BRUCE** `-**LEE** was `-**BORN** on a (`-**27**th); and, `-**DIED** on (**7/20**) = (20 + 7) = (`-**27**)!!!~'

`-**DEATH/DAY** # `-**NUMBER** in `-**REVERSE** = (94 (-) 19 (-) 5 (-) 4) = (`-**66**) = 2(6's) = (`-**26**) = "ONE `-YEAR `-AWAY from `-AGE of `-DEATH for SINGER/SONGWRITER KURT COBAIN (`-**27**)"!!!~'

(122 (-) 108) = (`-**14**)!!!~'

(122 + 108) = (`-**230**) = (23 + 0) = (`-**23**) = -a PROPHETIC # `-NUMBER!!!~'

(230 (-) 14) = (`-**216**) = (16 x 2) = (`-**32**) = -a PROPHETIC # `-NUMBER!!!~'

(230 + 14) = (`-**244**) = (24 + 4) = (`-**28**) = **"ONE `-YEAR `-AWAY from `-AGE of `-DEATH for SINGER/SONGWRITER KURT COBAIN (`-27)"!!!~'**

SINGER/SONGWRITER KURT COBAIN `-**DIED** (`-**44**) DAYS AWAY from `-**HIS `-BIRTHDAY!!!~'** (`-**44**) = 2(4's) = (`-**24**) = **"THREE `-YEARS `-AWAY from `-AGE of `-DEATH for SINGER/SONGWRITER KURT COBAIN (`-27)"!!!~'**

`-**DEATH/YEAR** = (`-**19/94**) = (19 + 94) = (`-**113**) = (13 x 1) = (`-**13**) = "A VERY PIVOTAL # `-NUMBER"!!!~'

(365 (-) 44) = (`-**321**) = RECIPROCAL (INVERSE/MIRROR) = (`-**123**) = (23 x 1) = (`-**23**) = -a PROPHETIC # `-NUMBER!!!~'

/|\ FRAGMENTED `-**BIRTH/DAY** # `-NUMBER = (2 + 2 + 0 + 1 + 9 + 6 + 7) = (`-**27**) = `-**AGE of `-DEATH for SINGER/SONGWRITER KURT COBAIN (`-27)"!!!~'** /|\

FRAGMENTED `-**BIRTH/DAY** # `-NUMBER = (2 + 2 + 0 + 1 + 9 + 6 + 7) = (`-**27**) = RECIPROCAL (INVERSE/MIRROR) = (`-**72**)!!!~'

FRAGMENTED `-**DEATH/DAY** # `-NUMBER = (4 + 5 + 1 + 9 + 9 + 4) = (`-**32**) = RECIPROCAL (INVERSE/MIRROR) = (`-**23**) = -a PROPHETIC # `-NUMBER!!!~'

(27 + 32) = (`-**59**) = (5 x 9) = (`-**45**) = `-**DEATH/DAY for SINGER/SONGWRITER KURT COBAIN (APRIL 5th)!!!~'**

`-**DIED** at the `-**AGE** of (`-**27**)!!!~'

SINGER/SONGWRITER AMY WINEHOUSE `-**BIRTHDAY** = (**9/14**/19/**83**) = (**9** + **14** + 19 + **83**) = (`-**125**) = (25 + 1) = (`-**26**) =

"ONE `-YEAR `-AWAY from `-AGE of `-DEATH for SINGER/ SONGWRITER AMY WINEHOUSE (`-27)"!!!~'

`-**BIRTH/DAY** = (**9/14**) = (9 + 14) = (`-**23**) = -a PROPHETIC # `-NUMBER!!!~'

`-**BIRTH/DAY** = (**9/14**) = RECIPROCAL (INVERSE/MIRROR) = (`-**419**) = (41 (-) 9) = (`-**32**) = -a PROPHETIC # `-NUMBER!!!~'

`-**BIRTH/YEAR** = (`-**19/83**) = (83 (-) 19) = (`-**64**) = (`-2) x (`-32) = (`-**232**) = **RECIPROCAL-SEQUENCING-NUMEROLOGY-RSN**!!!~'

`-**BIRTH/YEAR** = (`-**83**) = (8 x 3) = (`-**24**) = "THREE `-YEARS `-AWAY from `-AGE of `-DEATH for SINGER/SONGWRITER AMY WINEHOUSE (`-27)"!!!~'

`-**BIRTH/YEAR** = (`-**83**) = (8 x 3) = (`-**24**) = RECIPROCAL (INVERSE/MIRROR) = (`-**42**) = "The `-**MARK**"!!!~'

"WAS `-**BORN** in (`-**9**) (SEPTEMBER); and, `-**DIED** in (`-**7**) (JULY)"; and, (**9/7**) = (SEPTEMBER 7th) = (`-**7**) DAYS AWAY from `-HER `-**BIRTH/DAY**!!!~' RECIPROCAL (INVERSE/ MIRROR) = (**7/9**) = (JULY 9th) = (`-**14**) DAYS AWAY from `-HER `-**DEATH/DAY**!!!~' (**7/14**) = (7 x 14) = (`-**98**) = (9 x 8) = (`-**72**) = RECIPROCAL (INVERSE/MIRROR) = (`-**27**) = `-**AGE of** `-**DEATH for SINGER/SONGWRITER AMY WINEHOUSE** (`-**27**)"!!!~'

(1**98**3) = (3 (-) 1) (9 + 8) = `-*EQUALS* = (`-**217**) = (27 x 1) = (`-**27**) = `-**AGE of** `-**DEATH for SINGER/SONGWRITER AMY WINEHOUSE** (`-**27**)"!!!~'

SINGER/SONGWRITER AMY WINEHOUSE `-**DEATH/DAY** = (**7/23**/20/**11**) = (**7** + **23** + 20 + **11**) = (`-**61**)!!!~'

`-**DAY** of `-**DEATH** = (`-**23**$^{rd}$) = (`-**23**) = "FOUR `-YEARS `-AWAY from `-AGE of `-DEATH for SINGER/SONGWRITER AMY WINEHOUSE (`-**27**)"!!!~'

`-**DAY** of `-**DEATH** = (`-**23**$^{rd}$) = (`-**23**) = -a PROPHETIC # `-NUMBER!!!~'

`-**DEATH/YEAR** = (**20/11**) = (20 + 11) = (`-**31**) = RECIPROCAL (INVERSE/MIRROR) = (`-**13**) = "A VERY PIVOTAL # `-NUMBER"!!!~'

(125 (-) 61) = (`-**64**) = (`-2) x (`-32) = (`-**232**) = **RECIPROCAL-SEQUENCING-NUMEROLOGY-RSN**!!!~'

(125 + 61) = (`-**186**) = (86 x 1) = (`-**86**) = RECIPROCAL (INVERSE/ MIRROR) = (`-**68**) = "The `-**MARK**"!!!~'

(186 (-) 64) = (`-**122**) = (22 + 1) = (`-**23**) = -a PROPHETIC # `-NUMBER!!!~'

(186 + 64) = (`-**250**) = (25 + 0) = (`-**25**) = "TWO `-YEARS `-AWAY from `-AGE of `-DEATH for SINGER/SONGWRITER AMY WINEHOUSE (`-**27**)"!!!~'

SINGER/SONGWRITER AMY WINEHOUSE `-**DIED** (`-**53**) DAYS AWAY from `-HER `-**BIRTHDAY**!!!~' (`-**53**) = `-**AGE** of `-**DEATH** (`-**27**) x (`-**2**) = (`-**54**)!!!~'

(365 (-) 53) = (`-**312**) = (32 x 1) = (`-**32**) = -a PROPHETIC # `-NUMBER!!!~'

/|\ FRAGMENTED `-**BIRTH/DAY** # `-**NUMBER** = (9 + 1 + 4 + 1 + 9 + 8 + 3) = (`-**35**) = RECIPROCAL (INVERSE/MIRROR) = (`-**53**) = "SINGER/SONGWRITER AMY WINEHOUSE `-**DIED** this `-**MANY** `-**DAYS** `-**AWAY** from `-**BIRTH/DAY**"!!!~' /|\

FRAGMENTED `-**DEATH/DAY** # `-**NUMBER** = (7 + 2 + 3 + 2 + 0 + 1 + 1) = (`-**16**) = RECIPROCAL (INVERSE/MIRROR) = (`-**61**) = `-**DEATH/DAY** # `-**NUMBER** for **SINGER/SONGWRITER AMY WINEHOUSE** (`-**61**)!!!~'

(35 + 16) = (`-**51**) = RECIPROCAL (INVERSE/MIRROR) = (`-**15**)!!!~'

`-**DIED** at the `-**AGE** of (`-**55**)!!!~'

AMERICAN ACTOR SMILEY BURNETTE `-**BIRTHDAY** = (**3**/**18**/19/**11**) = (**3** + **18** + 19 + **11**) = (`-**51**) = **"FOUR `-YEARS `-AWAY from `-AGE of `-DEATH for AMERICAN ACTOR SMILEY BURNETTE** (`-**55**)"!!!~'

`-**BIRTH/DAY** = (**3/18**) = (3 x 18) = (`-**54**) = **"ONE `-YEAR `-AWAY from `-AGE of `-DEATH for AMERICAN ACTOR SMILEY BURNETTE** (`-**55**)"!!!~'

"WAS `-**BORN** in (`-**3**) (MARCH); and, `-**DIED** in (`-**2**) (FEBRUARY)"; and, (**3/2**) = (MARCH 2nd) = (`-**16**) DAYS AWAY from `-HIS `-**BIRTH/DAY**!!!~' RECIPROCAL (INVERSE/ MIRROR) = (**2/3**) = (FEBRUARY 3$^{rd}$) = (`-**13**) DAYS AWAY from `-HIS `-**DEATH/DAY**!!!~' (**16/13**) = (**ALL-IN-ONE-#-NUMBER**) = (6 (-) 1) (1 + 3) = (`-**54**) = **"ONE `-YEAR `-AWAY from `-AGE of `-DEATH for AMERICAN ACTOR SMILEY BURNETTE** (`-**55**)"!!!~'

(**1911**) = (1 + 1 + 1) (9) = `-*EQUALS* = (`-**39**) = `-**BIRTH/DAY** = (**3/18**) = (31 + 8) = (`-**39**)!!!~'

(**19**67) = (1 + 9) (+) (6 + 7) = (10) (+) (13) = `-*EQUALS* = (`-**23**) = -a PROPHETIC # `-NUMBER!!!~`

AMERICAN ACTOR SMILEY BURNETTE `-**DEATH/DAY** = (**2**/**16**/19/**67**) = (**2** + **16** + 19 + **67**) = (`-**104**) = (41 + 0) = (`-**41**) = `-**BIRTH/DAY** # `-**NUMBER** for AMERICAN ACTOR RUFE DAVIS (`-**41**)!!!~`

`-**DEATH/DAY** = (**2/16**) = (2 x 16) = (`-**32**) = -a PROPHETIC # `-NUMBER!!!~`

(104 (-) 51) = (`-**53**) = "TWO `-YEARS `-AWAY from `-AGE of `-DEATH for AMERICAN ACTOR SMILEY BURNETTE (`-**55**)"!!!~`

(104 + 51) = (`-**155**) = (55 x 1) = (`-**55**) = `-AGE of `-DEATH for AMERICAN ACTOR SMILEY BURNETTE (`-**55**)"!!!~`

AMERICAN ACTOR SMILEY BURNETTE `-**DIED** (`-**30**) DAYS AWAY from `-HIS `-BIRTHDAY!!!~`

`-**DEATH/YEAR** = (`-**19/67**) = (19 + 67) = (`-**86**) = RECIPROCAL (INVERSE/MIRROR) = (`-**68**) = "The `-**MARK**"!!!~`

(365 (-) 30) = (`-**335**) = RECIPROCAL (INVERSE/MIRROR) = (`-**533**) = (**ALL-IN-ONE-#-NUMBER**) = (5 (-) 3) (3) = (`-**23**) = -a PROPHETIC # `-NUMBER!!!~`

FRAGMENTED `-**BIRTH/DAY** # `-**NUMBER** = (3 + 1 + 8 + 1 + 9 + 1 + 1) = (`-**24**) = RECIPROCAL (INVERSE/MIRROR) = (`-**42**) = "The `-**MARK**"!!!~`

FRAGMENTED `-**DEATH/DAY** # `-**NUMBER** = (2 + 1 + 6 + 1 + 9 + 6 + 7) = (`-**32**) = RECIPROCAL (INVERSE/MIRROR) = (`-**23**) = -a PROPHETIC # `-NUMBER!!!~`

(32 + 23) = (`-**55**) = `-AGE of `-DEATH for AMERICAN ACTOR SMILEY BURNETTE (`-**55**)"!!!~'

(24 + 32) = (`-**56**) = (5 x 6) = (`-**30**) = "AMERICAN ACTOR SMILEY BURNETTE `-**DIED** this `-**MANY** `-**DAYS** `-**AWAY** from `-**HIS** `-**BIRTH/DAY** (`-**30**)"!!!~'

(24 + 32) = (`-**56**) = "ONE `-YEAR `-AWAY from `-AGE of `-DEATH for AMERICAN ACTOR SMILEY BURNETTE (`-**55**)"!!!~'

`-**DIED** at the `-**AGE** of (`-**66**)!!!~'

AMERICAN ACTOR RUFE DAVIS `-**BIRTHDAY** = (**12**/**2**/19/**08**) = (**12** + **2** + 19 + **08**) = (`-**41**) = RECIPROCAL (INVERSE/ MIRROR) = (`-**14**)!!!~'

(`-**41**) + (`-**14**) = (`-**55**) = `-AGE of `-DEATH for AMERICAN ACTOR SMILEY BURNETTE (`-**55**)"!!!~'

`-**BIRTH/DAY** = (**12**/**2**) = (22 + 1) = (`-**23**) = -a PROPHETIC # `-NUMBER!!!~'

"WAS `-**BORN** in (`-**12**) (DECEMBER); and, `-**DIED** in (`-**12**) (DECEMBER)"; and, (**12**/**12**) = (DECEMBER 12th) = (`-**10**) DAYS AWAY from `-HIS `-**BIRTH/DAY**!!!~' RECIPROCAL (INVERSE/ MIRROR) = (**12**/**12**) = (DECEMBER 12th) = (`-**1**) DAY AWAY from `-HIS `-**DEATH/DAY**!!!~' (**10**/**1**) = (11 + 0) = (`-**11**) = `-**DIED** this `-**MANY** `-**DAYS** `-**AWAY** from `-**HIS** `-**BIRTH/DAY** for AMERICAN ACTOR RUFE DAVIS (`-**11**)!!!~'

(19_08) = (9 + 0) (1 + 8) = `-*EQUALS* = (`-**99**) = "FLIP the (`-**9**) OVER to a (`-**6**)" = (`-**66**) = `-**AGE of** `-**DEATH for AMERICAN ACTOR RUFE DAVIS** (`-**66**)"!!!~'

(1_9_74) = (7 (-) 1) (9 (-) 4) = `-*EQUALS* = (`-**65**) = **"ONE `-YEAR `-AWAY from** `-**AGE of** `-**DEATH for AMERICAN ACTOR RUFE DAVIS** (`-**66**)"!!!~'

AMERICAN ACTOR RUFE DAVIS `-**DEATH/DAY** = (1_2/1_3/19/7_4) = (**12** + **13** + 19 + **74**) = (`-**118**)!!!~'

`-**DEATH/DAY** = (**12/13**) = (23 x 1 x 1) = (`-**23**) = -a PROPHETIC # `-NUMBER!!!~'

(118 (-) 41) = (`-**77**)!!!~'

(118 + 41) = (`-**159**) = RECIPROCAL (INVERSE/MIRROR) = (`-**951**) = "FLIP the (`-**9**) OVER to a (`-**6**)" = (`-**651**) = (65 + 1) = (`-**66**) = `-**AGE of** `-**DEATH for AMERICAN ACTOR RUFE DAVIS** (`-**66**)"!!!~'

AMERICAN ACTOR RUFE DAVIS `-**DIED** (`-**11**) DAYS AWAY from `-**HIS** `-**BIRTHDAY!!!~'**

`-**DEATH/YEAR** = (`-**19/74**) = (74 (-) 19) = (`-**55**) = `-**AGE of** `-**DEATH for AMERICAN ACTOR SMILEY BURNETTE** (`-**55**)"!!!~'

`-**DEATH/DAY** # `-**NUMBER** in `-**REVERSE** = (74 (-) 19 (-) 13 (-) 12) = (`-**30**) = AMERICAN ACTOR SMILEY BURNETTE `-**DIED** this `-**MANY** `-**DAYS** `-**AWAY** from `-**HIS** `-**BIRTH/DAY** (`-**30**)!!!~' (30 + 11) = (`-**41**) = `-**BIRTH/DAY** # `-**NUMBER** of AMERICAN ACTOR RUFE DAVIS (`-**41**)!!!~'

(365 (-) 11) = (`-**354**) = (54 x 3) = (`-**162**) = "FLIP the (`-**2**) OVER to a (`-**7**)" = (`-**167**) = (67 (-) 1) = (`-**66**) = `-**AGE of `-DEATH for AMERICAN ACTOR RUFE DAVIS (`-**66**)"!!!~'

FRAGMENTED `-**BIRTH/DAY** # `-NUMBER = (1 + 2 + 2 + 1 + 9 + 0 + 8) = (`-**23**) = RECIPROCAL (INVERSE/MIRROR) = (`-**32**) = -a PROPHETIC # `-NUMBER!!!~'

FRAGMENTED `-**DEATH/DAY** # `-NUMBER = (1 + **2** + 1 + **3** + 1 + 9 + 7 + 4) = (`-**28**) = RECIPROCAL (INVERSE/MIRROR) = (`-**82**)!!!~'

(23 + 28) = (`-**51**) = `-**BIRTH/DAY** # `-**NUMBER** for AMERICAN ACTOR SMILEY BURNETTE (`-**51**)"!!!~'

`-**DIED** at the `-**AGE** of (`-**71**)!!!~'

/|\ AMERICAN ACTRESS PAT WOODELL `-**BIRTHDAY** = (**7**/**12**/19/**44**) = (**7** + **12** + 19 + **44**) = (`-**82**) = RECIPROCAL (INVERSE/MIRROR) = (`-**28**) = `-**EQUALS** = FRAGMENTED `-**BIRTH/DAY** # `-NUMBER (`-**28**); and, FRAGMENTED `-**DEATH/DAY** # `-NUMBER (`-**28**)!!!~'

`-**BIRTH/DAY** = (**7/12**) = (72 (-) 1) = (`-**71**) = `-**AGE of `-DEATH for AMERICAN ACTRESS PAT WOODELL (`-**71**)"!!!~' /|\

"WAS `-**BORN** in (`-**7**) (JULY); and, `-**DIED** in (`-**9**) (SEPTEMBER)"; and, (**7/9**) = (JULY 9th) = (`-**3**) DAYS AWAY from `-HER `-**BIRTH/DAY**!!!~' RECIPROCAL (INVERSE/MIRROR) = (**9/7**) = (SEPTEMBER 7th) = (`-**22**) DAYS AWAY from `-HER `-**DEATH/DAY**!!!~' (**3/22**) = (32 x 2) = (`-**64**) = (`-2) x (`-32) = (`-**232**) = **RECIPROCAL-SEQUENCING-NUMEROLOGY-RSN**!!!~'

(1944) = "FLIP the (`-9) OVER to a (`-6)" = (1644) = (6 + 1) (4 (-) 4) = `-EQUALS = (`-70) = "ONE `-YEAR `-AWAY from `-AGE of `-DEATH for AMERICAN ACTRESS PAT WOODELL (`-71)"!!!~'

(2015) = (5 + 2) (1 + 0) = `-EQUALS = (`-71) = `-AGE of `-DEATH for AMERICAN ACTRESS PAT WOODELL (`-71)"!!!~'

AMERICAN ACTRESS PAT WOODELL `-DEATH/DAY = (9/29/20/15) = (9 + 29 + 20 + 15) = (`-73) = "TWO `-YEARS `-AWAY from `-AGE of `-DEATH for AMERICAN ACTRESS PAT WOODELL (`-71)"!!!~'

`-DEATH/DAY = (9/29) = (`-929) = RECIPROCAL-SEQUENCING-NUMEROLOGY-RSN!!!~'

`-DEATH/DAY = (9/29) = (`-929) = "FLIP the (`-2) OVER to a (`-7)" = (`-979) = (79 (-) 9) = (`-70) = "ONE `-YEAR `-AWAY from `-AGE of `-DEATH for AMERICAN ACTRESS PAT WOODELL (`-71)"!!!~'

(82 (-) 73) = (`-9)!!!~'

(82 + 73) = (`-155) = (55 x 1) = (`-55) = `-AGE of `-DEATH for AMERICAN ACTOR SMILEY BURNETTE (`-55)"!!!~'

(155 + 9) = (`-164) = (ALL-IN-ONE-#-NUMBER) = (1 + 6) (4) = (`-74) = "THREE `-YEARS `-AWAY from `-AGE of `-DEATH for AMERICAN ACTRESS PAT WOODELL (`-71)"!!!~'

AMERICAN ACTRESS PAT WOODELL `-DIED (`-79) DAYS AWAY from `-HER `-BIRTHDAY!!!~' (`-79) = `-BORN in (`-7); and, `-DIED in (`-9)!!!~'

`-**BIRTH/YEAR** = (`-**1944**) = (19 + 44) = (`-**63**) = (7 x 9) = (`-**79**) = "SEE `-**ABOVE**"!!!~'

(365 (-) 79) = (`-**286**) = (28 x 6) = (`-**168**) = (68 x 1) = (`-**68**) = "The `-**MARK**"!!!~'

/|\ FRAGMENTED `-**BIRTH/DAY** # `-**NUMBER** = (7 + 1 + 2 + 1 + 9 + 4 + 4) = (`-**28**) = RECIPROCAL (INVERSE/MIRROR) = (`-**82**) = `-**BIRTH/DAY** # `-**NUMBER** for AMERICAN ACTRESS PAT WOODELL (`-**82**)!!!~'

FRAGMENTED `-**BIRTH/DAY** # `-**NUMBER** = (`-**28**) = `-**EQUALS** = FRAGMENTED `-**DEATH/DAY** # `-**NUMBER** = (`-**28**)!!!~'

FRAGMENTED `-**DEATH/DAY** # `-**NUMBER** = (9 + 2 + 9 + 2 + 0 + 1 + 5) = (`-**28**) = RECIPROCAL (INVERSE/MIRROR) = (`-**82**) = `-**BIRTH/DAY** # `-**NUMBER** for AMERICAN ACTRESS PAT WOODELL (`-**82**)!!!~' /|\

(28 + 28) = (`-**56**) = "ONE `-**YEAR** `-**AWAY** from `-**AGE** of `-**DEATH** for AMERICAN ACTOR SMILEY BURNETTE (`-**55**)"!!!~'

`-**DIED** at the `-**AGE** of (`-**96**)!!!~'

AMERICAN ACTOR FRANK CADY `-**BIRTHDAY** = (**9/8**/19/**15**) = (**9** + **8** + 19 + **15**) = (`-**51**) = RECIPROCAL (INVERSE/MIRROR) = (`-**15**)!!!~'

AMERICAN ACTOR FRANK CADY `-**BIRTH/DAY** # `-**NUMBER** = (`-**51**) = `-**EQUALS** the `-**SAME** `-**EXACT**

165

`-BIRTH/DAY # `-NUMBER as for AMERICAN ACTOR SMILEY BURNETTE (`-51)"!!!~'

(`-51) + (`-15) = (`-66) = `-AGE of `-DEATH for AMERICAN ACTOR RUFE DAVIS (`-66)"!!!~'

`-BIRTH/DAY = (9/8) = "TWO `-YEARS `-AWAY from `-AGE of `-DEATH for AMERICAN ACTOR FRANK CADY (`-96)"!!!~'

`-BIRTH/DAY for AMERICAN ACTOR FRANK CADY = (9/8) = "FLIP the (`-9) OVER to a (`-6)" = (6/8) = `-EQUALS = the `-EXACT `-DEATH/DAY for AMERICAN ACTOR FRANK CADY (JUNE 8th)!!!~'

"WAS `-BORN in (`-9) (SEPTEMBER); and, `-DIED in (`-6) (JUNE)"; and, (9/6) = `-AGE of `-DEATH (`-96) = (SEPTEMBER 6th) = (`-2) DAYS AWAY from `-HIS `-BIRTH/DAY!!!~' RECIPROCAL (INVERSE/MIRROR) = (6/9) = (JUNE 9th) = (`-1) DAY AWAY from `-HIS `-DEATH/DAY!!!~' (2/1) = RECIPROCAL (INVERSE/MIRROR) = (1/2) = (`-12) = `-DEATH/YEAR for AMERICAN ACTOR FRANK CADY (`-20/12)!!!~'

(1915) = (9 x 1) (1 + 5) = `-EQUALS = (`-96) = `-AGE of `-DEATH for AMERICAN ACTOR FRANK CADY (`-96)"!!!~'

(2012) = (20) (12) = (20 + 12) = `-EQUALS = (`-32) = -a PROPHETIC # `-NUMBER!!!~'

AMERICAN ACTOR FRANK CADY `-DEATH/DAY = (6/8/20/12) = (6 + 8 + 20 + 12) = (`-46) = (`-23) x (`-2) = (`-232) = RECIPROCAL-SEQUENCING-NUMEROLOGY-RSN!!!~'

`-DEATH/DAY = (6/8) = (`-68) = "The `-MARK"!!!~'

`-**DEATH/YEAR** = (`-**20/12**) = (20 + 12) = (`-**32**) = -a PROPHETIC # `-NUMBER!!!~'

(51 (-) 46) = (`-**5**)!!!~'

(51 + 46) = (`-**97**) = "ONE `-YEAR `-AWAY from `-AGE of `-DEATH for AMERICAN ACTOR FRANK CADY (`-**96**)"!!!~'

(97 (-) 5) = (`-**92**) = AMERICAN ACTOR FRANK CADY `-**DIED** (`-**92**) DAYS AWAY from `-HIS `-**BIRTH/DAY!!!~'**

AMERICAN ACTOR FRANK CADY `-**DIED** (`-**92**) DAYS AWAY from `-HIS `-**BIRTHDAY!!!~'** (`-**92**) = "FLIP the (`-**2**) OVER to a (`-**7**)" = (`-**97**) = "ONE `-YEAR `-AWAY from `-AGE of `-DEATH for AMERICAN ACTOR FRANK CADY (`-**96**)"!!!~'

AMERICAN ACTOR FRANK CADY `-**DIED** (`-**92**) DAYS AWAY from `-HIS `-**BIRTHDAY!!!~'** (`-**92**) = "FLIP the (`-**2**) OVER to a (`-**7**)" = (`-**97**) = `-**DIED in the** `-**YEAR of** (`-**97**) = RECIPROCAL (INVERSE/MIRROR) = (`-**79**) = AMERICAN ACTRESS PAT WOODELL `-**DIED** (`-**79**) DAYS AWAY from `-HER `-**BIRTHDAY!!!~'** (`-**79**) = `-**BORN** in (`-**7**); and, `-**DIED** in (`-**9**) for AMERICAN ACTRESS PAT WOODELL!!!~'

AMERICAN ACTOR FRANK CADY /|\ `-**AGE of** `-**DEATH** = (`-**96**) = "WAS `-**BORN in** (`-**9**); and, `-**DIED in** (`-**6**)"!!!~'

(365 (-) 92) = (`-**273**) = (**ALL-IN-ONE-#-NUMBER**) = (2 + 7) (3) = (`-**93**) = "THREE `-YEARS `-AWAY from `-AGE of `-DEATH for AMERICAN ACTOR FRANK CADY (`-**96**)"!!!~'

FRAGMENTED `-**BIRTH/DAY** # `-NUMBER = (9 + 8 + 1 + 9 + 1 + 5) = (`-**33**)!!!~'

FRAGMENTED `-**DEATH/DAY** # `-**NUMBER** = (6 + 8 + 2 + 0 + 1 + 2) = (`-**19**) = RECIPROCAL (INVERSE/MIRROR) = (`-**91**) = **"FIVE `-YEARS `-AWAY from `-AGE of `-DEATH for AMERICAN ACTOR FRANK CADY (`-96)"**!!!~'

(33 + 19) = (`-**52**) = **"ONE `-AWAY from `-BIRTH/DAY # `-NUMBER for AMERICAN ACTOR FRANK CADY (`-51)"**!!!~'

`-**DIED** at the `-**AGE** of (`-**81**)!!!~'

AMERICAN ACTOR TOM LESTER `-**BIRTHDAY** = (**9/23**/19/**38**) = (**9** + **23** + 19 + **38**) = (`-**89**) = RECIPROCAL (INVERSE/MIRROR) = (`-**98**)!!!~'

(`-**89**) = **"EIGHT `-YEARS `-AWAY from `-AGE of `-DEATH for AMERICAN ACTOR TOM LESTER (`-81)"**!!!~'

`-**DAY** of `-**BIRTH** = (`-**23**) = -a PROPHETIC # `-NUMBER!!!~'

`-**BIRTH/DAY** = (**9/23**) = (9 + 23) = (`-**32**) = -a PROPHETIC # `-NUMBER!!!~'

`-**BIRTH/YEAR** = (19 + 19) = (`-**38**)!!!~'

(1 x 9) (1 x 9) = (`-**99**) = (9 x 9) = (`-**81**) = `-**AGE of `-DEATH for AMERICAN ACTOR TOM LESTER (`-81)"**!!!~'

"WAS `-BORN** in (`-9**) (SEPTEMBER); and, `-**DIED** in (`-**4**) (APRIL)"; and, (**9/4**) = (SEPTEMBER 4th) = (`-**19**) DAYS AWAY from `-HIS `-**BIRTH/DAY**!!!~' RECIPROCAL (INVERSE/MIRROR) = (**4/9**) = (APRIL 9[th]) = (`-**11**) DAY AWAY from `-HIS `-**DEATH/DAY**!!!~' (**19/11**) = (**ALL-IN-ONE-#-NUMBER**) = (1

(-) 9) (1 x 1) = (`-81) = `-AGE of `-DEATH for AMERICAN ACTOR TOM LESTER (`-81)!!!~'

(1938) = (98) (-) (13) = `-EQUALS = (`-85) = "FOUR `-YEARS `-AWAY from `-AGE of `-DEATH for AMERICAN ACTOR TOM LESTER (`-81)"!!!~'

AMERICAN ACTOR TOM LESTER `-DEATH/DAY = (4/20/20/20) = (4 + 20 + 20 + 20) = (`-64) = (`-2) x (`-32) = (`-232) = RECIPROCAL-SEQUENCING-NUMEROLOGY-RSN!!!~'

`-DEATH/DAY = (4/20) = (4 x 20) = (`-80) = "ONE `-YEAR `-AWAY from `-AGE of `-DEATH for AMERICAN ACTOR TOM LESTER (`-81)"!!!~'

`-DEATH/DAY = (4/20) = (42 + 0) = (`-42) = "The `-MARK"!!!~'

(89 (-) 64) = (`-25)!!!~'

(89 + 64) = (`-153) = (53 x 1) = (`-53) = RECIPROCAL (INVERSE/ MIRROR) = (`-35) = FRAGMENTED `-BIRTH/DAY # `-NUMBER for AMERICAN ACTOR TOM LESTER (`-35)!!!~'

(153 (-) 25) = (`-128) = RECIPROCAL (INVERSE/MIRROR) = (`-821) = (82 (-) 1) = (`-81) = `-AGE of `-DEATH for AMERICAN ACTOR TOM LESTER (`-81)"!!!~'

AMERICAN ACTOR TOM LESTER `-DIED (`-156) DAYS AWAY from `-HIS `-BIRTHDAY!!!~' (`-156) = (56 + 1) = (`-57) = `-BIRTH/YEAR = (19 + 38) = (`-57)!!!~'

(365 (-) 156) = (`-209) = (29 + 0) = (`-29) = (2 x 9) = (`-18) = RECIPROCAL (INVERSE/MIRROR) = (`-81) = `-AGE of `-DEATH for AMERICAN ACTOR TOM LESTER (`-81)"!!!~'

FRAGMENTED `-**BIRTH/DAY** # `-**NUMBER** = (9 + 2 + 3 + 1 + 9 + 3 + 8) = (`-**35**) = RECIPROCAL (INVERSE/MIRROR) = (`-**53**)!!!~'

FRAGMENTED `-**DEATH/DAY** # `-**NUMBER** = (4 + 2 + 0 + 2 + 0 + 2 + 0) = (`-**10**) = RECIPROCAL (INVERSE/MIRROR) = (`-**01**)!!!~'

(35 + 10) = (`-**45**) = RECIPROCAL (INVERSE/MIRROR) = (`-**54**)!!!~'

(45 + 54) = (`-**99**) = (9 x 9) = (`-**81**) = `-**AGE of** `-**DEATH for AMERICAN ACTOR TOM LESTER** (`-**81**)"!!!~'

`-**DIED** at the `-**AGE** of (`-**99**) = RECIPROCAL (INVERSE/ MIRROR) = (`-**66**)!!!~'

AMERICAN ACTOR EDDIE ALBERT `-**BIRTHDAY** = (**4/22**/19/**06**) = (**4** + **22** + 19 + **06**) = (`-**51**) = RECIPROCAL (INVERSE/MIRROR) = (`-**15**)!!!~'

AMERICAN ACTOR EDDIE ALBERT **BIRTH/DAY** # `-**NUMBER** = (`-**51**) = AMERICAN ACTOR FRANK CADY `-**BIRTH/DAY** # `-**NUMBER** = (`-**51**) = `-*EQUALS* the `-**EXACT** `-**SAME** `-**BIRTH/DAY** # `-**NUMBER** as for AMERICAN ACTOR SMILEY BURNETTE = (`-**51**)"!!!~'

(`-**51**) + (`-**15**) = (`-**66**) = `-**AGE of** `-**DEATH for AMERICAN ACTOR RUFE DAVIS** (`-**66**)"!!!~'

`-**BIRTH/YEAR** = (`-1**906**) = (96 x 1 + 0) = (`-**96**) = `-**AGE of** `-**DEATH for AMERICAN ACTOR FRANK CADY** (`-**96**)"!!!~'

`-**BIRTH/YEAR** = (`-1**906**) = (96 x 1 + 0) = (`-**96**) = **"THREE `-YEARS `-AWAY from `-AGE of `-DEATH for AMERICAN ACTOR EDDIE ALBERT (`-99)"!!!~'**

"WAS `-**BORN** in (`-**4**) (APRIL); and, `-**DIED** in (`-**5**) (MAY)"; and, (**4/5**) = (APRIL 5th) = (`-**17**) DAYS AWAY from `-HIS `-**BIRTH/ DAY!!!~'** RECIPROCAL (INVERSE/MIRROR) = (**5/4**) = (MAY 4th) = (`-**22**) DAY AWAY from `-HIS `-**DEATH/DAY!!!~'** (**17/22**) = (`-**39**) = 3(9's) = (`-**999**) = RECIPROCAL (INVERSE/MIRROR) = (`-**666**)!!!~'

(1**906**) = "FLIP the (`-**6**) OVER to a (`-**9**)" = (**19**09) = (1 x 9) (0 + 9) = `-*EQUALS* = (`-**99**) = `-**AGE of `-DEATH for AMERICAN ACTOR EDDIE ALBERT (`-99)"!!!~'**

AMERICAN ACTOR EDDIE ALBERT `-**DEATH/DAY** = (**5/26**/20/**05**) = (**5** + **26** + 20 + **05**) = (`-**56**) = AMERICAN ACTOR TOM LESTER `-**DIED** (`-**156**) DAYS AWAY from `-**HIS `-BIRTHDAY!!!~'**

`-**DEATH/DAY** = (**5/26**) = "FLIP the (`-**6**) OVER to a (`-**9**)" = (**5/29**) = RECIPROCAL (INVERSE/MIRROR) = (**92/5**) = (92 + 5) = (`-**97**) = **"TWO `-YEARS `-AWAY from `-AGE of `-DEATH for AMERICAN ACTOR EDDIE ALBERT (`-99)"!!!~'**

`-**DEATH/DAY** = (**5/26**) = (5 + 26) = (`-**31**) = RECIPROCAL (INVERSE/MIRROR) = (`-**13**) = "A VERY PIVOTAL # `-NUMBER"!!!~'

(56 (-) 51) = (`-**5**)!!!~'

(56 + 51) = (`-**107**) = **"EIGHT `-YEARS `-AWAY from `-AGE of `-DEATH for AMERICAN ACTOR EDDIE ALBERT (`-99)"!!!~'**

(107 (-) 5) = (`-**102**) = "THREE `-YEARS `-AWAY from `-AGE of `-DEATH for AMERICAN ACTOR EDDIE ALBERT (`-**99**)"!!!~'

(107 + 5) = (`-**112**) = (12 + 1) = (`-**13**) = "A VERY PIVOTAL # `-NUMBER"!!!~'

AMERICAN ACTOR EDDIE ALBERT `-**DIED** (`-**34**) DAYS AWAY from `-**HIS** `-**BIRTHDAY**!!!~'

(365 (-) 34) = (`-**331**) = (31 x 3) = (`-**93**) = "SIX `-YEARS `-AWAY from `-AGE of `-DEATH for AMERICAN ACTOR EDDIE ALBERT (`-**99**)"!!!~'

(365 (-) 34) = (`-**331**) = (33 x 1) = (`-**33**) x `-*TIMES* (`-**3**) = (`-**99**) = `-AGE of `-DEATH for AMERICAN ACTOR EDDIE ALBERT (`-**99**)"!!!~'

FRAGMENTED `-**BIRTH/DAY** # `-NUMBER = (4 + 2 + 2 + 1 + 9 + 0 + 6) = (`-**24**) = RECIPROCAL (INVERSE/MIRROR) = (`-**42**) = "The `-**MARK**"!!!~'

FRAGMENTED `-**DEATH/DAY** # `-NUMBER = (5 + 2 + 6 + 2 + 0 + 0 + 5) = (`-**20**) = RECIPROCAL (INVERSE/MIRROR) = (`-**02**)!!!~'

(24 + 20) = (`-**44**) = `-PLUS (**+**) `-**DEATH/DAY** # `-NUMBER (`-**56**) = (`-**100**) = "The `-**SWIVEL** `-**POINT**" & ='s "ONE `-YEAR `-AWAY from `-AGE of `-DEATH for AMERICAN ACTOR EDDIE ALBERT (`-**99**)"!!!~'

`-**DIED** at the `-**AGE** of (`-**70**)!!!~'

AMERICAN ACTRESS SUZANNE PLESHETTE `-**BIRTHDAY** = (**1/31**/19/**37**) = (**1** + **31** + 19 + **37**) = (`-**88**)!!!~'

`-**BIRTH/DAY** = (**1/31**) = (31 + 1) = (`-**32**) = -a PROPHETIC # `-NUMBER!!!~'

`-**BIRTH/DAY** = (**1/31**) = (31 x 1) = (`-**31**) = RECIPROCAL (INVERSE/MIRROR) = (`-**13**) = "A VERY PIVOTAL # `-NUMBER"!!!~'

`-**BIRTH/YEAR** = (`-**37**) = RECIPROCAL (INVERSE/MIRROR) = (`-**73**) = "**THREE `-YEARS `-AWAY from `-AGE of `-DEATH for AMERICAN ACTRESS SUZANNE PLESHETTE (`-70)**"!!!~'

"WAS `-**BORN** in (`-**1**) (JANUARY); and, `-**DIED** in (`-**1**) (JANUARY)"; and, (**1/1**) = (JANUARY 1ˢᵗ) = (`-**30**) DAYS AWAY from `-HER `-**BIRTH/DAY!!!~'** RECIPROCAL (INVERSE/ MIRROR) = (**1/1**) = (JANUARY 1ˢᵗ) = (`-**18**) DAY AWAY from `-HER `-**DEATH/DAY!!!~'** (**30/18**) = RECIPROCAL (INVERSE/ MIRROR) = (**18/30**) = (**ALL-IN-ONE-#-NUMBER**) = (1 (-) 8) (3 + 0) = (`-**73**) = "**THREE `-YEARS `-AWAY from `-AGE of `-DEATH for AMERICAN ACTRESS SUZANNE PLESHETTE (`-70)**"!!!~'

(1**93**7) = (93) (-) (17) = `-*EQUALS* = (`-**76**) = "**SIX `-YEARS `-AWAY from `-AGE of `-DEATH for AMERICAN ACTRESS SUZANNE PLESHETTE (`-70)**"!!!~'

AMERICAN ACTRESS SUZANNE PLESHETTE `-**DEATH/ DAY** = (**1/19**/20/**08**) = (**1** + **19** + 20 + **08**) = (`-**48**) = (4 x 8) = (`-**32**) = -a PROPHETIC # `-NUMBER!!!~'

`-**DEATH/DAY** = (**1/19**) = (19 + 1) = (`-**20**) = "FLIP the (`-**2**) OVER to a (`-**7**)" = (`-**70**) = `-**AGE of `-DEATH for AMERICAN ACTRESS SUZANNE PLESHETTE (`-70)**"!!!~'

(88 (-) 48) = (`-**40**)!!!~'

(88 + 48) = (`-**136**) = (**ALL-IN-ONE-#-NUMBER**) = (1 + 6) (3) = (`-**73**) = "THREE `-YEARS `-AWAY from `-AGE of `-DEATH for AMERICAN ACTRESS SUZANNE PLESHETTE (`-**70**)"!!!~'

(136 + 40) = (`-**176**) = (76 x 1) = (`-**76**) = "SIX `-YEARS `-AWAY from `-AGE of `-DEATH for AMERICAN ACTRESS SUZANNE PLESHETTE (`-**70**)"!!!~'

AMERICAN ACTRESS SUZANNE PLESHETTE `-**DIED** (`-**12**) DAYS AWAY from `-**HER** `-**BIRTHDAY**!!!~' (`-**12**) = RECIPROCAL (INVERSE/MIRROR) = (`-**21**) = "FLIP the (`-**2**) OVER to a (`-**7**)" = (`-**71**) = "ONE `-YEAR `-AWAY from `-AGE of `-DEATH for AMERICAN ACTRESS SUZANNE PLESHETTE (`-**70**)"!!!~' `-**SHE** `-DIED in the `-YEAR of (`-**71**)!!!~'

(365 (-) 12) = (`-**353**) = **RECIPROCAL-SEQUENCING-NUMEROLOGY-RSN**!!!~'

(`-**35**) x `-*TIMES* (`-**2**) = (`-**70**) = `-AGE of `-DEATH for AMERICAN ACTRESS SUZANNE PLESHETTE (`-**70**)"!!!~'

FRAGMENTED `-**BIRTH/DAY** # `-NUMBER = (1 + 3 + 1 + 1 + 9 + 3 + 7) = (`-**25**) = RECIPROCAL (INVERSE/MIRROR) = (`-**52**)!!!~'

`-**BIRTH/DAY** = (**1**/**31**)

`-**DEATH/DAY** = (**1**/**19**)

(1 + 31 + 1 + 19) = (`-**52**)!!!~'

FRAGMENTED `-**DEATH/DAY** # `-NUMBER = (1 + 1 + 9 + 2 + 0 + 0 + 8) = (`-**21**) = RECIPROCAL (INVERSE/MIRROR) = (`-**12**) = "AMERICAN ACTRESS SUZANNE PLESHETTE

`-DIED this `-MANY `-DAYS `-AWAY from `-HER `-BIRTH/ DAY (`-12)"!!!~'

(25 + 21) = (`-46) = (`-23) x (`-2) = (`-232) = **RECIPROCAL-SEQUENCING-NUMEROLOGY-RSN!!!~'**

`-DIED at the `-AGE of (`-74)!!!~'

AMERICAN ACTOR ED LAUTER `-**BIRTHDAY** = (**10/30**/19/**38**) = (**10** + **30** + 19 + **38**) = (`-**97**) = RECIPROCAL (INVERSE/MIRROR) = (`-**79**) = **"FIVE `-YEARS `-AWAY from `-AGE of `-DEATH for AMERICAN ACTOR ED LAUTER (`-74)"!!!~'**

`-BIRTH/DAY** = (**10/30**) = (13 + 0 + 0) = (`-13**) = "A VERY PIVOTAL # `-NUMBER"!!!~'

"WAS `-**BORN** in (`-**10**) (OCTOBER); and, `-**DIED** in (`-**10**) (OCTOBER)"; and, (**10/10**) = (OCTOBER 10th) = (`-**20**) DAYS AWAY from `-HIS `-**BIRTH/DAY!!!~'** RECIPROCAL (INVERSE/ MIRROR) = (**10/10**) = (OCTOBER 10[th]) = (`-**6**) DAY AWAY from `-HIS `-**DEATH/DAY!!!~'** (**20/6**) = "FLIP the (`-**2**) OVER to a (`-**7**)" = (70/6) = (70 + 6) = (`-**76**) = **"TWO `-YEARS `-AWAY from `-AGE of `-DEATH for AMERICAN ACTOR ED LAUTER (`-74)"!!!~'**

(1**93**8) = (93) (-) (18) = `-*EQUALS* = (`-**75**) = **"ONE `-YEAR `-AWAY from `-AGE of `-DEATH for AMERICAN ACTOR ED LAUTER (`-74)"!!!~'**

AMERICAN ACTOR ED LAUTER `-**DEATH/DAY** = (**10/16**/20/**13**) = (**10** + **16** + 20 + **13**) = (`-**59**)!!!~'

`-**DEATH/DAY** = (**10/16**) = (10 + 16) = (`-**26**) = "FLIP the (`-**2**) OVER to a (`-**7**)" = (`-**76**) = "**TWO** `-**YEARS** `-**AWAY** from `-**AGE** of `-**DEATH** for AMERICAN ACTOR ED LAUTER (`-**74**)"!!!~'

(97 (-) 59) = (`-**38**) = `-**BORN** in (`-**38**)!!!~'

(97 + 59) = (`-**156**) = (**ALL-IN-ONE-#-NUMBER**) = (1 + 6) (5) = (`-**75**) = "**ONE** `-**YEAR** `-**AWAY** from `-**AGE** of `-**DEATH** for AMERICAN ACTOR ED LAUTER (`-**74**)"!!!~'

(156 + 38) = (`-**194**) = (19 x 4) = (`-**76**) = "**TWO** `-**YEARS** `-**AWAY** from `-**AGE** of `-**DEATH** for AMERICAN ACTOR ED LAUTER (`-**74**)"!!!~'

AMERICAN ACTOR ED LAUTER `-**DIED** (`-**14**) DAYS AWAY from `-**HIS** `-**BIRTHDAY**!!!~'

(365 (-) 14) = (`-**351**) = (35 x 1) = (`-**35**) x `-*TIMES* (`-**2**) = (`-**70**) = "**FOUR** `-**YEARS** `-**AWAY** from `-**AGE** of `-**DEATH** for AMERICAN ACTOR ED LAUTER (`-**74**)"!!!~'

FRAGMENTED `-**BIRTH/DAY** # `-**NUMBER** = (1 + 0 + 3 + 0 + 1 + 9 + 3 + 8) = (`-**25**) = RECIPROCAL (INVERSE/MIRROR) = (`-**52**)!!!~'

(`-**25**) + (`-**52**) = (`-**77**) = "**THREE** `-**YEARS** `-**AWAY** from `-**AGE** of `-**DEATH** for AMERICAN ACTOR ED LAUTER (`-**74**)"!!!~'

FRAGMENTED `-**DEATH/DAY** # `-**NUMBER** = (1 + 0 + 1 + 6 + 2 + 0 + 1 + 3) = (`-**14**) = "**AMERICAN ACTOR ED LAUTER** `-**DIED** this `-**MANY** `-**DAYS** `-**AWAY** from `-**HIS** `-**BIRTH/ DAY** (`-**14**)"!!!~'

FRAGMENTED `-**DEATH/DAY** # `-**NUMBER** = (1 + 0 + 1 + 6 + 2 + 0 + 1 + 3) = (`-**14**) = RECIPROCAL (INVERSE/MIRROR) = (`-**41**)!!!~'

(`-**14**) + (`-**41**) = (`-**55**) = (`-**23**) + (`-**32**)!!!~'

(25 + 14) = (`-**39**) = RECIPROCAL (INVERSE/MIRROR) = (`-**93**)!!!~'

(93 + 39) = (`-**132**) = (32 x 1) = (`-**32**) = -a PROPHETIC # `-NUMBER!!!~'

`-**DIED** at the `-**AGE** of (`-**63**)!!!~'

BRITISH ACTRESS AUDREY HEPBURN `-**BIRTHDAY** = (**5/4**/19/**29**) = (**5** + **4** + 19 + **29**) = (`-**57**) = RECIPROCAL (INVERSE/MIRROR) = (`-**75**)!!!~'

`-**BIRTH/DAY** = (**5/4**) = (5 x 4) = (`-**20**) = `-**DAY** of `-**DEATH** (`-**20**th)!!!~'

`-**BIRTH/YEAR** = (`-**1929**) = (929 x 1) = (`-**929**) = **RECIPROCAL-SEQUENCING-NUMEROLOGY-RSN**!!!~'

(`-**92**) = RECIPROCAL (INVERSE/MIRROR) = (`-**29**)!!!~'

(92 (-) 29) = (`-**63**) = `-**AGE of `-DEATH for BRITISH ACTRESS AUDREY HEPBURN** (`-**63**)!!!~'

"WAS `-**BORN** in (`-**5**) (MAY); and, `-**DIED** in (`-**1**) (JANUARY)"; and, (**5/1**) = (MAY 1st) = (`-**3**) DAYS AWAY from `-HER `-**BIRTH/ DAY**!!!~' RECIPROCAL (INVERSE/MIRROR) = (**1/5**) = (JANUARY 5th) = (`-**15**) DAY AWAY from `-HER `-**DEATH/**

DAY!!!~' (3/15) = (31 x 5) = (`-**155**) = (**ALL-IN-ONE-#-NUMBER**) = (1 + 5) (5) = (`-**65**) = "**TWO `-YEARS `-AWAY from `-AGE of `-DEATH for BRITISH ACTRESS AUDREY HEPBURN (`-63)!!!~'**

(1929) = "FLIP the (`-9) OVER to a (`-6)" = (1626) = (6) (6 (-) 2 (-) 1) = `-*EQUALS* = (`-**63**) = `-**AGE of `-DEATH for BRITISH ACTRESS AUDREY HEPBURN (`-63)!!!~'**

BRITISH ACTRESS AUDREY HEPBURN `-**DEATH/DAY** = (1/20/19/93) = (**1** + **20** + 19 + **93**) = (`-**133**) = (33 (-) 1) = (`-**32**) = -a PROPHETIC # `-NUMBER!!!~'

/|\ `-**DEATH/YEAR** = (`-**93**) = "FLIP the (`-**9**) OVER to a (`-**6**)" = (`-**63**) = `-**AGE of `-DEATH for BRITISH ACTRESS AUDREY HEPBURN (`-63)!!!~' /|**

(133 (-) 57) = (`-**76**) = (7 x 6) = (`-**42**) = "**The `-MARK**"!!!~'

(133 + 57) = (`-**190**) = "FLIP the (`-9) OVER to a (`-6)" = (`-**160**) = (16 + 0) = (`-**16**) = RECIPROCAL (INVERSE/MIRROR) = (`-**61**) = "**TWO `-YEARS `-AWAY from `-AGE of `-DEATH for BRITISH ACTRESS AUDREY HEPBURN (`-63)!!!~'**

(190 + 76) = (`-**266**) = (66 (-) 2) = (`-**64**) = "**ONE `-YEAR `-AWAY from `-AGE of `-DEATH for BRITISH ACTRESS AUDREY HEPBURN (`-63)!!!~'**

BRITISH ACTRESS AUDREY HEPBURN `-**DIED** (`-**104**) DAYS AWAY from `-**HER `-BIRTHDAY!!!~'**

(365 (-) 104) = (`-**261**) = (61 + 2) = (`-**63**) = `-**AGE of `-DEATH for BRITISH ACTRESS AUDREY HEPBURN (`-63)!!!~'**

FRAGMENTED `-**BIRTH/DAY** # `-**NUMBER** = (5 + 4 + 1 + 9 + 2 + 9) = (`-**30**) = RECIPROCAL (INVERSE/MIRROR) = (`-**03**)!!!~' `-**DIED** at the `-**AGE** of (`-**63**)!!!~'

FRAGMENTED `-**DEATH/DAY** # `-**NUMBER** = (1 + 2 + 0 + 1 + 9 + 9 + 3) = (`-**25**) = RECIPROCAL (INVERSE/MIRROR) = (`-**52**) = (`-**52**) x `-**TIMES** (`-**2**) = (`-**104**) = "**BRITISH ACTRESS AUDREY HEPBURN** `-**DIED** this `-**MANY** `-**DAYS** `-**AWAY** from `-**HER** `-**BIRTH/DAY** (`-**104**)"!!!~'

(30 + 25) = (`-**55**) = (`-**23**) + (`-**32**)!!!~'

`-**DIED** at the `-**AGE** of (`-**96**)!!!~'

AMERICAN ACTRESS KATHARINE HEPBURN `-**BIRTHDAY** = (**5**/**12**/19/**07**) = (**5** + **12** + 19 + **07**) = (`-**43**) = RECIPROCAL (INVERSE/MIRROR) = (`-**34**)!!!~'

`-**BIRTH/YEAR** = (`-**1907**) = (97 (-) 1 + 0) = (`-**96**) = `-**AGE** of `-**DEATH** for AMERICAN ACTRESS KATHARINE HEPBURN (`-**96**)!!!~'

"WAS `-**BORN** in (`-**5**) (MAY); and, `-**DIED** in (`-**6**) (JUNE)"; and, (**5/6**) = (MAY 6th) = (`-**6**) DAYS AWAY from `-HER `-**BIRTH/ DAY!!!~'** RECIPROCAL (INVERSE/MIRROR) = (**6/5**) = (JUNE 5th) = (`-**24**) DAY AWAY from `-HER `-**DEATH/DAY!!!~'** (**6/24**) = "FLIP the (`-**6**) OVER to a (`-**9**)" = (**9/24**) = (92 + 4) = (`-**96**) = `-**AGE** of `-**DEATH** for AMERICAN ACTRESS KATHARINE HEPBURN (`-**96**)!!!~'

(1**907**) = (90) (1 (-) 7) = `-*EQUALS* = (`-**96**) = `-**AGE** of `-**DEATH** for AMERICAN ACTRESS KATHARINE HEPBURN (`-**96**)!!!~'

AMERICAN ACTRESS KATHARINE HEPBURN `-**DEATH/ DAY** = (**6**/**29**/20/**03**) = (**6** + **29** + 20 + **03**) = (`-**58**) = (5 + 8) = (`-**13**) = "A VERY PIVOTAL # `-NUMBER"!!!~'

`-**DEATH/DAY** = (`-**6/29**) = RECIPROCAL (INVERSE/ MIRROR) = (**92/6**) = (92 + 6) = (`-**98**) = "TWO `-YEARS `-AWAY from `-AGE of `-DEATH for AMERICAN ACTRESS KATHARINE HEPBURN (`-**96**)!!!~'

`-**DEATH/DAY** = (`-**6/29**) = "FLIP the (`-**6**) OVER to a (`-**9**)" = (`-**929**) = BRITISH ACTRESS AUDREY HEPBURN (`-**63**)!!!~'

`-**DEATH/YEAR** = (`-**20/03**) = (20 + 03) = (`-**23**) = -a PROPHETIC # `-NUMBER!!!~'

(58 (-) 43) = (`-**15**)!!!~'

(58 + 43) = (`-**101**) = "FIVE `-YEARS `-AWAY from `-AGE of `-DEATH for AMERICAN ACTRESS KATHARINE HEPBURN (`-**96**)!!!~'

(101 (-) 15) = (`-**86**) = RECIPROCAL (INVERSE/MIRROR) = (`-**68**) = "The `-**MARK**"!!!~'

AMERICAN ACTRESS KATHARINE HEPBURN `-**DIED** (`-**48**) DAYS AWAY from `-HER `-BIRTHDAY!!!~' (`-**48**) = (4 x 8) = (`-**32**) = -a PROPHETIC # `-NUMBER!!!~'

(365 (-) 48) = (`-**317**) = (`-**31.7**) = ROUNDED UP = (`-**32**) = -a PROPHETIC # `-NUMBER!!!~'

FRAGMENTED `-**BIRTH/DAY** # `-**NUMBER** = (5 + 1 + 2 + 1 + 9 + 0 + 7) = (`-**25**) = RECIPROCAL (INVERSE/MIRROR) = (`-**52**)!!!~'

`-**BIRTH/DAY** = (**5**/1**2**)

`-**DEATH/DAY** = (**6**/**29**)

(5 + 12 + 6 + 29) = (`-**52**)!!!~'

FRAGMENTED `-**DEATH/DAY** # `-**NUMBER** = (6 + 2 + 9 + 2 + 0 + 0 + 3) = (`-**22**)!!!~'

(25 + 22) = (`-**47**) = RECIPROCAL (INVERSE/MIRROR) = (`-**74**)!!!~'

(25 + 52 + 22) = (`-**99**) = "FLIP the (`-**9**) OVER to a (`-**6**)" = (`-**96**) = `-**AGE of `-DEATH for AMERICAN ACTRESS KATHARINE HEPBURN (`-96)!!!~'**

`-**DIED** at the `-**AGE** of (`-**65**)!!!~'

RUSSIAN/AMERICAN ACTOR YUL BRYNNER `-**BIRTHDAY** = (**7**/**11**/19/**20**) = (**7** + **11** + 19 + **20**) = (`-**57**) = RECIPROCAL (INVERSE/MIRROR) = (`-**75**)!!!~'

`-**BIRTH/DAY** = (**7**/**11**) = (**ALL-IN-ONE-#-NUMBER**) = (7 (-) 1) (1) = (`-**61**) = "**FOUR `-YEARS `-AWAY from `-AGE of `-DEATH for RUSSIAN/AMERICAN ACTOR YUL BRYNNER (`-65)**"!!!~'

"WAS `-**BORN** in (`-**7**) (JULY); and, `-**DIED** in (`-**10**) (OCTOBER)"; and, (**7**/**10**) = (JULY 10th) = (`-**1**) DAY AWAY from `-HIS `-**BIRTH/DAY**!!!~' RECIPROCAL (INVERSE/MIRROR) = (**10**/**7**) = (OCTOBER 7[th]) = (`-**3**) DAYS AWAY from `-HIS `-**DEATH/DAY**!!!~' (**1**/**3**) = (`-**13**) = "**A VERY PIVOTAL # `-NUMBER**"!!!~'

(1920) = "FLIP the (`-9) OVER to a (`-6)" = (1620) = (6) (1 + 2 + 0) = `-EQUALS = (`-63) = "TWO `-YEARS `-AWAY from `-AGE of `-DEATH for RUSSIAN/AMERICAN ACTOR YUL BRYNNER (`-65)"!!!~'

RUSSIAN/AMERICAN ACTOR YUL BRYNNER `-DEATH/DAY = (10/10/19/85) = (10 + 10 + 19 + 85) = (`-124) = (24 (-) 1) = (`-23) = -a PROPHETIC # `-NUMBER!!!~'

`-DEATH/DAY = (10/10) = (10 + 10) = (`-20) = "FLIP the (`-2) OVER to a (`-7)" = (`-70) = "FIVE `-YEARS `-AWAY from `-AGE of `-DEATH for RUSSIAN/AMERICAN ACTOR YUL BRYNNER (`-65)"!!!~'

`-DEATH/YEAR = (`-19/85) = (85 (-) 19) = (`-66) = "ONE `-YEAR `-AWAY from `-AGE of `-DEATH for RUSSIAN/AMERICAN ACTOR YUL BRYNNER (`-65)"!!!~'

(124 (-) 57) = (`-67) = (6 x 7) = (`-42) = "The `-MARK"!!!~'

(124 + 57) = (`-181) = RECIPROCAL-SEQUENCING-NUMEROLOGY-RSN!!!~'

(181 + 67) = (`-248) = RECIPROCAL (INVERSE/MIRROR) = (`-842) = (ALL-IN-ONE-#-NUMBER) = (8 (-) 2) (4) = (`-64) = "ONE `-YEAR `-AWAY from `-AGE of `-DEATH for RUSSIAN/AMERICAN ACTOR YUL BRYNNER (`-65)"!!!~'

RUSSIAN/AMERICAN ACTOR YUL BRYNNER `-DIED (`-91) DAYS AWAY from `-HIS `-BIRTHDAY!!!~' (`-91) = "FLIP the (`-9) OVER to a (`-6)" = (`-61) = "FOUR `-YEARS `-AWAY from `-AGE of `-DEATH for RUSSIAN/AMERICAN ACTOR YUL BRYNNER (`-65)"!!!~'

(365 (-) 91) = (`-**274**) = (**ALL-IN-ONE-#-NUMBER**) = (2 + 4) (7)
= (`-**67**) = "**TWO `-YEARS `-AWAY from `-AGE of `-DEATH for
RUSSIAN/AMERICAN ACTOR YUL BRYNNER (`-65)**"!!!~'

FRAGMENTED `-**BIRTH/DAY** # `-**NUMBER** = (7 + 1 + 1 + 1
+ 9 + 2 + 0) = (`-**21**) = RECIPROCAL (INVERSE/MIRROR) =
(`-**12**)!!!~'

FRAGMENTED `-**DEATH/DAY** # `-**NUMBER** = (1 + 0 + 1 + 0
+ 1 + 9 + 8 + 5) = (`-**25**) = RECIPROCAL (INVERSE/MIRROR)
= (`-**52**)!!!~'

(21 + 25) = (`-**46**) = (`-**23**) x (`-**2**) =
RECIPROCAL-SEQUENCING-NUMEROLOGY-RSN!!!~'

`-**DEATH/DAY** # `-**NUMBER** in `-**REVERSE** = (85
(-) 19 (-) 10 (-) 10) = (`-**46**) = (`-**23**) x (`-**2**) = (`-**232**) =
RECIPROCAL-SEQUENCING-NUMEROLOGY-RSN!!!~'

(`-**46**) = RECIPROCAL (INVERSE/MIRROR) = (`-**64**)!!!~'

(12 + 52) = (`-**64**) = "**ONE `-YEAR `-AWAY from `-AGE of
`-DEATH for RUSSIAN/AMERICAN ACTOR YUL BRYNNER
(`-65)**"!!!~'

`-**DIED** at the `-**AGE** of (`-**50**)!!!~'

AMERICAN ACTOR STEVE MCQUEEN `-**BIRTHDAY**
= (**3/24**/19/**30**) = (**3** + **24** + 19 + **30**) = (`-**76**) = RECIPROCAL
(INVERSE/MIRROR) = (`-**67**)!!!~'

`-**BIRTH/DAY** = (**3/24**) = (**ALL-IN-ONE-#-NUMBER**) = (3 + 2) (4) = (`-**54**) = "FOUR `-YEARS `-AWAY from `-AGE of `-DEATH for AMERICAN ACTOR STEVE MCQUEEN (`-**50**)"!!!~'

`-**BIRTH/DAY** = (**3/24**) = (3 + 24) = (`-**27**)!!!~'

`-**DEATH/DAY** = (**11/7**) = (**ALL-IN-ONE-#-NUMBER**) = (1 + 1) (7) = (`-**27**)!!!~'

`-**BIRTH/YEAR** = (`-**19/30**) = (19 + 30) = (`-**49**) = "ONE `-YEAR `-AWAY from `-AGE of `-DEATH for AMERICAN ACTOR STEVE MCQUEEN (`-**50**)"!!!~'

"WAS `-**BORN** in (`-**3**) (MARCH); and, `-**DIED** in (`-**11**) (NOVEMBER)"; and, (**3/11**) = (MARCH 11th) = (`-**13**) DAYS AWAY from `-HIS `-**BIRTH/DAY!!!~'** RECIPROCAL (INVERSE/MIRROR) = (**11/3**) = (NOVEMBER 3rd) = (`-**4**) DAYS AWAY from `-HIS `-**DEATH/DAY!!!~'** (**13/4**) = (13 x 4) = (`-**52**) = "TWO `-YEARS `-AWAY from `-AGE of `-DEATH for AMERICAN ACTOR STEVE MCQUEEN (`-**50**)"!!!~'

(**193**0) = (9 (-) 3 (-) 1) (0) = `-*EQUALS* = (`-**50**) = `-AGE of `-DEATH for AMERICAN ACTOR STEVE MCQUEEN (`-**50**)"!!!~'

AMERICAN ACTOR STEVE MCQUEEN `-**DEATH/DAY** = (**11/7**/19/**80**) = (**11** + **7** + 19 + **80**) = (`-**117**) = `-**DEATH/DAY** for AMERICAN ACTOR STEVE MCQUEEN (**11/7**)!!!~'

RUSSIAN/AMERICAN ACTOR YUL BRYNNER `-**BIRTHDAY** = (**7/11**) = RECIPROCAL (INVERSE/MIRROR) = (**11/7**) = AMERICAN ACTOR STEVE MCQUEEN `-**DEATH/DAY** = (**11/7**)!!!~'

(117 (-) 76) = (`-**41**)!!!~'

(117 + 76) = (`-**193**) = (19 x 3) = (`-**57**) = **"SEVEN `-YEARS `-AWAY from `-AGE of `-DEATH for AMERICAN ACTOR STEVE MCQUEEN (`-50)"!!!~'**

(193 (-) 41) = (`-**152**) = (52 (-) 1) = (`-**51**) = **"ONE `-YEAR `-AWAY from `-AGE of `-DEATH for AMERICAN ACTOR STEVE MCQUEEN (`-50)"!!!~'**

(193 + 41) = (`-**234**) = **PROPHETIC-LINEAR-PROGRESSION-PLP!!!~'**

AMERICAN ACTOR STEVE MCQUEEN `-**DIED** (`-**137**) DAYS AWAY from `-**HIS `-BIRTHDAY!!!~'** (`-**137**) = (**ALL-IN-ONE-#-NUMBER**) = (1 + 3) (7) = (`-**47**) = **"THREE `-YEARS `-AWAY from `-AGE of `-DEATH for AMERICAN ACTOR STEVE MCQUEEN (`-50)"!!!~'**

(365 (-) 137) = (`-**228**) = (**ALL-IN-ONE-#-NUMBER**) = (2 + 2) (8) = (`-**48**) = **"TWO `-YEARS `-AWAY from `-AGE of `-DEATH for AMERICAN ACTOR STEVE MCQUEEN (`-50)"!!!~'**

FRAGMENTED `-**BIRTH/DAY** # `-**NUMBER** = (3 + 2 + 4 + 1 + 9 + 3 + 0) = (`-**22**) = "FLIP the (`-**2**) OVER to a (`-**7**)" = (`-**27**) = FRAGMENTED `-**DEATH/DAY** # `-**NUMBER!!!~'**

`-**DEATH/DAY** = (**11/7**) = (**ALL-IN-ONE-#-NUMBER**) = (1 + 1) (7) = (`-**27**)!!!~'

FRAGMENTED `-**DEATH/DAY** # `-**NUMBER** = (1 + 1 + 7 + 1 + 9 + 8 + 0) = (`-**27**) = RECIPROCAL (INVERSE/MIRROR) = (`-**72**)!!!~'

(22 + 27) = (`-**49**) = "ONE `-YEAR `-AWAY from `-AGE of `-DEATH for AMERICAN ACTOR STEVE MCQUEEN (`-**50**)"!!!~'

`-**DEATH/DAY** # `-**NUMBER** in `-**REVERSE** = (80 (-) 19 (-) 7 (-) 11) = (`-**43**) = RECIPROCAL (INVERSE/MIRROR) = (`-**34**) = "SEE `-**ABOVE**"!!!~'

(72 (-) 22) = (`-**50**) = `-AGE of `-DEATH for AMERICAN ACTOR STEVE MCQUEEN (`-**50**)"!!!~'

`-**DIED** at the `-**AGE** of (`-**83**)!!!~'

AMERICAN ACTOR PAUL NEWMAN `-**BIRTHDAY** = (**1**/**26**/19/**25**) = (**1** + **26** + 19 + **25**) = (`-**71**) = RECIPROCAL (INVERSE/MIRROR) = (`-**17**)!!!~'

(71 + 17) = (`-**88**) = "FIVE `-YEARS `-AWAY from `-AGE of `-DEATH for AMERICAN ACTOR PAUL NEWMAN (`-**83**)"!!!~'

`-**BIRTH/DAY** = (**1/26**) = RECIPROCAL (INVERSE/MIRROR) = (**62/1**) = (**ALL-IN-ONE-#-NUMBER**) = (6 + 2) (1) = (`-**81**) = "TWO `-YEARS `-AWAY from `-AGE of `-DEATH for AMERICAN ACTOR PAUL NEWMAN (`-**83**)"!!!~'

`-**BIRTH/DAY** = (**1/26**) = (26 (-) 1) = (`-**25**) = `-**BIRTH/YEAR**!!!~'

`-**DAY** of `-**BIRTH** = (`-**26**)!!!~'

`-**DAY** of `-**DEATH** = (`-**26**)!!!~'

(26 + 26) = (`-**52**) = RECIPROCAL (INVERSE/MIRROR) = (`-**25**) = `-**BIRTH/YEAR!!!**~'

"WAS `-**BORN** in (`-**1**) (JANUARY); and, `-**DIED** in (`-**9**) (SEPTEMBER)"; and, (**1/9**) = (JANUARY 9th) = (`-**17**) DAYS AWAY from `-HIS `-**BIRTH/DAY!!!**~' RECIPROCAL (INVERSE/ MIRROR) = (**9/1**) = (SEPTEMBER 1st) = (`-**25**) DAYS AWAY from `-HIS `-**DEATH/DAY!!!**~' (**17/25**) = (**ALL-IN-ONE-#-NUMBER**) = (1 + 7) (5 (-) 2) = (`-**83**) = `-**AGE** of `-**DEATH** for AMERICAN ACTOR PAUL NEWMAN (`-**83**)"!!!~'

(**19**25) = (9 (-) 1) (5 (-) 2) = `-*EQUALS* = (`-**83**) = `-**AGE** of `-**DEATH** for AMERICAN ACTOR PAUL NEWMAN (`-**83**)"!!!~'

AMERICAN ACTOR PAUL NEWMAN `-**DEATH/DAY** = (**9/26**/20/**08**) = (**9** + **26** + 20 + **08**) = (`-**63**) = (6 x 3) = (`-**18**) = RECIPROCAL (INVERSE/MIRROR) = (`-**81**) = "TWO `-YEARS `-AWAY from `-AGE of `-DEATH for AMERICAN ACTOR PAUL NEWMAN (`-**83**)"!!!~'

`-**DEATH/DAY** = (**9/26**) = (92 (-) 6) = (`-**86**) = "THREE `-YEARS `-AWAY from `-AGE of `-DEATH for AMERICAN ACTOR PAUL NEWMAN (`-**83**)"!!!~'

`-**DEATH/YEAR** = (`-**2**0/0**8**) = RECIPROCAL (INVERSE/ MIRROR) = (**8**0/0**2**) = (82 + 0 + 0) = (`-**82**) = "ONE `-YEAR `-AWAY from `-AGE of `-DEATH for AMERICAN ACTOR PAUL NEWMAN (`-**83**)"!!!~'

(71 (-) 63) = (`-**8**)!!!~'

(71 + 63) = (`-**134**) = (34 + 1) = (`-**35**) = RECIPROCAL (INVERSE/ MIRROR) = (`-**53**)!!!~'

(134 (-) 8) = (`-**126**) = (26 x 1) = (`-**26**) = `-**DAY** of `-**BIRTH** (`-**26**<sup>th</sup>); and, `-**DAY** of `-**DEATH** (`-**26**th)!!!~'

(134 + 8) = (`-**142**) = (42 x 1) = (`-**42**) = "The `-**MARK**"!!!~'

AMERICAN ACTOR PAUL NEWMAN `-**DIED** (`-**122**) DAYS AWAY from `-**HIS** `-**BIRTHDAY**!!!~' (`-**122**) = (22 + 1) = (`-**23**) = -a PROPHETIC # `-**NUMBER**!!!~'

(365 (-) 122) = (`-**243**) = (43 x 2) = (`-**86**) = "**THREE `-YEARS `-AWAY from `-AGE of `-DEATH for AMERICAN ACTOR PAUL NEWMAN (`-83)**"!!!~'

/|\ FRAGMENTED `-**BIRTH/DAY** # `-**NUMBER** = (1 + 2 + 6 + 1 + 9 + 2 + 5) = (`-**26**) = `-**DAY** of `-**BIRTH** (`-**26**th); and, `-**DAY** of `-**DEATH** (`-**26**th)!!!~'

FRAGMENTED `-**BIRTH/DAY** # `-**NUMBER** = (1 + 2 + 6 + 1 + 9 + 2 + 5) = (`-**26**) = RECIPROCAL (INVERSE/MIRROR) = (`-**62**)!!!~' /|\

(26 + 62) = (`-**88**) = "**FIVE `-YEARS `-AWAY from `-AGE of `-DEATH for AMERICAN ACTOR PAUL NEWMAN (`-83)**"!!!~'

/|\ FRAGMENTED `-**DEATH/DAY** # `-**NUMBER** = (9 + 2 + 6 + 2 + 0 + 0 + 8) = (`-**27**) = RECIPROCAL (INVERSE/MIRROR) = (`-**72**)!!!~'

`-**BIRTH/DAY** = (**1/26**) = (26 + 1) = (`-**27**)!!!~' /|\

(26 + 27) = (`-**53**) = RECIPROCAL (INVERSE/MIRROR) = (`-**35**)"!!!~'

(53 + 35) = (`-**88**) = "FIVE `-YEARS `-AWAY from `-AGE of `-DEATH for AMERICAN ACTOR PAUL NEWMAN (`-**83**)"!!!~'

`-**DIED** at the `-**AGE** of (`-**81**)!!!~'

AMERICAN ACTOR CHARLES BRONSON `-**BIRTHDAY** = (**11**/**3**/19/**21**) = (**11** + **3** + 19 + **21**) = (`-**54**) = RECIPROCAL (INVERSE/MIRROR) = (`-**45**)!!!~'

(54 + 45) = (`-**99**) = (9 x 9) = (`-**81**) = `-**AGE** of `-**DEATH** for AMERICAN ACTOR CHARLES BRONSON (`-**81**)"!!!~'

`-**BORN** in (`-**11**); and, `-**DIED** in (`-**8**) = (**11/8**) = RECIPROCAL (INVERSE/MIRROR) = (**8/11**) = (81 x 1) = (`-**81**) = `-**AGE** of `-**DEATH** for AMERICAN ACTOR CHARLES BRONSON (`-**81**)"!!!~'

`-**BIRTH/DAY** = (**11/3**) = (13 x 1) = (`-**13**) = "A VERY PIVOTAL # `-NUMBER"!!!~'

"WAS `-**BORN** in (`-**11**) (NOVEMBER); and, `-**DIED** in (`-**8**) (AUGUST)"; and, (**11/8**) = (NOVEMBER 8th) = (`-**5**) DAYS AWAY from `-HIS `-**BIRTH/DAY!!!**~' RECIPROCAL (INVERSE/ MIRROR) = (**8/11**) = (AUGUST 11[th]) = (`-**19**) DAYS AWAY from `-HIS `-**DEATH/DAY!!!**~' (**5/19**) = RECIPROCAL (INVERSE/ MIRROR) = (**91/5**) = (**ALL-IN-ONE-#-NUMBER**) = (9 (-) 1) (5) = (`-**85**) = "FOUR `-YEARS `-AWAY from `-AGE of `-DEATH for AMERICAN ACTOR CHARLES BRONSON (`-**81**)"!!!~'

(**19**21) = (9 (-) 1) (2 (-) 1) = `-*EQUALS* = (`-**81**) = `-**AGE** of `-**DEATH** for AMERICAN ACTOR CHARLES BRONSON (`-**81**)"!!!~'

AMERICAN ACTOR CHARLES BRONSON `-**DEATH/DAY**
= (**8**/**30**/20/**03**) = (**8** + **30** + 20 + **03**) = (`-**61**)!!!~'

`-**DEATH/DAY** = (**8/30**) = (83 + 0) = (`-**83**) = "TWO `-YEARS
`-AWAY from `-AGE of `-DEATH for AMERICAN ACTOR
CHARLES BRONSON (`-**81**)"!!!~'

`-**DEATH/YEAR** = (`-**2**0/0**3**) = (20 + 03) = (`-**23**) = -a PROPHETIC
`-NUMBER!!!~'

(61 (-) 54) = (`-**7**)!!!~'

(61 + 54) = (`-**115**) = (11 x 5) = (`-**55**) = (`-**23**) + (`-**32**)!!!~'

(115 (-) 7) = (`-**108**) = RECIPROCAL (INVERSE/MIRROR) =
(`-**801**) = (80 + 1) = (`-**81**) = `-**AGE of `-DEATH for AMERICAN
ACTOR CHARLES BRONSON (`-**81**)"!!!~'

(115 + 7) = (`-**122**) = (22 + 1) = (`-**23**) = -a PROPHETIC #
`-NUMBER!!!~'

AMERICAN ACTOR CHARLES BRONSON `-**DIED** (`-**65**)
DAYS AWAY from `-HIS `-BIRTHDAY!!!~' (`-**65**) = (6 x 5) =
(`-**30**)!!!~'

(365 (-) 65) = (`-**300**)!!!~'

/|\ FRAGMENTED `-**BIRTH/DAY** # `-NUMBER = (1 + 1 + 3 + 1
+ 9 + 2 + 1) = (`-**18**) = RECIPROCAL (INVERSE/MIRROR) = (`-
81) = `-**AGE of `-DEATH for AMERICAN ACTOR CHARLES
BRONSON (`-**81**)"!!!~' /|\

FRAGMENTED `-**DEATH/DAY** # `-NUMBER = (8 + 3 + 0 +
2 + 0 + 0 + 3) = (`-**16**) = RECIPROCAL (INVERSE/MIRROR)
= (`-**61**)!!!~'

(16 + 61) = (`-77) = "FOUR `-YEARS `-AWAY from `-AGE of `-DEATH for AMERICAN ACTOR CHARLES BRONSON (`-81)"!!!~'

(18/16) = (86 x 1 x 1) = (`-86) = RECIPROCAL (INVERSE/ MIRROR) = (`-68) = "The `-MARK"!!!~'

(18 + 16) = (`-34) = RECIPROCAL (INVERSE/MIRROR) = (`-43)"!!!~'

(43 + 34) = (`-77) = "FOUR `-YEARS `-AWAY from `-AGE of `-DEATH for AMERICAN ACTOR CHARLES BRONSON (`-81)"!!!~'

`-DIED at the `-AGE of (`-74) = (7 x 4) = (`-28) = "YEAR of `-BIRTH (`-28)"!!!~'

AMERICAN ACTOR JAMES COBURN `-BIRTHDAY = (8/31/19/28) = (8 + 31 + 19 + 28) = (`-86) = RECIPROCAL (INVERSE/MIRROR) = (`-68) = "The `-MARK"!!!~'

`-BORN in (`-11); and, `-DIED in (`-8) = (11/8) = RECIPROCAL (INVERSE/MIRROR) = (8/11) = (81 x 1) = (`-81) = `-AGE of `-DEATH for AMERICAN ACTOR CHARLES BRONSON (`-81)"!!!~'

`-BORN in (`-8); and, `-DIED in (`-11) = (8/11) = RECIPROCAL (INVERSE/MIRROR) = (11/8) = `-DEATH/DAY for AMERICAN ACTOR JAMES COBURN (11/18)!!!~'

`-BIRTH/DAY = (8/31) = (ALL-IN-ONE-#-NUMBER) = (8 (-) 1) (3) = (`-73) = "ONE `-YEAR `-AWAY from `-AGE of `-DEATH for AMERICAN ACTOR JAMES COBURN (`-74)"!!!~'

"WAS `-**BORN** in (`-**8**) (AUGUST); and, `-**DIED** in (`-**11**) (NOVEMBER)"; and, (**8/11**) = (AUGUST 11th) = (`-**20**) DAYS AWAY from `-HIS `-**BIRTH/DAY!!!**~' RECIPROCAL (INVERSE/ MIRROR) = (**11/8**) = (NOVEMBER 8<sup>th</sup>) = (`-**10**) DAYS AWAY from `-HIS `-**DEATH/DAY!!!**~' (**20/10**) = "FLIP the (`-**2**) OVER to a (`-**7**)" = (**70/10**) = (70 + 1 + 0) = (`-**71**) = "**THREE `-YEARS `-AWAY from `-AGE of `-DEATH for AMERICAN ACTOR JAMES COBURN (`-74)"!!!**~'

(19**2**8) = (9 (-) 2) (8 (-) 1) = `-*EQUALS* = (`-**77**) = "**THREE `-YEARS `-AWAY from `-AGE of `-DEATH for AMERICAN ACTOR JAMES COBURN (`-74)"!!!**~'

(19**2**8) = (9 + 8) (1 + 2) = (**17**) (**3**) = (73 + 1) = `-*EQUALS* = (`-**74**) = `-**AGE of `-DEATH for AMERICAN ACTOR JAMES COBURN (`-74)"!!!**~'

AMERICAN ACTOR JAMES COBURN `-**DEATH/DAY** = (**11/18**/20/**02**) = (**11** + **18** + 20 + **02**) = (`-**51**)!!!~'

`-**DEATH/DAY** = (**11/18**) = RECIPROCAL (INVERSE/ MIRROR) = (**81/11**) = (**ALL-IN-ONE-#-NUMBER**) = (8 (-) 1) (1 + 1) = (`-**72**) = "**TWO `-YEARS `-AWAY from `-AGE of `-DEATH for AMERICAN ACTOR JAMES COBURN (`-74)"!!!**~'

`-**DEATH/YEAR** = (`-**20/02**) = (`-**20**) = RECIPROCAL (INVERSE/MIRROR) = (`-**02**)!!!~'

(86 (-) 51) = (`-**35**)!!!~'

(86 + 51) = (`-**137**) = RECIPROCAL (INVERSE/MIRROR) = (`-**731**) = (73 + 1) = (`-**74**) = `-**AGE of `-DEATH for AMERICAN ACTOR JAMES COBURN (`-74)"!!!**~'

(137 (-) 35) = (`-**102**) = RECIPROCAL (INVERSE/MIRROR) = (`-**201**) = "FLIP the (`-**2**) OVER to a (`-**7**)" = (`-**701**) = (70 + 1) = (`-**71**) = "THREE `-YEARS `-AWAY from `-AGE of `-DEATH for AMERICAN ACTOR JAMES COBURN (`-**74**)"!!!~'

(137 + 35) = (`-**172**) = (72 + 1) = (`-**73**) = "ONE `-YEAR `-AWAY from `-AGE of `-DEATH for AMERICAN ACTOR JAMES COBURN (`-**74**)"!!!~'

AMERICAN ACTOR JAMES COBURN `-**DIED** (`-**79**) DAYS AWAY from `-HIS `-BIRTHDAY!!!~' (`-**79**) = "FIVE `-YEARS `-AWAY from `-AGE of `-DEATH for AMERICAN ACTOR JAMES COBURN (`-**74**)"!!!~'

(365 (-) 79) = (`-**286**) = (28 x 6) = (`-**168**) = "The `-**MARK**"!!!~'

FRAGMENTED `-**BIRTH/DAY** # `-NUMBER = (8 + 3 + 1 + 1 + 9 + 2 + 8) = (`-**32**) = RECIPROCAL (INVERSE/MIRROR) = (`-**23**) = -a PROPHETIC # `-NUMBER!!!~'

FRAGMENTED `-**DEATH/DAY** # `-NUMBER = (1 + 1 + 1 + 8 + 2 + 0 + 0 + 2) = (`-**15**) = RECIPROCAL (INVERSE/MIRROR) = (`-**51**)!!!~'

(32 + 15) = (`-**47**) = RECIPROCAL (INVERSE/MIRROR) = (`-**74**) = `-AGE of `-DEATH for AMERICAN ACTOR JAMES COBURN (`-**74**)"!!!~'

(23 + 51) = (`-**74**) = `-AGE of `-DEATH for AMERICAN ACTOR JAMES COBURN (`-**74**)"!!!~'

/|\ `-**BIRTH/DAY** = (**8/31**) = (**8**) **3**(**1's**)!!!~'

= *RECIPROCAL (INVERSE/MIRROR)* =

`-**DEATH/DAY** = (**11/18**) = RECIPROCAL (INVERSE/ MIRROR) = (**81/11**) = (**8**) **3**(**1's**)!!!~' /|\

`-**DIED** at the `-**AGE** of (`-**89**)!!!~'

AMERICAN ACTOR JAMES STEWART `-**BIRTHDAY** = (**5/20**/19/**08**) = (**5** + **20** + 19 + **08**) = (`-**52**) = RECIPROCAL (INVERSE/MIRROR) = (`-**25**) = (5 + 20) = `-**BIRTH/DAY** (MAY **20**th)!!!~'

`-**AGE** of `-**DEATH** = (`-**89**) = (8 x 9) = (`-**72**) = `-**DEATH/DAY** (**7/2**) of AMERICAN ACTOR JAMES STEWART = (**JULY 2**nd)!!!~'

`-**BIRTH/DAY** = (**5/20**) = (5 + 20) = (`-**25**) = RECIPROCAL (INVERSE/MIRROR) = (`-**52**) = `-**BIRTH/DAY** # `-**NUMBER** for AMERICAN ACTOR JAMES STEWART (`-**52**)!!!~'

`-**BIRTH/YEAR** = (`-**19/08**) = RECIPROCAL (INVERSE/ MIRROR) = (`-**80/91**) = (89 x 1 + 0) = (`-**89**) = `-**AGE** of `-**DEATH** (`-**89**)!!!~'

"WAS `-**BORN** in (`-**5**) (MAY); and, `-**DIED** in (`-**7**) (JULY)"; and, (**5/7**) = (MAY 7th) = (`-**13**) DAYS AWAY from `-HIS `-**BIRTH/ DAY**!!!~' RECIPROCAL (INVERSE/MIRROR) = (**7/5**) = (JULY 5th) = (`-**3**) DAYS AWAY from `-HIS `-**DEATH/DAY**!!!~' (**13/3**) = (13 x 3) = (`-**39**) = RECIPROCAL (INVERSE/MIRROR) = (`-**93**) = "FOUR `-**YEARS** `-**AWAY from** `-**AGE** of `-**DEATH** for AMERICAN ACTOR JAMES STEWART (`-**89**)"!!!~'

(**19**08) = (1 x 9) (0 + 8) = ('-**98**) = RECIPROCAL (INVERSE/ MIRROR) = '-***EQUALS*** = ('-**89**) = '-AGE of '-DEATH for AMERICAN ACTOR JAMES STEWART ('-**89**)"!!!~'

AMERICAN ACTOR JAMES STEWART '-**DEATH/DAY** = (**7**/**2**/19/**97**) = (**7** + **2** + 19 + **97**) = ('-**125**) = (25 x 1) = ('-**25**) = RECIPROCAL (INVERSE/MIRROR) = ('-**52**) = '-**BIRTH/DAY** # '-**NUMBER** for AMERICAN ACTOR JAMES STEWART ('-**52**)!!!~'

'-**DEATH/DAY** = (**7**/**2**) = (8 x 9) = ('-**89**) = '-AGE of '-DEATH for AMERICAN ACTOR JAMES STEWART ('-**89**)"!!!~'

'-**DEATH/DAY** # '-**NUMBER** in '-**REVERSE** = (97 (-) 19 (-) 2 (-) 7) = ('-**69**) = "**YIN/YANG**" = "The '-**CYCLE** of '-**LIFE**"!!!~'

'-**DEATH/YEAR** = ('-**19/97**) = (97 (-) 19) = ('-**78**) = RECIPROCAL (INVERSE/MIRROR) = ('-**87**) = "**TWO '-YEARS '-AWAY** from '-AGE of '-DEATH for AMERICAN ACTOR JAMES STEWART ('-**89**)"!!!~'

(125 (-) 52) = ('-**73**) = "FLIP the ('-**7**) OVER to a ('-**2**)" = ('-**23**) = -a PROPHETIC # '-NUMBER!!!~'

(125 + 52) = ('-**177**) = (**ALL-IN-ONE-#-NUMBER**) = (1 + 7) (7) = ('-**87**) = "**TWO '-YEARS '-AWAY** from '-AGE of '-DEATH for AMERICAN ACTOR JAMES STEWART ('-**89**)"!!!~'

AMERICAN ACTOR JAMES STEWART '-**DIED** ('-**43**) DAYS AWAY from '-**HIS** '-**BIRTHDAY**!!!~'

(365 (-) 43) = ('-**322**) = (32 x 2) = ('-**64**) = ('-**2**) x ('-**32**) = ('-**232**) = **RECIPROCAL-SEQUENCING-NUMEROLOGY-RSN**!!!~'

FRAGMENTED `-**BIRTH/DAY** # `-**NUMBER** = (5 + 2 + 0 + 1 + 9 + 0 + 8) = (`-**25**) = (5 + 20) = `-**BIRTH/DAY** (**MAY 20**th)!!!~'

/|\ FRAGMENTED `-**BIRTH/DAY** # `-**NUMBER** = (5 + 2 + 0 + 1 + 9 + 0 + 8) = (`-**25**) = RECIPROCAL (INVERSE/MIRROR) = (`-**52**) = `-**BIRTH/DAY** # `-**NUMBER for AMERICAN ACTOR JAMES STEWART** (`-**52**)!!!~'

FOR; AMERICAN ACTOR JAMES STEWART `-**DEATH/DAY** # `-**NUMBER** = `-*EQUALED* = (`-**125**) = (25 x 1) = (`-**25**)!!!~' /|\

FRAGMENTED `-**DEATH/DAY** # `-**NUMBER** = (7 + 2 + 1 + 9 + 9 + 7) = (`-**35**) = RECIPROCAL (INVERSE/MIRROR) = (`-**53**)!!!~'

(35 + 53) = (`-**88**) = "**ONE** `-**YEAR** `-**AWAY from** `-**AGE of** `-**DEATH for AMERICAN ACTOR JAMES STEWART** (`-**89**)"!!!~'

(25 + 35) = (`-**60**) = RECIPROCAL (INVERSE/MIRROR) = (`-**06**)!!!~'

`-**DIED** at the `-**AGE** of (`-**52**)!!!~'

FILM ACTRESS GRACE KELLY `-**BIRTHDAY** = (**11**/**12**/19/**29**) = (**11** + **12** + 19 + **29**) = (`-**71**) = RECIPROCAL (INVERSE/ MIRROR) = (`-**17**)!!!~'

(71 (-) 17) = (`-**54**) = "**TWO** `-**YEARS** `-**AWAY from** `-**AGE of** `-**DEATH for FILM ACTRESS GRACE KELLY** (`-**52**)!!!~'

`-**BIRTH/DAY** = (**11**/**12**) = (11 + 12) = (`-**23**) = -a PROPHETIC # `-**NUMBER!!!**~'

`-BIRTH/YEAR** = (`-1929**) = (19 + 29) = (`-**48**) = **"FOUR `-YEARS `-AWAY from `-AGE of `-DEATH for FILM ACTRESS GRACE KELLY (`-52)!!!~'**

"WAS `-**BORN** in (`-**11**) (NOVEMBER); and, `-**DIED** in (`-**9**) (SEPTEMBER)"; and, (**11/9**) = (NOVEMBER 9th) = (`-**3**) DAYS AWAY from `-HER `-**BIRTH/DAY!!!~'** RECIPROCAL (INVERSE/MIRROR) = (**9/11**) = (SEPTEMBER 11th) = (`-**3**) DAY AWAY from `-HER `-**DEATH/DAY!!!~'** (**3/3**) = (5 (-) 2) = (`-**3**) = **`-AGE of `-DEATH (`-52)!!!~'**

(1**9**2**9**) = "FLIP the (`-**9**) OVER to a (`-**6**)" = (1**6**2**6**) = (1 (-) 6) (2 (-) 6) = `-*EQUALS* = (`-**54**) = **"TWO `-YEARS `-AWAY from `-AGE of `-DEATH for FILM ACTRESS GRACE KELLY (`-52)!!!~'**

FILM ACTRESS GRACE KELLY `-**DEATH/DAY** = (**9/14**/19/**82**) = (**9** + **14** + 19 + **82**) = (`-**124**) = (24 (-) 1) = (`-**23**) = -a PROPHETIC # `-NUMBER!!!~'

(`-**124**) = RECIPROCAL (INVERSE/MIRROR) = (`-**421**) = (**ALL-IN-ONE-#-NUMBER**) = (4 + 1) (2) = (`-**52**) = **`-AGE of `-DEATH for FILM ACTRESS GRACE KELLY (`-52)!!!~'**

`-**DEATH/DAY** = (`-**9/14**) = (**ALL-IN-ONE-#-NUMBER**) = (9 (-) 4) (1) = (`-**51**) = **"ONE `-YEAR `-AWAY from `-AGE of `-DEATH for FILM ACTRESS GRACE KELLY (`-52)!!!~'**

`-**DEATH/DAY** = (`-**9/14**) = (9 + 14) = (`-**23**) = -a PROPHETIC # `-NUMBER!!!~'

(124 (-) 71) = (`-**53**) = **"ONE `-YEAR `-AWAY from `-AGE of `-DEATH for FILM ACTRESS GRACE KELLY (`-52)!!!~'**

(124 + 71) = (`-**195**) = RECIPROCAL (INVERSE/MIRROR) = (`-**591**) = (59 (-) 1) = (`-**58**) = "SIX `-YEARS `-AWAY from `-AGE of `-DEATH for FILM ACTRESS GRACE KELLY (`-**52**)!!!~'

(195 (-) 53) = (`-**142**) = (**ALL-IN-ONE-#-NUMBER**) = (1 + 4) (2) = (`-**52**) = `-AGE of `-DEATH for FILM ACTRESS GRACE KELLY (`-**52**)!!!~'

(195 + 53) = (`-**248**) = (48 + 2) = (`-**50**) = "TWO `-YEARS `-AWAY from `-AGE of `-DEATH for FILM ACTRESS GRACE KELLY (`-**52**)!!!~'

FILM ACTRESS GRACE KELLY `-**DIED** (`-**59**) DAYS AWAY from `-HER `-BIRTHDAY!!!~' (`-**59**) = `-BIRTH/DAY # `-NUMBER (`-**71**) (+) `-DEATH/DAY # `-NUMBER (`-**124**) = RECIPROCAL (INVERSE/MIRROR) = (`-**195**) = (95 x 1) = (`-**95**)!!!~'

(365 (-) 59) = (`-**306**) = (36 + 0) = (`-**36**) = RECIPROCAL (INVERSE/ MIRROR) = (`-**63**) = (19 (-) 82) = `-**DEATH/YEAR**!!!~'

/|\ FRAGMENTED `-**BIRTH/DAY** # `-NUMBER = (1 + 1 + 1 + 2 + 1 + 9 + 2 + 9) = (`-**26**) = RECIPROCAL (INVERSE/MIRROR) = (`-**62**)!!!~'

(**26** x `-**TIMES** (`-**2**) = (`-**52**) = `-AGE of `-DEATH for FILM ACTRESS GRACE KELLY (`-**52**)!!!~' /|\

FRAGMENTED `-**DEATH/DAY** # `-NUMBER = (9 + 1 + 4 + 1 + 9 + 8 + 2) = (`-**34**) = RECIPROCAL (INVERSE/MIRROR) = (`-**43**)!!!~'!!!~'

(26 + 34) = (`-**60**) = RECIPROCAL (INVERSE/MIRROR) = (`-**06**)!!!~'

(60 (-) 6) = (`-**54**) = "TWO `-YEARS `-AWAY from `-AGE of `-DEATH for FILM ACTRESS GRACE KELLY (`-**52**)!!!~'

(60 (-) 6) = (`-**54**) = RECIPROCAL (INVERSE/MIRROR) = (`-**45**) = (5 x 9) = (`-**59**) = FILM ACTRESS GRACE KELLY `-**DIED** this `-**MANY** `-**DAYS** `-**AWAY** from `-**HER** `-**BIRTH/DAY**!!!~'

`-**DIED** at the `-**AGE** of (`-**79**)!!!~'

ENGLISH/AMERICAN ACTRESS ELIZABETH TAYLOR `-**BIRTHDAY** = (**2**/**27**/19/**32**) = (**2** + **27** + 19 + **32**) = (`-**80**) = "ONE `-YEAR `-AWAY from `-AGE of `-DEATH for ENGLISH/AMERICAN ACTRESS ELIZABETH TAYLOR (`-**79**)"!!!~'

`-**BIRTH/DAY** = (**2**/**27**) = (2 + 27) = (`-**29**) = "FLIP the (`-**2**) OVER to a (`-**7**)" = (`-**79**) = `-AGE of `-DEATH for ENGLISH/AMERICAN ACTRESS ELIZABETH TAYLOR (`-**79**)"!!!~'

`-**BIRTH/YEAR** = (`-**32**) = -a PROPHETIC # `-NUMBER!!!~'

`-**DEATH/DAY** = (**3**/**23**) = (`-**323**) = **R**ECIPROCAL-**S**EQUENCING-**N**UMEROLOGY-**RSN**!!!~'

(`-**32**) = RECIPROCAL (INVERSE/MIRROR) = (`-**23**) = "WAS `-**BORN** in (`-**2**); and, `-**DIED** in (`-**3**)"!!!~'

"WAS `-**BORN** in (`-**2**) (FEBRUARY); and, `-**DIED** in (`-**3**) (MARCH)"; and, (**2/3**) = (FEBRUARY 3rd) = (`-**24**) DAYS AWAY from `-HER `-**BIRTH/DAY**!!!~' RECIPROCAL (INVERSE/MIRROR) = (**3/2**) = (MARCH 2nd) = (`-**21**) DAY AWAY from `-HER `-**DEATH/DAY**!!!~' (**24/21**) = (**ALL-IN-ONE-#-NUMBER**) = (2 + 4) (2 + 1) = (`-**63**) = (7 x 9) = (`-**79**) = `-AGE of `-**DEATH** for

ENGLISH/AMERICAN ACTRESS ELIZABETH TAYLOR (`-79)"!!!~'

(1932) = (9 (-) 2) (1 + 3) = `-EQUALS = (`-74) = "FIVE `-YEARS `-AWAY from `-AGE of `-DEATH for ENGLISH/AMERICAN ACTRESS ELIZABETH TAYLOR (`-79)"!!!~'

ENGLISH/AMERICAN ACTRESS ELIZABETH TAYLOR `-DEATH/DAY = (3/23/20/11) = (3 + 23 + 20 + 11) = (`-57) = "SEE `-BELOW"!!!~'

`-DEATH/DAY = (3/23) = "FLIP the (`-2) OVER to a (`-7)" = (3/73) = (73 + 3) = (`-76) = "FLIP the (`-6) OVER to a (`-9)" = (`-79) = `-AGE of `-DEATH for ENGLISH/AMERICAN ACTRESS ELIZABETH TAYLOR (`-79)"!!!~'

`-DAY of `-DEATH = (`-23$^{rd}$) = (`-23) = -a PROPHETIC # `-NUMBER!!!~'

`-DEATH/YEAR = (`-20/11) = (20 + 11) = (`-31) = RECIPROCAL (INVERSE/MIRROR) = (`-13) = "A VERY PIVOTAL # `-NUMBER"!!!~'

(80 (-) 57) = (`-23) = -a PROPHETIC # `-NUMBER!!!~'

(80 + 57) = (`-137) = RECIPROCAL (INVERSE/MIRROR) = (`-731) = (73 + 1) = (`-74) = "FIVE `-YEARS `-AWAY from `-AGE of `-DEATH for ENGLISH/AMERICAN ACTRESS ELIZABETH TAYLOR (`-79)"!!!~'

(137 + 23) = (`-160) = (**ALL-IN-ONE-#-NUMBER**) = (1 + 6) (0) = (`-70) = "NINE `-YEARS `-AWAY from `-AGE of `-DEATH for ENGLISH/AMERICAN ACTRESS ELIZABETH TAYLOR (`-79)"!!!~'

ENGLISH/AMERICAN ACTRESS ELIZABETH TAYLOR `-**DIED** (`-**24**) DAYS AWAY from `-**HER** `-**BIRTHDAY!!!**~' (`-**24**) = "FLIP the (`-**2**) OVER to a (`-**7**)" = (`-**74**) = **"FIVE `-YEARS `-AWAY from `-AGE of `-DEATH for ENGLISH/AMERICAN ACTRESS ELIZABETH TAYLOR (`-79)"!!!**~'

(365 (-) 24) = (`-**341**) = (34 + 1) = (`-**35**) = (5 x 7) = (`-**57**) = `-**DEATH/ DAY # `-NUMBER for ENGLISH/AMERICAN ACTRESS ELIZABETH TAYLOR (`-57)"!!!**~'

FRAGMENTED `-**BIRTH/DAY** # `-**NUMBER** = (2 + 2 + 7 + 1 + 9 + 3 + 2) = (`-**26**) = RECIPROCAL (INVERSE/MIRROR) = (`-**62**)!!!~'

(26 + 26) = (`-**52**) = "FLIP the (`-**2**) OVER to a (`-**7**)" = (`-**57**) = `-**DEATH/DAY** # `-**NUMBER** for **ENGLISH/AMERICAN ACTRESS ELIZABETH TAYLOR (`-57)!!!**~'

(26 + 26) = (`-**52**) = "FLIP the (`-**2**) OVER to a (`-**7**)" = (`-**57**) = RECIPROCAL (INVERSE/MIRROR) = (`-**75**) = **"FOUR `-YEARS `-AWAY from `-AGE of `-DEATH for ENGLISH/ AMERICAN ACTRESS ELIZABETH TAYLOR (`-79)"!!!**~'

FRAGMENTED `-**DEATH/DAY** # `-**NUMBER** = (3 + 2 + 3 + 2 + 0 + 1 + 1) = (`-**12**) = RECIPROCAL (INVERSE/MIRROR) = (`-**21**)!!!~'

(26 + 12) = (`-**38**) = RECIPROCAL (INVERSE/MIRROR) = (`-**83**) = **"FOUR `-YEARS `-AWAY from `-AGE of `-DEATH for ENGLISH/AMERICAN ACTRESS ELIZABETH TAYLOR (`-79)"!!!**~'

(62 + 21) = (`-**83**) = (8 x 3) = (`-**24**) = **ENGLISH/AMERICAN ACTRESS ELIZABETH TAYLOR** `-**DIED** this `-**MANY** `-**DAYS** `-**AWAY** from `-**HER** `-**BIRTH/DAY**!!!~'

`-**DIED** at the `-**AGE** of (`-**58**) = (5 + 8) = (`-**13**) = "A VERY PIVOTAL # `-NUMBER"!!!~'

FILM ACTOR RICHARD BURTON `-**BIRTHDAY** = (**11**/**10**/19/**25**) = (**11** + **10** + 19 + **25**) = (`-**65**) = RECIPROCAL (INVERSE/MIRROR) = (`-**56**) = "**TWO** `-**YEARS** `-**AWAY** from `-**AGE** of `-**DEATH** for FILM ACTOR RICHARD BURTON (`-**58**)"!!!~'

`-**AGE** of `-**DEATH** = (`-**58**) = RECIPROCAL (INVERSE/ MIRROR) = (`-**85**) = `-**DEATH/DAY** of (**8/5**) for FILM ACTOR RICHARD BURTON = (**AUGUST 5**[th])!!!~'

"WAS `-**BORN** in (`-**11**) (NOVEMBER); and, `-**DIED** in (`-**8**) (AUGUST)"; and, (**11/8**) = (NOVEMBER 8th) = (`-**2**) DAYS AWAY from `-HIS `-**BIRTH/DAY**!!!~' RECIPROCAL (INVERSE/ MIRROR) = (**8/11**) = (AUGUST 11[th]) = (`-**6**) DAYS AWAY from `-HIS `-**DEATH/DAY**!!!~' (**2/6**) = (`-**26**) = RECIPROCAL (INVERSE/MIRROR) = (`-**62**) = (62 (-) 26) = (`-**36**) = RECIPROCAL (INVERSE/MIRROR) = (`-**63**) = (9 x 7) = (`-**97**) = **FILM ACTOR RICHARD BURTON** `-**DIED** this `-**MANY** `-**DAYS** `-**AWAY** from `-**HIS** `-**BIRTH/DAY**!!!~'

(**2/6**) = (`-**26**) = FRAGMENTED `-**BIRTH/DAY** # `-**NUMBER** for **ENGLISH/AMERICAN ACTRESS ELIZABETH TAYLOR** (`-**26**)!!!~'

(19_25) = "FLIP the (`-**9**) OVER to a (`-**6**)" = (16_25) = (6 (-) 1) (2 + 5) = (`-**57**) = "**ONE `-YEAR `-AWAY from `-AGE of `-DEATH for FILM ACTOR RICHARD BURTON (`-58)**"!!!~'

FILM ACTOR RICHARD BURTON `-**DEATH/DAY** = (**8**/**5**/19/**84**) = (**8** + **5** + 19 + **84**) = (`-**116**) = (`-**116**) / `-*DIVIDED by* (`-**2**) = (`-**58**) = `-**AGE of `-DEATH for FILM ACTOR RICHARD BURTON (`-58)**"!!!~'

`-**DEATH/DAY** = (`-**85**) = (8 + 5) = (`-**13**) = "A VERY PIVOTAL # `-NUMBER"!!!~'

`-**DEATH/YEAR** = (`-**84**) = `-**NEAR `-DEATH/DAY** = (`-**85**)!!!~'

`-**DEATH/DAY** # `-**NUMBER** in `-**REVERSE** = (84 (-) 19 (-) 5 (-) 8) = (`-**52**) = RECIPROCAL (INVERSE/MIRROR) = (`-**25**) = `-**BIRTH/YEAR** for FILM ACTOR RICHARD BURTON (`-**25**)"!!!~'

`-**DEATH/YEAR** = (`-**19/84**) = (84 (-) 19) = (`-**65**) = `-**BIRTH/ DAY** # `-**NUMBER** for FILM ACTOR RICHARD BURTON (`-**65**)"!!!~'

(116 (-) 65) = (`-**51**) = "**SEVEN `-YEARS `-AWAY from `-AGE of `-DEATH for FILM ACTOR RICHARD BURTON (`-58)**"!!!~'

(116 + 65) = (`-**181**) = (`-**18**) = RECIPROCAL (INVERSE/ MIRROR) = (`-**81**)!!!~'

(81 (-) 18) = (`-**63**) = (9 x 7) = (`-**97**) = **FILM ACTOR RICHARD BURTON `-DIED this `-MANY `-DAYS `-AWAY from `-HIS `-BIRTH/DAY!!!~'**

(181 (-) 51) = (`-**130**) = (13 + 0) = (`-**13**) = "A VERY PIVOTAL # `-NUMBER"!!!~'

(181 + 51) = (`-**232**) = **RECIPROCAL-SEQUENCING-NUMEROLOGY-RSN!!!~'**

FILM ACTOR RICHARD BURTON `-**DIED** (`-**97**) DAYS AWAY from `-**HIS** `-**BIRTHDAY!!!~'**

(365 (-) 97) = (`-**268**) = (68 x 2) = (`-**136**) = (36 x 1) = (`-**36**) = RECIPROCAL (INVERSE/MIRROR) = (`-**63**) = (9 x 7) = (`-**97**) = **FILM ACTOR RICHARD BURTON** `-**DIED** this `-**MANY** `-**DAYS** `-**AWAY** from `-**HIS** `-**BIRTH/DAY!!!~'**

FRAGMENTED `-**BIRTH/DAY** # `-**NUMBER** = (1 + 1 + 1 + 0 + 1 + 9 + 2 + 5) = (`-**20**) = RECIPROCAL (INVERSE/MIRROR) = (`-**02**)!!!~'

FRAGMENTED `-**DEATH/DAY** # `-**NUMBER** = (8 + 5 + 1 + 9 + 8 + 4) = (`-**35**) = RECIPROCAL (INVERSE/MIRROR) = (`-**53**) = **"FIVE `-YEARS `-AWAY from `-AGE of `-DEATH for FILM ACTOR RICHARD BURTON (`-58)"!!!~'**

(20 + 35) = (`-**55**) = (`-**23**) + (`-**32**)!!!~'

`-**DIED** at the `-**AGE** of (`-**83**)!!!~'

AMERICAN ACTRESS GINGER ROGERS `-**BIRTHDAY** = (**7/16**/19/**11**) = (**7** + **16** + 19 + **11**) = (`-**53**) = RECIPROCAL (INVERSE/MIRROR) = (`-**35**)!!!~'

(53 + 35) = (`-**88**) = **"FIVE `-YEARS `-AWAY from `-AGE of `-DEATH for AMERICAN ACTRESS GINGER ROGERS (`-83)"!!!~'**

`-**BIRTH/DAY** = (**7/16**) = "FLIP the (`-**6**) OVER to a (`-**9**)" = (**7/19**) = RECIPROCAL (INVERSE/MIRROR) = (**91/7**) = (91 (-) 7) =

(`-84) = "ONE `-YEAR `-AWAY from `-AGE of `-DEATH for AMERICAN ACTRESS GINGER ROGERS (`-83)"!!!~'

`-BIRTH/DAY = (7/16) = (71 + 6) = (`-77) = "SIX `-YEARS `-AWAY from `-AGE of `-DEATH for AMERICAN ACTRESS GINGER ROGERS (`-83)"!!!~'

`-BIRTH/DAY = (7/16) = (7 + 16) = (`-23) = -a PROPHETIC # `-NUMBER!!!~'

"WAS `-BORN in (`-7) (JULY); and, `-DIED in (`-4) (APRIL)"; and, (7/4) = (JULY 4th) = (`-12) DAYS AWAY from `-HER `-BIRTH/DAY!!!~' RECIPROCAL (INVERSE/MIRROR) = (4/7) = (APRIL 7th) = (`-18) DAY AWAY from `-HER `-DEATH/DAY!!!~' (12/18) = RECIPROCAL (INVERSE/MIRROR) = (18/12) = (82 x 1 + 1) = (`-83) = `-AGE of `-DEATH for AMERICAN ACTRESS GINGER ROGERS (`-83)"!!!~'

(1911) = (9 (-) 1) (1 + 1) = `-EQUALS = (`-82) = "ONE `-YEAR `-AWAY from `-AGE of `-DEATH for AMERICAN ACTRESS GINGER ROGERS (`-83)"!!!~'

AMERICAN ACTRESS GINGER ROGERS `-DEATH/DAY = (4/25/19/95) = (4 + 25 + 19 + 95) = (`-143) = (43 x 1) = (`-43)!!!~'

`-DEATH/DAY = (`-4/25) = (4) (2 (-) 5) = (`-43)!!!~'

(43 + 43) = (`-86) = RECIPROCAL (INVERSE/MIRROR) = (`-68) = "The `-MARK"!!!~'

`-DEATH/DAY = (`-4/25) = (ALL-IN-ONE-#-NUMBER) = (4 x 2) (5) = (`-85) = "TWO `-YEARS `-AWAY from `-AGE of `-DEATH for AMERICAN ACTRESS GINGER ROGERS (`-83)"!!!~'

`-DEATH/YEAR = (`-19/95) = (95 (-) 19) = (`-76) = `-BIRTH/
DAY for AMERICAN ACTRESS GINGER ROGERS (`-7/16) =
(76 x 1) = (`-76)!!!~'

`-DEATH/DAY = (`-4/25) = (ALL-IN-ONE-#-NUMBER) = (4)
(2 + 5) = (`-47)!!!~'

`-DEATH/DAY # `-NUMBER in `-REVERSE = (95 (-) 19 (-) 25
(-) 4) = (`-47) = RECIPROCAL (INVERSE/MIRROR) = (`-74) =
"WAS `-BORN in (`-7); and, `-DIED in (`-4)"!!!~'

(143 (-) 53) = (`-90) = "SEVEN `-YEARS `-AWAY from `-AGE
of `-DEATH for AMERICAN ACTRESS GINGER ROGERS
(`-83)"!!!~'

(143 + 53) = (`-196) = (ALL-IN-ONE-#-NUMBER) = (1 (-) 9) (6)
= (`-86) = "THREE `-YEARS `-AWAY from `-AGE of `-DEATH
for AMERICAN ACTRESS GINGER ROGERS (`-83)"!!!~'

(196 + 90) = (`-286) = (86 (-) 2) = (`-84) = "ONE `-YEAR `-AWAY
from `-AGE of `-DEATH for AMERICAN ACTRESS GINGER
ROGERS (`-83)"!!!~'

AMERICAN ACTRESS GINGER ROGERS `-DIED (`-82) DAYS
AWAY from `-HER `-BIRTHDAY!!!~' (`-82) = "ONE `-YEAR
`-AWAY from `-AGE of `-DEATH for AMERICAN ACTRESS
GINGER ROGERS (`-83)"!!!~'

(365 (-) 82) = (`-283) = (28 x 3) = (`-84) = "ONE `-YEAR `-AWAY
from `-AGE of `-DEATH for AMERICAN ACTRESS GINGER
ROGERS (`-83)"!!!~'

FRAGMENTED `-BIRTH/DAY # `-NUMBER = (7 + 1 + 6 + 1 + 9
+ 1 + 1) = (`-26) = RECIPROCAL (INVERSE/MIRROR) = (`-62)!!!~'

(26 + 26) = (`-**52**) = RECIPROCAL (INVERSE/MIRROR) = (`-**25**) = `-**DAY** of `-**DEATH** (`-**25**th)!!!~'

`-**BIRTH/DAY** = (**7/16**)

`-**DEATH/DAY** = (**4/25**)

(7 + 16 + 4 + 25) = (`-**52**) = RECIPROCAL (INVERSE/MIRROR) = (`-**25**) = `-**DAY** of `-**DEATH** (`-**25**th)!!!~'

(26 + 62) = (`-**88**) = "**FIVE `-YEARS `-AWAY from `-AGE of `-DEATH for AMERICAN ACTRESS GINGER ROGERS (`-83)**"!!!~'

/|\ FRAGMENTED `-**DEATH/DAY** # `-**NUMBER** = (4 + 2 + 5 + 1 + 9 + 9 + 5) = (`-**35**) = RECIPROCAL (INVERSE/MIRROR) = (`-**53**) = `-**BIRTH/DAY** # `-**NUMBER for AMERICAN ACTRESS GINGER ROGERS** (`-**53**)!!!~'

AMERICAN ACTRESS GINGER ROGERS `-DEATH/DAY** # `-NUMBER** = (`-**143**) = (**ALL-IN-ONE-#-NUMBER**) = (1 + 4) (3) = (`-**53**)!!!~' /|\

(26 + 35) = (`-**61**) = RECIPROCAL (INVERSE/MIRROR) = (`-**16**)!!!~'

`-**DIED** at the `-**AGE** of (`-**88**)!!!~'

AMERICAN ACTOR FRED ASTAIRE `-**BIRTHDAY** = (**5/10**/18/**99**) = (**5** + **10** + 18 + **99**) = (`-**132**) = (32 x 1) = (`-**32**) = -a PROPHETIC # `-NUMBER!!!~'

`-AGE of `-DEATH = (`-88) = (8 x 8) = (`-64) = `-DEATH/ DAY = (`-6/22) = (6) (2 + 2) = (`-64) = (`-2) x (`-32) = (`-232) = RECIPROCAL-SEQUENCING-NUMEROLOGY-RSN!!!~'

`-BIRTH/DAY # `-NUMBER in `-REVERSE = (99 (-) 18 (-) 10 (-) 5) = (`-66) = RECIPROCAL (INVERSE/MIRROR) = (`-99) = `-BIRTH/YEAR for AMERICAN ACTOR FRED ASTAIRE (`-99)!!!~'

"WAS `-BORN in (`-5) (MAY); and, `-DIED in (`-6) (JUNE)"; and, (5/6) = (MAY 6th) = (`-4) DAYS AWAY from `-HIS `-BIRTH/ DAY!!!~' RECIPROCAL (INVERSE/MIRROR) = (6/5) = (JUNE 5th) = (`-17) DAYS AWAY from `-HIS `-DEATH/DAY!!!~' (4/17) = RECIPROCAL (INVERSE/MIRROR) = (17/4) = (ALL-IN-ONE-#-NUMBER) = (1 + 7) (4) = (`-84) = "FOUR `-YEARS `-AWAY from `-AGE of `-DEATH for AMERICAN ACTOR FRED ASTAIRE (`-88)"!!!~'

(17/4) = (17 x 4) = (`-68) = "The `-MARK"!!!~'

(1899) = (1 + 8) (9 + 9) = (`-9/18) = (9 (-) 1) (8) = `-EQUALS = (`-88) = `-AGE of `-DEATH for AMERICAN ACTOR FRED ASTAIRE (`-88)"!!!~'

AMERICAN ACTOR FRED ASTAIRE `-DEATH/DAY = (6/22/19/87) = (6 + 22 + 19 + 87) = (`-134)!!!~'

/|\ `-DEATH/DAY = (6/22) = (6 + 22) = (`-28) = 2(8's) = (`-88) = `-AGE of `-DEATH for AMERICAN ACTOR FRED ASTAIRE (`-88)"!!!~'

`-DEATH/DAY = (6/22) = (6 x 22) = (`-132) = `-BIRTH/DAY # `-NUMBER for AMERICAN ACTOR FRED ASTAIRE (`-132)!!!~'

`-**DEATH/YEAR** = (`-**19/87**) = (87 (-) 19) = (`-**68**) = "The `-**MARK**"!!!~' /|\

(134 (-) 132) = (`-**2**)!!!~'

(134 + 132) = (`-**266**) = (**ALL-IN-ONE-#-NUMBER**) = (2 + 6) (6) = (`-**86**) = "TWO `-YEARS `-AWAY from `-AGE of `-DEATH for AMERICAN ACTOR FRED ASTAIRE (`-**88**)"!!!~'

(`-**266**) = (26 x 6) = (`-**156**) = (56 x 1) = (`-**56**) = "WAS `-**BORN** in (`-**5**); and, `-**DIED** in (`-**6**) for AMERICAN ACTOR FRED ASTAIRE (`-**56**)"!!!~'

(266 + 2) = (`-**268**) = (**ALL-IN-ONE-#-NUMBER**) = (2 + 6) (8) = (`-**88**) = `-AGE of `-DEATH for AMERICAN ACTOR FRED ASTAIRE (`-**88**)"!!!~'

(266 (-) 2) = (`-**264**) = (**64** / `-*DIVIDED by* (`-**2**) = (`-**32**) = -a PROPHETIC # `-NUMBER!!!~'

AMERICAN ACTOR FRED ASTAIRE `-**DIED** (`-**43**) DAYS AWAY from `-**HIS** `-**BIRTHDAY**!!!~' (`-**43**) x (`-**2**) = (`-**86**) = RECIPROCAL (INVERSE/MIRROR) = (`-**68**) = "The `-**MARK**"!!!~'

(365 (-) 43) = (`-**322**) = (32 x 2) = (`-**64**) = (`-**2**) x (`-**32**) = (`-**232**) = **RECIPROCAL-SEQUENCING-NUMEROLOGY-RSN**!!!~'

/|\ FRAGMENTED `-**BIRTH/DAY** # `-NUMBER = (5 + 1 + 0 + 1 + 8 + 9 + 9) = (`-**33**) = (1 + 32) = (`-**132**) = `-**BIRTH/DAY** # `-**NUMBER** for AMERICAN ACTOR FRED ASTAIRE (`-**132**) = `-**DEATH/DAY** (*6 x 22*) = (`-**132**)!!!~' /|\

209

/|\ FRAGMENTED `-**DEATH/DAY** # `-**NUMBER** = (**6** + **2** + **2** + 1 + 9 + 8 + 7) = (`-**35**) = RECIPROCAL (INVERSE/MIRROR) = (`-**53**)!!!~'

(35 + 53) = (`-**88**) = `-**AGE of** `-**DEATH for AMERICAN ACTOR FRED ASTAIRE** (`-**88**)"!!!~' /|\

(33 + 35) = (`-**68**) = "The `-**MARK**"!!!~'

`-**DIED** at the `-**AGE** of (`-**43**)!!!~'

AMERICAN ACTRESS NATALIE WOOD `-**BIRTHDAY** = (**7/20**/19/**38**) = (**7** + **20** + 19 + **38**) = (`-**84**) = RECIPROCAL (INVERSE/MIRROR) = (`-**48**) = "**FIVE** `-**YEARS** `-**AWAY from** `-**AGE of** `-**DEATH for AMERICAN ACTRESS NATALIE WOOD** (`-**43**)"!!!~'

(84 + 48) = (`-**132**) = (32 x 1) = (`-**32**) = -a PROPHETIC # `-**NUMBER!!!**~'

`-**BIRTH/DAY** = (**7/20**) = (7 + 20) = (`-**27**) = `-**DEATH/DAY** = (**11/29**) = RECIPROCAL (INVERSE/MIRROR) = (**29/11**) = (29 (-) 1 (-) 1) = (`-**27**)!!!~'

"WAS `-**BORN** in (`-**7**) (JULY); and, `-**DIED** in (`-**11**) (NOVEMBER)"; and, (**7/11**) = (JULY 11th) = (`-**9**) DAYS AWAY from `-HER `-**BIRTH/DAY!!!**~' RECIPROCAL (INVERSE/ MIRROR) = (**11/7**) = (NOVEMBER 7th) = (`-**22**) DAY AWAY from `-HER `-**DEATH/DAY!!!**~' (**9/22**) = (**92** / `-**DIVIDED** `-**by** (`-**2**) = (`-**46**) = "**THREE** `-**YEARS** `-**AWAY from** `-**AGE of** `-**DEATH for AMERICAN ACTRESS NATALIE WOOD** (`-**43**)"!!!~'

(`-92) = RECIPROCAL (INVERSE/MIRROR) = (`-29) = "**DAY of `-DEATH** (`-29ᵗʰ)"!!!~'

(19**38**) = (1 + 3) (9 (-) 8) = `-*EQUALS* = (`-**41**) = "**TWO `-YEARS `-AWAY from `-AGE of `-DEATH for AMERICAN ACTRESS NATALIE WOOD** (`-**43**)"!!!~'

AMERICAN ACTRESS NATALIE WOOD `-**DEATH/DAY** = (**11/29**/19/**81**) = (**11** + **29** + 19 + **81**) = (`-**140**) = (40 x 1) = (`-**40**) = "**THREE `-YEARS `-AWAY from `-AGE of `-DEATH for AMERICAN ACTRESS NATALIE WOOD** (`-**43**)"!!!~'

`-**DEATH/DAY** = (`-**11/29**) = (11 + 29) = (`-**40**) = "**THREE `-YEARS `-AWAY from `-AGE of `-DEATH for AMERICAN ACTRESS NATALIE WOOD** (`-**43**)"!!!~'

(43 + 43) = (`-**86**) = RECIPROCAL (INVERSE/MIRROR) = (`-**68**) = "**The `-MARK**"!!!~'

(140 (-) 84) = (`-**56**) = RECIPROCAL (INVERSE/MIRROR) = (`-**65**)!!!~'

(140 + 84) = (`-**224**) = (**ALL-IN-ONE-#-NUMBER**) = (2 + 2) (4) = (`-**44**) = "**ONE `-YEAR `-AWAY from `-AGE of `-DEATH for AMERICAN ACTRESS NATALIE WOOD** (`-**43**)"!!!~'

(224 + 56) = (`-**280**) = (**80** / `-*DIVIDED* `-*by* (`-**2**) = (`-**40**) = "**THREE `-YEARS `-AWAY from `-AGE of `-DEATH for AMERICAN ACTRESS NATALIE WOOD** (`-**43**)"!!!~'

(224 (-) 56) = (`-**168**) = "**The `-MARK**"!!!~'

AMERICAN ACTRESS NATALIE WOOD `-**DIED** (`-**132**) DAYS AWAY from `-**HER `-BIRTHDAY**!!!~' (`-**132**) = (32 x 1) = (`-**32**) = -a PROPHETIC # `-**NUMBER**!!!~'

(365 (-) 132) = ('-**233**) = RECIPROCAL (INVERSE/MIRROR) = ('-**332**) = ('-32) x ('-**3**) = RECIPROCAL-**S**EQUENCING-**N**UMEROLOGY-**RSN**!!!~'

(365 (-) 132) = ('-**233**) = (23 x 3) = ('-**69**) = "**YIN/YANG**" = "The '-**CYCLE** of '-**LIFE**"!!!~'

FRAGMENTED '-**BIRTH/DAY** # '-**NUMBER** = (7 + 2 + 0 + 1 + 9 + 3 + 8) = ('-**30**) = RECIPROCAL (INVERSE/MIRROR) = ('-**03**)!!!~'

(30 + 03) = ('-**33**) = (1 + 32) = ('-**132**) = **AMERICAN ACTRESS NATALIE WOOD** '-**DIED** this '-**MANY** '-**DAYS** '-**AWAY** from '-**HER** '-**BIRTH/DAY**!!!~'

'-**BIRTH/DAY** = (**7/20**)

'-**DEATH/DAY** = (**11/29**)

(7 + 20 + 11 + 29) = ('-**67**) = (6 x 7) = ('-**42**) = "The '-**MARK**"!!!~'

FRAGMENTED '-**DEATH/DAY** # '-**NUMBER** = (1 + 1 + 2 + 9 + 1 + 9 + 8 + 1) = ('-**32**) = (1 x 32) = ('-**132**) = **AMERICAN ACTRESS NATALIE WOOD** '-**DIED** this '-**MANY** '-**DAYS** '-**AWAY** from '-**HER** '-**BIRTH/DAY**!!!~'

FRAGMENTED '-**DEATH/DAY** # '-**NUMBER** = (1 + 1 + 2 + 9 + 1 + 9 + 8 + 1) = ('-**32**) = RECIPROCAL (INVERSE/MIRROR) = ('-**23**) = -a PROPHETIC # '-**NUMBER**!!!~'

(30 + 32) = ('-**62**) = '-**DEATH/YEAR** = (19 (-) 81)!!!~'

(30 + 32) = (`-**62**) = RECIPROCAL (INVERSE/MIRROR) = (`-**26**) = "FLIP the (`-**6**) OVER to a (`-**9**)" = (`-**29**) = `-**DAY** of `-**DEATH** (`-**29**ᵗʰ)!!!~'

`-**DIED** at the `-**AGE** of (`-**86**)!!!~'

AMERICAN ACTOR JAMES CAGNEY `-**BIRTHDAY** = (**7**/**17**/18/**99**) = (**7** + **17** + 18 + **99**) = (`-**141**) = **RECIPROCAL-SEQUENCING-NUMEROLOGY-RSN**!!!~'

`-**AGE** of `-**DEATH** = (`-**86**) = `-**DEATH/YEAR** = (`-**86**)!!!~'

`-**BIRTH/DAY** = (`-**7/17**) = **RECIPROCAL-SEQUENCING-NUMEROLOGY-RSN**!!!~'

`-**BIRTH/DAY** = (`-**7/17**) = (**ALL-IN-ONE-#-NUMBER**) = (7 + 1) (7) = (`-**87**) = "ONE `-**YEAR** `-**AWAY** from `-**AGE** of `-**DEATH** for AMERICAN ACTOR JAMES CAGNEY (`-**86**)"!!!~'

`-**BIRTH/YEAR** = (`-**18/99**) = (99 (-) 18) = (`-**81**) = "FIVE `-**YEARS** `-**AWAY** from `-**AGE** of `-**DEATH** for AMERICAN ACTOR JAMES CAGNEY (`-**86**)"!!!~'

"WAS `-**BORN** in (`-**7**) (JULY); and, `-**DIED** in (`-**3**) (MARCH)"; and, (**7/3**) = (JULY 3ʳᵈ) = (`-**14**) DAYS AWAY from `-HIS `-**BIRTH/DAY**!!!~' RECIPROCAL (INVERSE/MIRROR) = (**3/7**) = (MARCH 7ᵗʰ) = (`-**23**) DAYS AWAY from `-HIS `-**DEATH/DAY**!!!~' (**14/23**) = (14 + 23) = (`-**37**) = RECIPROCAL (INVERSE/MIRROR) = (`-**73**) = "WAS `-**BORN** in (`-**7**); and, `-**DIED** in (`-**3**)"!!!~'

(**18**99) = (1 + 8) (9 + 9) = (`-**9/18**) = "FLIP the (`-**9**) OVER to a (`-**6**)" = (`-**6/18**) = RECIPROCAL (INVERSE/MIRROR) = (`-**18/6**) =

(86 x 1) = (`-**86**) = `-**AGE** of `-**DEATH** for **AMERICAN ACTOR JAMES CAGNEY** (`-**86**)"!!!~'

AMERICAN ACTOR JAMES CAGNEY `-**DEATH/DAY** = (**3**/**30**/19/**86**) = (**3** + **30** + 19 + **86**) = (`-**138**) = RECIPROCAL (INVERSE/MIRROR) = (`-**831**) = (83 + 1) = (`-**84**) = "TWO `-YEARS `-AWAY from `-AGE of `-DEATH for AMERICAN ACTOR JAMES CAGNEY (`-**86**)"!!!~'

`-**DEATH/YEAR** = (`-**19/86**) = (86 (-) 19) = (`-**67**) = (6 x 7) = (`-**42**) = "The `-**MARK**"!!!~'

(141 (-) 138) = (`-**3**)!!!~'

(141 + 138) = (`-**279**) = (79 x 2) = (`-**158**) = RECIPROCAL (INVERSE/MIRROR) = (`-**851**) = (85 + 1) = (`-**86**) = `-**AGE** of `-**DEATH** for **AMERICAN ACTOR JAMES CAGNEY** (`-**86**)"!!!~'

(279 + 3) = (`-**282**) = **RECIPROCAL-SEQUENCING-NUMEROLOGY-RSN**!!!~'

(279 + 3) = (`-**282**) = (82 + 2) = (`-**84**) = "TWO `-YEARS `-AWAY from `-AGE of `-DEATH for AMERICAN ACTOR JAMES CAGNEY (`-**86**)"!!!~'

(279 + 3) = (`-**282**) = `-*DIVIDED* `-*by* (`-**2**) = (`-**141**) = `-**BIRTH/DAY # `-NUMBER** for **AMERICAN ACTOR JAMES CAGNEY** (`-**141**)!!!~'

AMERICAN ACTOR JAMES CAGNEY `-**DIED** (`-**109**) DAYS AWAY from `-**HIS `-BIRTHDAY**!!!~' (`-**109**) = (10 x 9) = (`-**90**) = "FOUR `-YEARS `-AWAY from `-AGE of `-DEATH for **AMERICAN ACTOR JAMES CAGNEY** (`-**86**)"!!!~'

(365 (-) 109) = (`-**256**) = (**ALL-IN-ONE-#-NUMBER**) = (2 + 6) (5)
= (`-**85**) = "ONE `-YEAR `-AWAY from `-AGE of `-DEATH for
AMERICAN ACTOR JAMES CAGNEY (`-**86**)"!!!~'

FRAGMENTED `-**BIRTH/DAY** # `-NUMBER = (7 + 1 + 7 + 1
+ 8 + 9 + 9) = (`-**42**) = "The `-**MARK**"!!!~'

FRAGMENTED `-**BIRTH/DAY** # `-NUMBER = (7 + 1 + 7 + 1
+ 8 + 9 + 9) = (`-**42**) = RECIPROCAL (INVERSE/MIRROR) =
(`-**24**) = `-**BIRTH/DAY** (7 + 17) = (`-**24**)!!!~'

FRAGMENTED `-**DEATH/DAY** # `-NUMBER = (3 + **3** + **0** + 1
+ 9 + 8 + 6) = (`-**30**) = "**DAY** of `-**DEATH** (`-**30**th)"!!!~'

FRAGMENTED `-**DEATH/DAY** # `-NUMBER = (3 + 3 + 0 +
1 + 9 + 8 + 6) = (`-**30**) = RECIPROCAL (INVERSE/MIRROR)
= (`-**03**)!!!~'

(42 + 30) = (`-**72**) = RECIPROCAL (INVERSE/MIRROR) =
(`-**27**)!!!~'

(72 + 27) = (`-**99**) = `-**BIRTH/YEAR** for AMERICAN ACTOR
JAMES CAGNEY (`-**99**)!!!~'

`-**DIED** at the `-**AGE** of (`-**57**)!!!~'

AMERICAN ACTOR HUMPHREY BOGART `-**BIRTHDAY**
= (**12/25**/18/**99**) = (**12** + **25** + 18 + **99**) = (`-**154**) = (54 + 1) = (`-**55**) = "TWO `-YEARS `-AWAY from `-AGE of `-DEATH for
AMERICAN ACTOR HUMPHREY BOGART (`-**57**)"!!!~'

`-**AGE** of `-**DEATH** = (`-**57**) = `-**DEATH/YEAR** = (`-**57**)!!!~'

`-**BIRTH/DAY** = (`-**12/25**) = (25 (-) 12) = (`-**13**) = "A VERY PIVOTAL # `-NUMBER"!!!-'

`-**DAY** of `-**BIRTH** = (`-**25**[th]) = RECIPROCAL (INVERSE/ MIRROR) = (`-**52**) = "FLIP the (`-**2**) OVER to a (`-**7**)" = (`-**57**) = `-**AGE of `-DEATH for AMERICAN ACTOR HUMPHREY BOGART** (`-**57**)"!!!-'

"WAS `-**BORN** in (`-**12**) (DECEMBER); and, `-**DIED** in (`-**1**) (JANUARY)"; and, (**12/1**) = (DECEMBER 1st) = (`-**24**) DAYS AWAY from `-HIS `-**BIRTH/DAY!!!-'** RECIPROCAL (INVERSE/MIRROR) = (**1/12**) = (JANUARY 12[th]) = (`-**2**) DAYS AWAY from `-HIS `-**DEATH/DAY!!!-'** (**24/2**) = (`-**242**) = **RECIPROCAL-SEQUENCING-NUMEROLOGY-RSN!!!-'**

(18**99**) = "FLIP the (`-**9**) OVER to a (`-**6**)" = (18**66**) = (1 (-) 6) (8 (-) 6) = (`-**5/2**) = "FLIP the (`-**2**) OVER to a (`-**7**)" = (`-**57**) = `-**AGE of `-DEATH for AMERICAN ACTOR HUMPHREY BOGART** (`-**57**)"!!!-'

AMERICAN ACTOR HUMPHREY BOGART `-**DEATH/DAY** = (**1/14**/19/**57**) = (**1** + **14** + 19 + **57**) = (`-**91**) = "FLIP the (`-**9**) OVER to a (`-**6**)" = (`-**61**) = **"FOUR `-YEARS `-AWAY from `-AGE of `-DEATH for AMERICAN ACTOR HUMPHREY BOGART** (`-**57**)"!!!-'

`-**DEATH/DAY** = (**1/14**) = (14 (-) 1) = (`-**13**) = "A VERY PIVOTAL # `-NUMBER"!!!-'

`-**DEATH/DAY** # `-**NUMBER in `-REVERSE** = (57 (-) 19 (-) 14 (-) 1) = (`-**23**) = -a PROPHETIC # `-NUMBER!!!-'

`-**DEATH/YEAR** = (`-**19/57**) = (19 + 57) = (`-**76**) = (7 x 6) = (`-**42**) = "The `-**MARK**"!!!-'

(154 (-) 91) = (`-**63**) = "SIX `-YEARS `-AWAY from `-AGE of `-DEATH for AMERICAN ACTOR HUMPHREY BOGART (`-**57**)"!!!~'

(154 + 91) = (`-**245**) = RECIPROCAL (INVERSE/MIRROR) = (`-**542**) = (54 + 2) = (`-**56**) = "ONE `-YEAR `-AWAY from `-AGE of `-DEATH for AMERICAN ACTOR HUMPHREY BOGART (`-**57**)"!!!~'

(245 (-) 63) = (`-**182**) = (**ALL-IN-ONE-#-NUMBER**) = (8 (-) 2) (1) = (`-**61**) = "FOUR `-YEARS `-AWAY from `-AGE of `-DEATH for AMERICAN ACTOR HUMPHREY BOGART (`-**57**)"!!!~'

AMERICAN ACTOR HUMPHREY BOGART `-**DIED** (`-**20**) DAYS AWAY from `-**HIS** `-**BIRTHDAY!!!**~'

(365 (-) 20) = (`-**345**) = RECIPROCAL (INVERSE/MIRROR) = (`-**543**) = (**ALL-IN-ONE-#-NUMBER**) = (5) (4 + 3) = (`-**57**) = `-AGE of `-DEATH for AMERICAN ACTOR HUMPHREY BOGART (`-**57**)"!!!~'

`-**BIRTH/DAY** = (**12/25**) = (12 + 25) = (`-**37**) = FRAGMENTED `-**BIRTH/DAY** # `-NUMBER (`-**37**)!!!~'

FRAGMENTED `-**BIRTH/DAY** # `-NUMBER = (1 + 2 + 2 + 5 + 1 + 8 + 9 + 9) = (`-**37**) = RECIPROCAL (INVERSE/MIRROR) = (`-**73**)!!!~'

FRAGMENTED `-**DEATH/DAY** # `-NUMBER = (1 + 1 + 4 + 1 + 9 + 5 + 7) = (`-**28**) = RECIPROCAL (INVERSE/MIRROR) = (`-**82**)!!!~'

(82 (-) 28) = (`-**54**) = "THREE `-YEARS `-AWAY from `-AGE of `-DEATH for AMERICAN ACTOR HUMPHREY BOGART (`-**57**)"!!!~'

(82 (-) 28) = (`-**54**) = (`-**154**) = `-**BIRTH/DAY** # `-**NUMBER** for AMERICAN ACTOR HUMPHREY BOGART (`-**154**)!!!~'

(37 + 28) = (`-**65**) = RECIPROCAL (INVERSE/MIRROR) = (`-**56**) = "ONE `-YEAR `-AWAY from `-AGE of `-DEATH for AMERICAN ACTOR HUMPHREY BOGART (`-**57**)"!!!~'

`-**DIED** at the `-**AGE** of (`-**89**)!!!~'

AMERICAN ACTRESS LAUREN BACALL `-**BIRTHDAY** = (**9/16**/19/**24**) = (**9** + **16** + 19 + **24**) = (`-**68**) = "The `-**MARK**"!!!~'

`-**AGE** of `-**DEATH**= (`-**89**) = (8 x 9) = (`-**72**) = `-**DEATH/DAY** = (**8/12**) = (**ALL-IN-ONE-#-NUMBER**) = (8 (-) 1) (2) = (`-**72**)!!!~'

`-**BIRTH/DAY** = (**9/16**) = (**ALL-IN-ONE-#-NUMBER**) = (9 (-) 1) 6) = (`-**86**) = "FLIP the (`-**6**) OVER to a (`-**9**)" = (`-**89**) = `-**AGE** of `-**DEATH** (`-**89**)!!!~'

`-**BIRTH/YEAR** = (`-**1924**) = (19 + 24) = (`-**43**) = RECIPROCAL (INVERSE/MIRROR) = (`-**34**) = `-**DEATH/YEAR** = (20 + 14) = (`-**34**)!!!~'

"WAS `-**BORN** in (`-**9**) (SEPTEMBER); and, `-**DIED** in (`-**8**) (AUGUST)"; and, (**9/8**) = (SEPTEMBER 8th) = (`-**8**) DAYS AWAY from `-HER `-**BIRTH/DAY**!!!~' RECIPROCAL (INVERSE/MIRROR) = (**8/9**) = (AUGUST 9[th]) = (`-**3**) DAY AWAY from `-HER `-**DEATH/DAY**!!!~' (**8/3**) = "SIX `-YEARS `-AWAY from `-AGE

of `-DEATH for AMERICAN ACTRESS LAUREN BACALL (`-89)"!!!~'

(19̲24) = (9 (-) 1) (2 + 4) = `-EQUALS = (`-86) = "FLIP the (`-6) OVER to a (`-9)" = (`-89) = `-AGE of `-DEATH for AMERICAN ACTRESS LAUREN BACALL (`-89)"!!!~'

AMERICAN ACTRESS LAUREN BACALL `-**DEATH/DAY** = (8/12̲/20/14̲) = (8̲ + 12̲ + 20 + 14̲) = (`-54̲) = RECIPROCAL (INVERSE/MIRROR) = (`-45̲) = "SEE `-**BELOW**"!!!~'

`-**BIRTH/DAY** = (9/16̲)!!!~'

`-**DEATH/DAY** = (8/12̲)!!!~'

(9 + 16 + 8 + 12) = (`-45̲) = "SEE `-**ABOVE**"!!!~'

`-**DEATH/DAY** = (`-8/12̲) = (81 + 2) = (`-83̲) = "SIX `-YEARS `-AWAY from `-AGE of `-DEATH for AMERICAN ACTRESS LAUREN BACALL (`-89̲)"!!!~'

`-**DEATH/DAY** = (`-8/12̲) = (8 x 12) = (`-96̲) = "SEVEN `-YEARS `-AWAY from `-AGE of `-DEATH for AMERICAN ACTRESS LAUREN BACALL (`-89̲)"!!!~'

`-**DEATH/DAY** = (`-8/12̲) = "FLIP the (`-2̲) OVER to a (`-7̲)" = (`-8/17̲) = (81 + 7) = (`-88̲) = "ONE `-YEAR `-AWAY from `-AGE of `-DEATH for AMERICAN ACTRESS LAUREN BACALL (`-89̲)"!!!~'

(68 (-) 54) = (`-14̲)!!!~'

(68 + 54) = (`-122̲) = (22 + 1) = (`-23̲) = -a PROPHETIC # `-NUMBER!!!~'

(122 + 14) = (`-**136**) = (36 (-) 1) = (`-**35**) = AMERICAN ACTRESS LAUREN BACALL `-**DIED** (`-**35**) DAYS AWAY from `-HER `-BIRTHDAY!!!~'

(122 + 14) = (`-**136**) = (`-**136**) / `-*DIVIDED* `-*by* (`-**2**) = (`-**68**) = "The `-**MARK**"!!!~'

(122 (-) 14) = (`-**108**) = RECIPROCAL (INVERSE/MIRROR) = (`-**801**) = (80 + 1) = (`-**81**) = "EIGHT `-YEARS `-AWAY from `-AGE of `-DEATH for AMERICAN ACTRESS LAUREN BACALL (`-**89**)"!!!~'

AMERICAN ACTRESS LAUREN BACALL `-**DIED** (`-**35**) DAYS AWAY from `-HER `-BIRTHDAY!!!~'

(365 (-) 35) = (`-**330**) = (3 x 30) = (`-**90**) = "ONE `-YEAR `-AWAY from `-AGE of `-DEATH for AMERICAN ACTRESS LAUREN BACALL (`-**89**)"!!!~'

FRAGMENTED `-**BIRTH/DAY** # `-NUMBER = (9 + 1 + 6 + 1 + 9 + 2 + 4) = (`-**32**) = RECIPROCAL (INVERSE/MIRROR) = (`-**23**) = -a PROPHETIC # `-NUMBER!!!~'

FRAGMENTED `-**DEATH/DAY** # `-NUMBER = (8 + 1 + 2 + 2 + 0 + 1 + 4) = (`-**18**) = RECIPROCAL (INVERSE/MIRROR) = (`-**81**) = "EIGHT `-YEARS `-AWAY from `-AGE of `-DEATH for AMERICAN ACTRESS LAUREN BACALL (`-**89**)"!!!~'

(32 + 18) = (`-**50**) = (5 + 0) = (`-**5**) = "The `-**HAND** of `-**GOD**"!!!~'

(81 (-) 23) = (`-**58**) = RECIPROCAL (INVERSE/MIRROR) = (`-**85**) = "FOUR `-YEARS `-AWAY from `-AGE of `-DEATH for AMERICAN ACTRESS LAUREN BACALL (`-**89**)"!!!~'

`-**DIED** at the `-**AGE** of (`-**88**)!!!~'

AMERICAN ACTOR JAMES ARNESS `-**BIRTHDAY** = (**5**/**26**/19/**23**) = (**5** + **26** + 19 + **23**) = (`-**73**) = RECIPROCAL (INVERSE/MIRROR) = (`-**37**)!!!~'

(73 (-) 37) = (`-**36**) = RECIPROCAL (INVERSE/MIRROR) = (`-**63**) = `-**DEATH/DAY for AMERICAN ACTOR JAMES ARNESS (JUNE 3ʳᵈ)**!!!~'

`-**DAY** of `-**BIRTH** = (`-**26**ᵗʰ) = RECIPROCAL (INVERSE/ MIRROR) = (`-**62**)!!!~'

(26 + 62) = (`-**88**) = `-**AGE of `-DEATH for AMERICAN ACTOR JAMES ARNESS** (`-**88**)"!!!~'

`-**BIRTH/DAY** = (**5/26**) = RECIPROCAL (INVERSE/MIRROR) = (**62/5**) = (6) (2 (-) 5) = (`-**63**) = `-**DEATH/DAY for AMERICAN ACTOR JAMES ARNESS (JUNE 3ʳᵈ)**!!!~'

`-**BIRTH/YEAR** = (`-**23**) = -a PROPHETIC # `-NUMBER!!!~'

`-**BIRTH/YEAR** = (`-**19/23**) = (19 + 23) = (`-**42**) = "The `-**MARK**"!!!~'

`-**BIRTH/DAY** = (`-**5/26**) = (5 + 26) = (`-**31**) = RECIPROCAL (INVERSE/MIRROR) = (`-**13**) = "A VERY PIVOTAL # `-NUMBER"!!!~'

`-**BIRTH/DAY** = (`-**5/26**) = RECIPROCAL (INVERSE/ MIRROR) = (`-**62/5**) = (**ALL-IN-ONE-#-NUMBER**) = (6 + 2) (5) = (`-**85**) = "**THREE `-YEARS `-AWAY from `-AGE of `-DEATH for AMERICAN ACTOR JAMES ARNESS** (`-**88**)"!!!~'

"WAS `-**BORN** in (`-**5**) (MAY); and, `-**DIED** in (`-**6**) (JUNE)"; and, (**5/6**) = (MAY 6ᵗʰ) = (`-**20**) DAYS AWAY from `-HIS `-**BIRTH/DAY!!!**~' RECIPROCAL (INVERSE/MIRROR) = (**6/5**) = (JUNE 5ᵗʰ) = (`-**2**) DAYS AWAY from `-HIS `-**DEATH/DAY!!!**~' (**20/2**) = (`-**202**) = **RECIPROCAL-SEQUENCING-NUMEROLOGY-RSN!!!**~'

(**19**23) = (1 (-) 9) (2 + 3) = `-*EQUALS* = (`-**85**) = "THREE `-YEARS `-AWAY from `-AGE of `-DEATH for AMERICAN ACTOR JAMES ARNESS (`-**88**)"!!!~'

AMERICAN ACTOR JAMES ARNESS `-**DEATH/DAY** = (**6/3**/20/**11**) = (**6** + **3** + 20 + **11**) = (`-**40**)!!!~'

`-**DEATH/DAY** = (**6/3**) = (6 x 3) = (`-**18**) = RECIPROCAL (INVERSE/MIRROR) = (`-**81**) = "SEVEN `-YEARS `-AWAY from `-AGE of `-DEATH for AMERICAN ACTOR JAMES ARNESS (`-**88**)"!!!~'

`-**DEATH/YEAR** = (`-**20/11**) = (20 + 11) = (`-**31**) = RECIPROCAL (INVERSE/MIRROR) = (`-**13**) = "A VERY PIVOTAL # `-NUMBER"!!!~'

(73 (-) 40) = (`-**33**)!!!~'

(73 + 40) = (`-**113**) = (13 x 1) = (`-**13**) = "A VERY PIVOTAL # `-NUMBER"!!!~'

(113 (-) 33) = (`-**80**) = "EIGHT `-YEARS `-AWAY from `-AGE of `-DEATH for AMERICAN ACTOR JAMES ARNESS (`-**88**)"!!!~'

(113 + 33) = (`-**146**) = (46 x 1) = (`-**46**) = (`-**23**) x (`-**2**) = (`-**232**) = **RECIPROCAL-SEQUENCING-NUMEROLOGY-RSN!!!**~'

AMERICAN ACTOR JAMES ARNESS `-**DIED** (`-**8**) DAYS AWAY from `-**HIS** `-**BIRTHDAY!!!~'** (`-**8**) = `-**DIED at the** `-**AGE of** (`-**88**)!!!~'

(365 (-) 8) = (`-**357**) = (**ALL-IN-ONE-#-NUMBER**) = (3 + 5) (7) = (`-**87**) = "**ONE** `-**YEAR** `-**AWAY from** `-**AGE of** `-**DEATH for AMERICAN ACTOR JAMES ARNESS** (`-**88**)"!!!~'

/|\ FRAGMENTED `-**BIRTH/DAY** # `-**NUMBER** = (5 + 2 + 6 + 1 + 9 + 2 + 3) = (`-**28**) = 2(8's) = (`-**88**) = `-**AGE of** `-**DEATH for AMERICAN ACTOR JAMES ARNESS** (`-**88**)"!!!~' /|\

FRAGMENTED `-**BIRTH/DAY** # `-**NUMBER** = (5 + 2 + 6 + 1 + 9 + 2 + 3) = (`-**28**) = RECIPROCAL (INVERSE/MIRROR) = (`-**82**) = "**SIX** `-**YEARS** `-**AWAY from** `-**AGE of** `-**DEATH for AMERICAN ACTOR JAMES ARNESS** (`-**88**)"!!!~'

(82 (-) 28) = (`-**54**) = `-**BIRTH/DAY** = (**5/26**) = (5) (2 (-) 6) = (`-**54**)!!!~'

FRAGMENTED `-**DEATH/DAY** # `-**NUMBER** = (6 + 3 + 2 + 0 + 1 + 1) = (`-**13**) = "A VERY PIVOTAL # `-NUMBER"!!!~'

FRAGMENTED `-**DEATH/DAY** # `-**NUMBER** = (6 + 3 + 2 + 0 + 1 + 1) = (`-**13**) = RECIPROCAL (INVERSE/MIRROR) = (`-**31**) = `-**BIRTH/DAY** = (5 + 26) = (`-**31**)!!!~'

(28 + 13) = (`-**41**) = RECIPROCAL (INVERSE/MIRROR) = (`-**14**)!!!~'

(41 + 14) = (`-**55**) = (`-**23**) + (`-**32**)!!!~'

`-**DIED** at the `-**AGE** of (`-**81**)!!!~'

AMERICAN ACTOR DENNIS WEAVER `-**BIRTHDAY** = (**6**/**4**/19/**24**) = (**6** + **4** + 19 + **24**) = (`-**53**) = RECIPROCAL (INVERSE/MIRROR) = (`-**35**)!!!~'

/|\ (53 (-) 35) = (`-**18**) = RECIPROCAL (INVERSE/MIRROR) = (`-**81**) = `-**AGE of** `-**DEATH for AMERICAN ACTOR DENNIS WEAVER** (`-**81**)"!!!~' /|\

`-**BIRTH/DAY** = (**6**/**4**) = (6 x 4) = (`-**24**) = `-**DAY of** `-**DEATH** (`-**24**th) **for AMERICAN ACTOR DENNIS WEAVER** (`-**24**) = `-**BIRTH/YEAR for AMERICAN ACTOR DENNIS WEAVER** = (`-**24**)!!!~'

`-**BIRTH/DAY** = (**6**/**4**) = (`-**64**) = (`-**2**) x (`-**32**) = (`-**232**) = **R**ECIPROCAL-**S**EQUENCING-**N**UMEROLOGY-**RSN**!!!~'

"WAS `-**BORN** in (`-**6**) (JUNE); and, `-**DIED** in (`-**2**) (FEBRUARY)"; and, (**6**/**2**) = (JUNE 2nd) = (`-**2**) DAYS AWAY from `-HIS `-**BIRTH/DAY**!!!~' RECIPROCAL (INVERSE/MIRROR) = (**2**/**6**) = (FEBRUARY 6th) = (`-**18**) DAYS AWAY from `-HIS `-**DEATH/DAY**!!!~' (**2**/**18**) = RECIPROCAL (INVERSE/MIRROR) = (**18**/**2**) = (82 (-) 1) = (`-**81**) = `-**AGE of** `-**DEATH for AMERICAN ACTOR DENNIS WEAVER** (`-**81**)"!!!~'

(**19**24) = (1 (-) 9) (2 (-) 4) = `-**EQUALS** = (`-**82**) = "**ONE** `-**YEAR** `-**AWAY from** `-**AGE of** `-**DEATH for AMERICAN ACTOR DENNIS WEAVER** (`-**81**)"!!!~'

AMERICAN ACTOR DENNIS WEAVER `-**DEATH/DAY** = (**2**/**24**/20/**06**) = (**2** + **24** + 20 + **06**) = (`-**52**)!!!~'

`-**DEATH/DAY** = (**2/24**) = (2) (2 x 4) = (`-**28**) = RECIPROCAL (INVERSE/MIRROR) = (`-**82**) = **"ONE `-YEAR `-AWAY from `-AGE of `-DEATH for AMERICAN ACTOR DENNIS WEAVER (`-81)"!!!~'**

`-**DEATH/YEAR** = (`-**20/06**) = (20 + 06) = (`-**26**) = `-**DEATH/ DAY** = (**2/24**) = (2) (2 + 4) = (`-**26**) = FRAGMENTED `-**BIRTH/ DAY** # `-**NUMBER** = (`-**26**)!!!~'

(26 + 26) = (`-**52**) = `-**DEATH/DAY** # `-**NUMBER for AMERICAN ACTOR DENNIS WEAVER** = (`-**52**)!!!~'

`-**BIRTH/DAY** # `-**NUMBER** = (`-**53**) = `-**NEAR `-DEATH/DAY** # `-**NUMBER** = (`-**52**)!!!~'

(53 (-) 52) = (`-**1**)!!!~'

(53 + 52) = (`-**105**) = (10 x 5) = (`-**50**) x `-*TIMES* (`-**2**) = (`-**100**)!!!~'

AMERICAN ACTOR DENNIS WEAVER `-**DIED** (`-**100**) DAYS AWAY from `-**HIS `-BIRTHDAY!!!~'**

(365 (-) 100) = (`-**265**) = (**ALL-IN-ONE-#-NUMBER**) = (2 + 6) (5) = (`-**85**) = **"FOUR `-YEARS `-AWAY from `-AGE of `-DEATH for AMERICAN ACTOR DENNIS WEAVER (`-81)"!!!~'**

`-**DEATH/YEAR** = (`-**20/06**) = (20 + 06) = (`-**26**) = `-**DEATH/ DAY** = (**2/24**) = (2) (2 + 4) = (`-**26**) = FRAGMENTED `-**BIRTH/ DAY** # `-**NUMBER** = (`-**26**)!!!~'

FRAGMENTED `-**BIRTH/DAY** # `-**NUMBER** = (6 + 4 + 1 + 9 + 2 + 4) = (`-**26**) = RECIPROCAL (INVERSE/MIRROR) = (`-**62**)!!!~'

(26 + 62) = (`-**88**) = "SEVEN `-YEARS `-AWAY from `-AGE of `-DEATH for AMERICAN ACTOR DENNIS WEAVER (`-**81**)"!!!~'

FRAGMENTED `-**DEATH/DAY** # `-**NUMBER** = (2 + 2 + 4 + 2 + 0 + 0 + 6) = (`-**16**) = RECIPROCAL (INVERSE/MIRROR) = (`-**61**)!!!~'

(16 + 61) = (`-**77**) = "FOUR `-YEARS `-AWAY from `-AGE of `-DEATH for AMERICAN ACTOR DENNIS WEAVER (`-**81**)"!!!~'

(26 + 16) = (`-**42**) = "The `-**MARK**"!!!~'

(26 + 16) = (`-**42**) = RECIPROCAL (INVERSE/MIRROR) = (`-**24**) = `-**DAY** of `-**DEATH** (`-**24**th) for AMERICAN ACTOR DENNIS WEAVER = (`-**24**) = `-**BIRTH/YEAR** for AMERICAN ACTOR DENNIS WEAVER = (`-**24**)!!!~'

`-**DIED** at the `-**AGE** of (`-**82**)!!!~'

AMERICAN ACTOR BURT REYNOLDS `-**BIRTHDAY** = (**2/11**/19/**36**) = (**2** + **11** + 19 + **36**) = (`-**68**) = "The `-**MARK**"!!!~' = RECIPROCAL (INVERSE/MIRROR) = (`-**86**) = "FOUR `-YEARS `-AWAY from `-AGE of `-DEATH for AMERICAN ACTOR BURT REYNOLDS (`-**82**)"!!!~'

(86 (-) 68) = (`-**18**) = RECIPROCAL (INVERSE/MIRROR) = (`-**81**) = "ONE `-YEAR `-AWAY from `-AGE of `-DEATH for AMERICAN ACTOR BURT REYNOLDS (`-**82**)"!!!~'

(68 + 86) = (`-**154**) = (54 x 1) = (`-**54**) = `-**DEATH/DAY** = (`-**9/6**) = (9 x 6) = (`-**54**)!!!~'

`-**BIRTH/DAY** = (**2/11**) = (2 + 11) = (`-**13**) = "A VERY PIVOTAL # `-NUMBER"!!!~'

`-**BIRTH/YEAR** = (`-**19/36**) = (19 + 36) = (`-**55**) = (`-**23**) + (`-**32**)!!!~'

"WAS `-**BORN** in (`-**2**) (FEBRUARY); and, `-**DIED** in (`-**9**) (SEPTEMBER)"; and, (**2/9**) = (FEBRUARY 9th) = (`-**2**) DAYS AWAY from `-HIS `-**BIRTH/DAY**!!!~' RECIPROCAL (INVERSE/ MIRROR) = (**9/2**) = (SEPTEMBER 2$^{nd}$) = (`-**4**) DAYS AWAY from `-HIS `-**DEATH/DAY**!!!~' (**2/4**) = RECIPROCAL (INVERSE/ MIRROR) = (**4/2**) = (`-**42**) = "The `-**MARK**"!!!~'

(**19**36) = (1 (-) 9) (3 (-) 6) = `-**_EQUALS_** = (`-**83**) = "ONE `-YEAR `-AWAY from `-AGE of `-DEATH for AMERICAN ACTOR BURT REYNOLDS (`-**82**)"!!!~'

AMERICAN ACTOR BURT REYNOLDS `-**DEATH/DAY** = (**9/6**/20/**18**) = (**9** + **6** + 20 + **18**) = (`-**53**) = RECIPROCAL (INVERSE/MIRROR) = (`-**35**)!!!~'

(53 (-) 35) = (`-**18**) = RECIPROCAL (INVERSE/MIRROR) = (`-**81**) = "ONE `-YEAR `-AWAY from `-AGE of `-DEATH for AMERICAN ACTOR BURT REYNOLDS (`-**82**)"!!!~'

(53 (-) 35) = (`-**18**) = `-**DEATH/YEAR** for AMERICAN ACTOR BURT REYNOLDS (`-**18**)!!!~'

`-**DEATH/YEAR** = (`-**20/18**) = (20 + 18) = (`-**38**) = RECIPROCAL (INVERSE/MIRROR) = (`-**83**) = "ONE `-YEAR `-AWAY from `-AGE of `-DEATH for AMERICAN ACTOR BURT REYNOLDS (`-**82**)"!!!~'

(68 (-) 53) = (`-**15**) = `-**DEATH/DAY** (**9/6**) = (9 + 6) = (`-**15**)!!!~'

(68 + 53) = (`-**121**) = **RECIPROCAL-SEQUENCING-NUMEROLOGY-RSN**!!!~'

AMERICAN ACTOR BURT REYNOLDS `-**DIED** (`-**158**) DAYS AWAY from `-HIS `-**BIRTHDAY**!!!~' (`-**158**) = (58 x 1) = (`-**58**) = RECIPROCAL (INVERSE/MIRROR) = (`-**85**) = "**THREE `-YEARS `-AWAY from `-AGE of `-DEATH for AMERICAN ACTOR BURT REYNOLDS** (`-**82**)"!!!~'

(365 (-) 158) = (`-**270**) = (**ALL-IN-ONE-#-NUMBER**) = (2 + 7) (0) = (`-**90**) = "**EIGHT `-YEARS `-AWAY from `-AGE of `-DEATH for AMERICAN ACTOR BURT REYNOLDS** (`-**82**)"!!!~'

FRAGMENTED `-**BIRTH/DAY** # `-**NUMBER** = (2 + 1 + 1 + 1 + 9 + 3 + 6) = (`-**23**) = RECIPROCAL (INVERSE/MIRROR) = (`-**32**) = -a PROPHETIC # `-NUMBER!!!~'

/|\ FRAGMENTED `-**DEATH/DAY** # `-**NUMBER** = (9 + 6 + 2 + 0 + 1 + 8) = (`-**26**) = RECIPROCAL (INVERSE/MIRROR) = (`-**62**)!!!~'

(26 + 62) = (`-**88**) = 2(8's) = (`-**28**) = RECIPROCAL (INVERSE/MIRROR) = (`-**82**) = `-**AGE of `-DEATH for AMERICAN ACTOR BURT REYNOLDS** (`-**82**)"!!!~' /|\

(23 + 26) = (`-**49**) = RECIPROCAL (INVERSE/MIRROR) = (`-**94**)!!!~'

(94 (-) 49) = (`-**45**) = RECIPROCAL (INVERSE/MIRROR) = (`-**54**) = `-**DEATH/DAY** = (`-**9/6**) = (9 x 6) = (`-**54**)!!!~'

/|\ `-**BIRTH/DAY** = (**2/11**)!!!~'

`-**DEATH/DAY** = (**9/6**)!!!~'

(2 + 11 + 9 + 6) = (`-**28**) = RECIPROCAL (INVERSE/MIRROR) = (`-**82**) = `-AGE of `-DEATH for AMERICAN ACTOR BURT REYNOLDS (`-**82**)"!!!~' /|\

`-**DIED** at the `-**AGE** of (`-**71**)!!!~'

/|\ AMERICAN ACTOR JACKIE GLEASON `-**BIRTHDAY** = (**2/26**/19/**16**) = (**2** + **26** + 19 + **16**) = (`-**63**) = RECIPROCAL (INVERSE/MIRROR) = (`-**36**) = `-**DEATH/DAY** # `-**NUMBER** = `-*EQUALS* = (`-**136**)!!!~' /|\

(63 (-) 36) = (`-**27**) = RECIPROCAL (INVERSE/MIRROR) = (`-**72**) = "ONE `-YEAR `-AWAY from `-AGE of `-DEATH for AMERICAN ACTOR JACKIE GLEASON (`-**71**)"!!!~'

(63 + 36) = (`-**99**) = RECIPROCAL (INVERSE/MIRROR) = (`-**66**) = `-**DEATH/DAY** = (**6/24**) = (6) (2 + 4) = (`-**66**)!!!~'

`-**BIRTH/DAY** = (**2/26**) = "FLIP the (`-**2**) OVER to a (`-**7**)" = (**7/76**) = (**ALL-IN-ONE-#-NUMBER**) = (77 (-) 6) = (`-**71**) = `-AGE of `-DEATH for AMERICAN ACTOR JACKIE GLEASON (`-**71**)"!!!~'

`-**BIRTH/DAY** = (**2/26**) = "FLIP the (`-**2**) OVER to a (`-**7**)" = (**7/26**) = (**ALL-IN-ONE-#-NUMBER**) = (7) (2 (-) 6) = (`-**74**) = "THREE `-YEARS `-AWAY from `-AGE of `-DEATH for AMERICAN ACTOR JACKIE GLEASON (`-**71**)"!!!~'

`-**BIRTH/DAY** = (**2/26**) = RECIPROCAL (INVERSE/MIRROR) = (**62/2**) = (62 + 2) = (`-**64**) = (`-**2**) x (`-**32**) = (`-**232**) = **RECIPROCAL-SEQUENCING-NUMEROLOGY-RSN**!!!~'

`-BIRTH/YEAR** = (`-19/16**) = (96 x 1 x 1) = (`-**96**) = `-**DEATH/ DAY** = (`-**6/24**) = "FLIP the (`-**6**) OVER to a (`-**9**)" = (`-**9/24**) = (9) (2 + 4) = (`-**96**)!!!~'

"WAS `-**BORN** in (`-**2**) (FEBRUARY); and, `-**DIED** in (`-**6**) (JUNE)"; and, (**2/6**) = (FEBRUARY 6th) = (`-**20**) DAYS AWAY from `-HIS `-**BIRTH/DAY**!!!~' RECIPROCAL (INVERSE/MIRROR) = (**6/2**) = (JUNE 2nd) = (`-**22**) DAYS AWAY from `-HIS `-**DEATH/ DAY**!!!~' (**20/22**) = (20 + 22) = (`-**42**) = "The `-**MARK**"!!!~'

/|\ (**1916**) = (1 + 9 + 1 + 6) = `-**EQUALS** = (`-**17**) = RECIPROCAL (INVERSE/MIRROR) = (`-**71**) = `-**AGE of `-DEATH for AMERICAN ACTOR JACKIE GLEASON** (`-**71**)"!!!~' /|\

/|\ AMERICAN ACTOR JACKIE GLEASON `-**DEATH/DAY** = (**6/24**/19/**87**) = (**6** + **24** + 19 + **87**) = (`-**136**) = (36 x 1) = (`-**36**) = RECIPROCAL (INVERSE/MIRROR) = (`-**63**) = `-**BIRTH/DAY** # `-**NUMBER for AMERICAN ACTOR JACKIE GLEASON** (`-**63**)!!!~' /|\

`-**DEATH/DAY** = (**6/24**) = (62 + 4) = (`-**66**) = "FIVE `-YEARS `-AWAY from `-AGE of `-DEATH for AMERICAN ACTOR JACKIE GLEASON** (`-**71**)"!!!~'

`-**DEATH/YEAR** = (`-**19/87**) = (87 (-) 19) = (`-**68**) = "The `-**MARK**"!!!~'

(136 (-) 63) = (`-**73**) = "TWO `-YEARS `-AWAY from `-AGE of `-DEATH for AMERICAN ACTOR JACKIE GLEASON** (`-**71**)"!!!~'

(136 + 63) = (`-**199**) = (19 x 9) = (`-**171**) = (71 x 1) = (`-**71**) = `-**AGE of `-DEATH for AMERICAN ACTOR JACKIE GLEASON** (`-**71**)"!!!~'

(199 + 73) = (`-**272**) = **RECIPROCAL-SEQUENCING-NUMEROLOGY-RSN!!!~'**

(199 + 73) = (`-**272**) = (72 (-) 2) = (`-**70**) = "**ONE `-YEAR `-AWAY from `-AGE of `-DEATH for AMERICAN ACTOR JACKIE GLEASON (`-71)**"!!!~'

(199 (-) 73) = (`-**126**) = (12 x 6) = (`-**72**) = "**ONE `-YEAR `-AWAY from `-AGE of `-DEATH for AMERICAN ACTOR JACKIE GLEASON (`-71)**"!!!~'

AMERICAN ACTOR JACKIE GLEASON `-**DIED** (`-**118**) DAYS AWAY from `-**HIS `-BIRTHDAY!!!~'** (`-**118**) = RECIPROCAL (INVERSE/MIRROR) = (`-**811**) = (**ALL-IN-ONE-#-NUMBER**) = (8 (-) 1) (1) = (`-**71**) = `-**AGE of `-DEATH for AMERICAN ACTOR JACKIE GLEASON (`-71)**"!!!~'

(`-**118**) = (18 x 1) = (`-**18**) x `-***TIMES*** (`-**2**) = (`-**36**) = `-*DEATH/DAY # `-NUMBER (`-136)*; and, (**RECIPROCAL/INVERSE/MIRROR**) = `-*BIRTH/DAY # `-NUMBER (`-**63**)!!!~'

(365 (-) 118) = (`-**247**) = RECIPROCAL (INVERSE/MIRROR) = (`-**742**) = (**ALL-IN-ONE-#-NUMBER**) = (7) (4 (-) 2) = (`-**72**) = "**ONE `-YEAR `-AWAY from `-AGE of `-DEATH for AMERICAN ACTOR JACKIE GLEASON (`-71)**"!!!~'

FRAGMENTED `-**BIRTH/DAY** # `-NUMBER = (2 + 2 + 6 + 1 + 9 + 1 + 6) = (`-**27**) = RECIPROCAL (INVERSE/MIRROR) = (`-**72**) = "**ONE `-YEAR `-AWAY from `-AGE of `-DEATH for AMERICAN ACTOR JACKIE GLEASON (`-71)**"!!!~'

FRAGMENTED `-**DEATH/DAY** # `-NUMBER = (6 + 2 + 4 + 1 + 9 + 8 + 7) = (`-**37**) = RECIPROCAL (INVERSE/MIRROR) =

(`-73) = "TWO `-YEARS `-AWAY from `-AGE of `-DEATH for AMERICAN ACTOR JACKIE GLEASON (`-71)"!!!~`

(27 + 37) = (`-64) = (`-2) x (`-32) = (`-232) = RECIPROCAL-SEQUENCING-NUMEROLOGY-RSN!!!~`

`-BIRTH/DAY = (2/26)!!!~`

`-DEATH/DAY = (6/24)!!!~`

(2 + 26 + 6 + 24) = (`-58) = RECIPROCAL (INVERSE/MIRROR) = (`-85)!!!~`

(85 (-) 58) = (`-27) = RECIPROCAL (INVERSE/MIRROR) = (`-72) = "ONE `-YEAR `-AWAY from `-AGE of `-DEATH for AMERICAN ACTOR JACKIE GLEASON (`-71)"!!!~`

`-DIED at the `-AGE of (`-24)!!!~`

AMERICAN ACTOR JAMES DEAN `-BIRTHDAY = (2/8/19/31) = (2 + 8 + 19 + 31) = (`-60) = RECIPROCAL (INVERSE/MIRROR) = (`-06)!!!~`

/|\ FRAGMENTED `-BIRTH/DAY # `-NUMBER = (2 + 8 + 1 + 9 + 3 + 1) = (`-24) = `-AGE of `-DEATH for AMERICAN ACTOR JAMES DEAN (`-24)"!!!~` /|\

`-BIRTH/DAY = (2/8) = (`-28) = "FOUR `-YEARS `-AWAY from `-AGE of `-DEATH for AMERICAN ACTOR JAMES DEAN (`-24)"!!!~`

`-BIRTH/YEAR = (`-31) = RECIPROCAL (INVERSE/MIRROR) = (`-13) = "A VERY PIVOTAL # `-NUMBER"!!!~`

`-BIRTH/YEAR = (`-19/31) = (19 + 31) = (`-50) / `-DIVIDED `-by (`-2) = (`-25) = "ONE `-YEAR `-AWAY from `-AGE of `-DEATH for AMERICAN ACTOR JAMES DEAN (`-24)"!!!~'

"WAS `-BORN in (`-2) (FEBRUARY); and, `-DIED in (`-9) = `-EQUALS; `-ALMOST, `-BIRTH/DAY = (`-2/8)"!!!~'

"WAS `-BORN in (`-2) (FEBRUARY); and, `-DIED in (`-9) (SEPTEMBER)"; and, (2/9) = (FEBRUARY 9th) = (`-1) DAY AWAY from `-HIS `-BIRTH/DAY!!!~' RECIPROCAL (INVERSE/ MIRROR) = (9/2) = (SEPTEMBER 2nd) = (`-28) DAYS AWAY from `-HIS `-DEATH/DAY!!!~' (1/28) = (28 (-) 1) = (`-27) = "THREE `-YEARS `-AWAY from `-AGE of `-DEATH for AMERICAN ACTOR JAMES DEAN (`-24)"!!!~'

(1931) = (1 (-) 9) (3 (-) 1) = `-EQUALS = (`-82) = RECIPROCAL (INVERSE/MIRROR) = (`-28) = "FOUR `-YEARS `-AWAY from `-AGE of `-DEATH for AMERICAN ACTOR JAMES DEAN (`-24)"!!!~'

AMERICAN ACTOR JAMES DEAN `-DEATH/DAY = (9/30/19/55) = (9 + 30 + 19 + 55) = (`-113) = (13 x 1) = (`-13) = "A VERY PIVOTAL # `-NUMBER" = RECIPROCAL (INVERSE/ MIRROR) = (`-31) = AMERICAN ACTOR JAMES DEAN was `-BORN in (`-31)!!!~'

`-DEATH/DAY = (9/30) = (9 x 30) = (`-270) = (27 + 0) = (`-27) = "THREE `-YEARS `-AWAY from `-AGE of `-DEATH for AMERICAN ACTOR JAMES DEAN (`-24)"!!!~'

`-DEATH/YEAR = (`-55) = (`-23) + (`-32)!!!~'

(113 (-) 60) = (`-53) = RECIPROCAL (INVERSE/MIRROR) = (`-35)!!!~'

(53 (-) 35) = (`-18) = "SIX `-YEARS `-AWAY from `-AGE of `-DEATH for AMERICAN ACTOR JAMES DEAN (`-24)"!!!~'

(113 + 60) = (`-173) = "FLIP the (`-7) OVER to a (`-2)" = (`-123) = (23 + 1) = (`-24) = `-AGE of `-DEATH for AMERICAN ACTOR JAMES DEAN (`-24)"!!!~'

(173 + 53) = (`-226) = (26 (-) 2) = (`-24) = `-AGE of `-DEATH for AMERICAN ACTOR JAMES DEAN (`-24)"!!!~'

(173 (-) 53) = (`-120) = (20 + 1) = (`-21) = "THREE `-YEARS `-AWAY from `-AGE of `-DEATH for AMERICAN ACTOR JAMES DEAN (`-24)"!!!~'

AMERICAN ACTOR JAMES DEAN `-DIED (`-131) DAYS AWAY from `-HIS `-BIRTHDAY!!!~' (`-131) = (31 (-) 1) = (`-30) = "SIX `-YEARS `-AWAY from `-AGE of `-DEATH for AMERICAN ACTOR JAMES DEAN (`-24)"!!!~'

AMERICAN ACTOR JAMES DEAN `-DEATH/DAY # `-NUMBER = (`-113) = "SWIPE the (`-3) to the `-LEFT" = (`-131) = `-DAYS from `-DEATH to `-BIRTH; while, being `-BORN in (`-31)!!!~'

(`-131) = (31 x 1) = (`-31) = RECIPROCAL (INVERSE/MIRROR) = (`-13) = "A VERY PIVOTAL # `-NUMBER"!!!~'

(`-131) = RECIPROCAL-SEQUENCING-NUMEROLOGY-RSN!!!~'

(`-131) = (31 x 1) = (`-31) = AMERICAN ACTOR JAMES DEAN was `-BORN in (`-31)!!!~'

(365 (-) 131) = (`-234) = PROPHETIC-LINEAR-PROGRESSION-PLP!!!~'

(365 (-) 131) = (`-**234**) = (23 + 4) = (`-**27**) = **"THREE `-YEARS `-AWAY from `-AGE of `-DEATH for AMERICAN ACTOR JAMES DEAN (`-24)"!!!~'**

/|\ FRAGMENTED `-**BIRTH/DAY** # `-**NUMBER** = (2 + 8 + 1 + 9 + 3 + 1) = (`-**24**) = `-**AGE of `-DEATH for AMERICAN ACTOR JAMES DEAN (`-24)"!!!~' /|**

FRAGMENTED `-**BIRTH/DAY** # `-**NUMBER** = (2 + 8 + 1 + 9 + 3 + 1) = (`-**24**) = RECIPROCAL (INVERSE/MIRROR) = (`-**42**) = **"The `-MARK"!!!~'**

FRAGMENTED `-**DEATH/DAY** # `-**NUMBER** = (9 + 3 + 0 + 1 + 9 + 5 + 5) = (`-**32**) = RECIPROCAL (INVERSE/MIRROR) = (`-**23**) = -a PROPHETIC # `-NUMBER!!!~'

(24 + 32) = (`-**56**) = RECIPROCAL (INVERSE/MIRROR) = (`-**65**)!!!~'

(24 + 32) = (`-**56**) / `-*DIVIDED* `-*by* (`-**2**) = (`-**28**) = `-**BIRTH/DAY (2/8) for AMERICAN ACTOR JAMES DEAN (FEBRUARY 8**th**)!!!~'**

UNCLE CAL (AUNT SANDRA'S **HUSBAND**) - **BIRTH** = (**7/24/19/32**) = (7 + 24 + 19 + 32) = (`-**82**) for `-**BIRTH/DAY #** `-**NUMBER** = RECIPROCAL (INVERSE/MIRROR) = (`-**28**) = 2(8's) = (`-**88**) = **"AGE of `-DEATH /|\ from the `-BIRTH/ DAY # `-NUMBER /|\ `-itself"!!!~'** `-**DAY of `-DEATH** = (**8/22**) (20/20)!!!~' (BIRTH = **82**/DEATH = **822**)!!!~' `-FRAGMENTED `-**BIRTH/DAY #** `-**NUMBER** = (7 + 2 + 4 + 1 + 9 + 3 + 2) = (`-**28**) = RECIPROCAL (INVERSE/MIRROR) = (`-**82**)!!!~' `-**BIRTH/ DAY # `-NUMBER** (`-**82**) (**-**) `-FRAGMENTED `-**BIRTH/DAY**

\# `-**NUMBER** (`-**28**) = (`-**54**) = AUNT SANDRA'S `-**BIRTH/ DAY** = (**5/4**) = (**MAY 4**th)!!!~' **DEATH/DAY** = (8/**22**/2**0**/2**0**) = (8 x 2 x 2 x 2 x 2) = (`-**128**) = (28 x 1) = (`-**28**) = RECIPROCAL (INVERSE/MIRROR) = (`-**82**)!!!~' **DEATH/DAY** = (8/**22**/2**0**/2**0**) = "FLIP the (`-**2**) OVER to a (`-**7**)" = (8/**77**/**7**0/**7**0) = **4**(**7's**) = (4 x 7) = (`-**28**) = RECIPROCAL (INVERSE/MIRROR) = (`-**82**)!!!~' FRAGMENTED `-**DEATH/DAY** \# `-**NUMBER** = (8 + 2 + 2 + 2 + 0 + 2 + 0) = (`-**16**)!!!~' `-**DEATH/DAY** \# `-**NUMBER** = (8 + 22 + 20 + 20) = (`-**70**)!!!~' (70 (-) 16) = (`-**54**) = **AUNT SANDRA'S `-BIRTH/ DAY**!!!~' **FRAGMENTED** `-DEATH/DAY \# `-NUMBER (`-**16**) **+** `-DEATH/DAY \# `-NUMBER (`-**70**) = (`-**86**) = RECIPROCAL (INVERSE/MIRROR) = (`-**68**) = "**The `-MARK**"!!!~' `-**BIRTH/ DAY** = (**7/24**) = (7 x 24) = (`-**168**)!!!~' `-**DEATH/DAY** = (**8/22**) = (8 x 22) = (`-**176**) = RECIPROCAL (INVERSE/MIRROR) = (`-**671**) = (67 + 1) = (`-**68**)!!!~' `-**DIED** (`-**29**) **DAYS** from `-**HIS `-BIRTH/ DAY** (`-**29**) = RECIPROCAL (INVERSE/MIRROR) = (`-**92**) = `-**DIED** at (**9/20**p.m.)!!!~' (365 (-) 29) = (`-**336**) = (33 x 6) = (`-**198**) = (**ALL-IN-ONE-\#-NUMBER**) = (1 (-) 9) (8) = (`-**88**) = "**AGE of `-DEATH for `-UNCLE CAL**"!!!~' `-**BIRTH/DAY** = (**7/24**) = (7) (2 x 4) = (`-**78**)!!!~' `-**DEATH/DAY** = (**8/22**) = "FLIP the (`-**2**) OVER to a (`-**7**)" = (**8/77**) = `-***RECIPROCALS**-*'!!!~' `-**DIED** in the `-**MONTH** of (`-**8**); and, was `-**BORN** in the `-**MONTH** of (`-**7**) = (**87/78**)!!!~' (78 + 87) = (`-**165**) = (65 x 1) = (`-**65**) = "**AGE of `-AUNT `-SANDRA at the `-TIME of `-UNCLE CAL'S `-DEATH** /|\ (`-**65**) `-YEARS `-OLD**"!!!~' `-**DEATH/DAY** = (**8/22**) = (82 x 2) = (`-**164**) = (64 + 1) = (`-**65**)!!!~' UNCLE CAL was `-**BORN** in (`-**32**) = RECIPROCAL (INVERSE/MIRROR) = (`-**23**) = AND; had `-**DIED**, (`-**23**) YEARS `-OLDER than `-**HIS `-WIFE** AUNT SANDRA!!!~'

I've `-CREATED a NEW TYPE of PHILOSOPHY (**R**eciprocal-**S**equencing-**N**umerology)/

(Reciprocal-Sequenced-Inversed-Realities) that `-PROVES without `-QUESTION the `-PRESENCE of GOD'S EXISTENCE in our DAILY `-LIVES & `-AFFAIRS!!!!!~'

FOUNDER & DISCOVERER/ORIGINATOR/AUTHOR: DWAYNE W. ANDERSON!!!~'

The `-LIST goes `-ON; and, `-ON!!!~' JUST `-WATCH the `-NEWS `-STATIONS; and, `-USE & `-CALCULATE these `-DEATHS with `-ALL of the `-FORMULAS `-PRESENTED within; and, by `-ALL; of the `-PENNED `-BOOKS of the `-PROPHET!!!~'

From the `-FRAGMENTED # `-NUMBERS, to the `-WHOLE # `-NUMBERS; `-ALL of these # `-NUMBERS, `-*ADD* `-*UP* to the `-AGE of `-DEATH, `-BIRTH/DAY, `-BIRTH/DAY #'s, `-DEATH/DAY, `-DEATH/DAY #'s, `-*TIMES* `-*BETWEEN* `-*BIRTH; and,* `-*DEATH*; `-SEAMLESSLY!!!~' `-ALL `-ARTICULATED by `-GOD'S `-HAND; or, `-SPIRIT!!!~' Now; `-LOOK at the # `-NUMBERS from `-BIRTH; and, `-YOU can `-EASILY; `-*IN* `-*FACT* `-*SEE*, the `-DEATH `-COMING!!!~'

The `-DEATH `-MYSTERY /|\ The `-HIDDEN `-LANGUAGES of the `-UNIVERSE!!!~'

The `-GOD `-BOOK of `-NUMEROLOGY!!!~'